Hotel Exile

Contents

List of Illustrations

Photographic credits are given in italics.

List of Illustrations

The Hotel Lutetia

Prologue

A hotel, explains the former concierge in the elegantly leathered library of the Hotel Lutetia in Paris, is not an actor in a drama. It is simply the stage on which dramas are played out. We, the staff, are invisible, like stagehands who work behind the scenes to allow the performance to proceed without a hitch. We do not interfere. We do not speak of the triumphs or calamities of our guests. What we may witness we cannot share, for the reputation of a grand hotel is based, above all, on discretion. So if you want to find the stories, you have to look outside the hotel, he says. We have nothing here.

A hotel is like a train station in slow motion: a place for people who are passing through, a temporary stop on the way to somewhere else. It mimics home, offering comfort without love. Sometimes, it is a place to hide, to conceal a secret life.

A hotel is a neutral territory upon which friends and enemies may meet. It does not judge its clients so long as they behave with appropriate discretion and pay their bills. Exiled politicians may meet here to thrash out the blueprint for a future that will never happen. They can book the President Salon for conferences where delegates fight for control of an agenda that will never be realized. They can drink coffee and argue among themselves for as long as they wish so long as they pay for the hire of the room, observed by discreet staff and enemy spies.

But a hotel, like a country, can be invaded and occupied, made to serve a purpose other than luxury or commerce. Staff must act with the same professional consideration whether they serve artists, businessmen, eccentric aristocrats or enemy soldiers. James Joyce or Admiral Canaris, does it matter who is ordering the wine?

And yet, there is a sense of contamination: a sense that, by serving the enemy, however unwillingly, a moral compromise has been made. When the hotel is again occupied, this time by the victims of the former conquerors, there is an opportunity for the building, and its staff, to be purified.

Épuration. A potent term containing within it a very Catholic sentiment – the purification of sins, set in contrast to the ideology of racial purification which has created this horror.

At the Hotel Lutetia, purification comes in two forms: the moral purification gained from serving those who have been starved and beaten, allowing them a taste of the luxury ordinarily reserved for the wealthy. And the physical purification administered to these same victims, who arrive at the hotel clad in filthy striped pyjamas, riddled with lice, to be greeted with a puff of DDT, the swift removal of their tattered rags and a hot, cleansing shower.

The origins of the English word 'hotel' lie first in French, *hôtel*, meaning 'a mansion, palace, large house' which derives from Old French *ostel / hostel*, 'a place where guests are received' – a house, home, dwelling, inn, lodging, shelter. This in turn derives from medieval Latin *hospitale*, 'inn, large house'. The words 'hospital' and 'hotel' therefore derive from the same origin, the Latin *hospes*, 'guest, host'.

So a hotel and a hospital are not so far apart.

The Hotel Lutetia is a Paris institution, the only 'grand' hotel on the city's bohemian Left Bank. Situated in the 6th *arrondissement*, planted elegantly between the Latin Quarter and the Champs de Mars, the Lutetia is close to the Senate, the elite École Normale Supérieure, the Jardin de Luxembourg and the famous cafés of boulevard Saint-Germain. Ever since it opened in 1910 the Lutetia has served as a meeting place for artists, intellectuals, musicians, politicians. André Gide took his lunch here, James Joyce lived in one of its rooms, Picasso and Matisse were regular guests. It has a darker history, too.

This is not the story of a famous Paris hotel. It is about three groups of people who are connected to a particular city, to that particular hotel, to one another, and to the grim ideology which dictates the course of their lives. These groups are linked – willingly or not – by race, nationality and language, and by their status as outsiders.

They all live in exile, in profoundly different ways. They are displaced, dislocated, their lives disrupted. They are temporary beings who live out of suitcases, their drama playing out in many hotel rooms. The Hotel Lutetia is the prism through which we view their lives.

There are three phases in our relationship with the Lutetia: in the first, the hotel fulfils its normal function by accommodating guests in its bedrooms and banqueting halls, providing them with service, food, drinks, sometimes a bed for the night or a platform to speak from. We cross its threshold as temporary guests, one group among many, anonymous and unremarked except by the Nazi spies stationed in the lobby or waiting in the bar, alert for eavesdropping opportunities after the meeting's end. In the second phase we take possession of the building and transform its function, changing it physically, inside and out. It is not ours; we have stolen it and imposed our will upon its staff. In the third, the hotel becomes a shelter, a place of healing – a hospital of sorts.

Exile in café (Wolf Franck), Paris 1935, by Fred Stein

PART I

Before: 1933–1939

Not everyone's life is like a house that belongs to him, and that he can go on decorating ever more richly with the furniture of his memory. Some people live in hotels, in many hotels. The years close behind them like hotel doors – and the only thing that remains is a little courage and no regrets.

Erich Maria Remarque – *Arch of Triumph*

Flight

It is a cold night in the spring of 1933 when Gisela Freund arrives at Frankfurt station. A handful of travellers hurry through the rain to catch the Paris express, which is ready to leave. As she approaches the train she hears the sound of boots against the wet cobbles. Turning, she glimpses the silhouettes of two uniformed SS men. Her heart starts beating violently. What if they spot her?

She is twenty-four years old, wearing a simple skirt and a brown suede jacket. In her hand, a small suitcase. Round her neck, a Leica camera which her father gave her when she passed her school exams.

As she enters a third-class compartment, she notes one other passenger, a middle-aged man seated next to the window, his hat pulled down over his eyes. He appears to be dozing. Closing the door as quietly as she can, Gisela puts her suitcase in the rack then seats herself opposite him, clutching her camera. She checks her watch: the train is about to depart.

The silence seems to make time stretch. Then comes the sound she has been dreading: heavy footsteps, voices, doors opening and closing. The man opposite seems to be watching her attentively.

The compartment door opens and an SS officer enters, bringing with him a rush of cold night air. He holds out his hand.

'Papers.'

He barely glances at the passport held out to him by the man. Turning toward the girl, he takes her passport and starts slowly leafing through it.

'A student? Where are you going?'

'Back to Paris for my studies.' She forces herself to take a neutral, bland tone. 'I'll be back in three months.'

His large hands continue to flick indecisively through the pages. Suddenly he looks at her. 'Are you Jewish?'

'Have you ever met a Jew called Gisela?'

I almost shouted it, imitating the authoritative voice of my father who, with his big moustache and martial manner, had often been mistaken for a high-ranking officer. I, too, looked the Nazi right in the eyes. He was barely older than me. Surprised, he handed back my passport, clicked his heels, raised his right hand: 'Heil Hitler!' The door closed behind him; the footsteps receded.

A few moments later the train moves off. Gisela falls back into her seat, lost in thought.

That morning she had bumped into an acquaintance who worked for the local council. It was he who warned her to leave.

The student group to which she belonged had printed a magazine that they distributed clandestinely at the university. In it they wrote critically of the new regime, and in their latest issue they had published the names of professors who had been dismissed, and described the fate of their comrade Anne, the only other girl in the group, arrested by the Gestapo while handing out the student newspaper. A few days later she was returned to her parents in a coffin.

'No doubt she had refused to give our names, because nobody came for us. I imagined with horror the torture she must have suffered. I admired her courage and wondered if in her place I would have had the strength to resist.'

Gisela, a keen photographer, had taken a powerful series of photographs of their comrades after they were beaten by the Nazis. The head of their group, a student named Karl, said she should think about leaving.

'Your photos should be seen abroad,' he told her. 'People need to know what is happening here.'

So here she is, on a night train to Paris, the photographs hidden on her body. In her camera is a second, unfinished film. What if they open it? In a moment of panic she hurries to the train toilet, empties her camera, throws the film down the pan, places the empty Leica in her suitcase. She tries to sleep.

Outside, everything is dark. On the windows, drops of rain slide one after the other, disappearing like the tears she wished she could shed.

'What was the point of our resistance? They had all the means to beat us. I felt suddenly exhausted and discouraged. It was cold in the train. Through my half-closed eyelids I could see the gaze of the man opposite me, silent and impenetrable.'

Prelude to Disaster

Across Europe this journey is being repeated, thousands of men and women clambering onto trains headed for Vienna, Prague, Amsterdam or Paris clutching a suitcase, each one engaged in a desperate performance aimed at convincing those who might be watching them that they are just normal passengers travelling to visit an elderly aunt, or taking a much-needed holiday, or making a journey on business. Shaking hands light up cigarettes, furtive glances dart toward the window as the whistle blows for departure. Acquaintances avert their eyes, pretending not to recognize their fellow travellers.

The author Heinrich Mann, elder brother of the now more famous Thomas, is a highly visible member of the anti-Nazi opposition. The countdown to his departure begins in early February 1933 with a public appeal, signed by him – along with Albert Einstein, the artist Käthe Kollwitz and many others – urging Socialists and Communists to form a united front against the Nazis. Shortly afterwards Mann is expelled from the Academy of Arts and his Berlin flat placed under surveillance.

On 19 February Mann attends a concert, then a dinner at which the host has already packed his bags and ordered the removal van for the following day. As he leaves the party the French Ambassador shakes the venerable author's hand. 'If you should cross Pariser Platz,' he murmurs, 'my door is always open.'

And now the moment has come. He takes only what he needs for his work. Since his partner, Nelly Kroeger, is not in any immediate danger they decide that she will stay behind to close up their apartments and settle their accounts. Having only recently taken out a lease on a new flat, Heinrich wonders at his own lack of foresight.

On 20 February, Nelly buys a train ticket to Frankfurt for the following day and checks in a small suitcase. On the morning of his departure Mann dresses with his usual attention to detail – bow tie, hat, gloves, scarf – and leaves for the station, carrying an umbrella and a briefcase. He and Nelly part as casually as possible – *Goodbye, darling! Have a wonderful trip!* – as if he is popping off to one of his conferences. Nelly waves him off on the platform, then she is left alone.

Two days later, Heinrich Mann crosses the Rhine into Strasbourg. On the same day, police arrive at his flat on Fasanenstrasse. They search the apartment, loot it and boast that the famous author has been arrested. Luckily, Mann's friends have already removed his desk, chair, books and numerous other items. The rest will be claimed by his landlord in lieu of unpaid rent.

He travels on to Toulon, where he is met by a friend. The idea of exile in the south of France is not such a terrible one for an author who has just embarked on a historical novel about the sixteenth-century French monarch Henri IV. Mann is fluent in French, steeped in the country's history and culture. If his long-suffering partner can sort out their finances, at least he will not have to worry too much about the practicalities of survival.

Poor Nelly: she is ill-equipped to deal with what her dearest Heinrich has left behind. After his departure she spends weeks fighting to extract money from a bank that will only recognize his name on the account; he rarely writes, and meanwhile she is fending off visits from the Gestapo from which she is saved only by the fact that her brother has recently joined the SS.

*

How to define the beginning of a cataclysm? Perhaps like this: a series of small, incremental changes that gradually creep up on complacent citizens, busy with lives that are at once so comfortable as to admit no possibility of change, and too filled with the personal dramas that distract us all to notice something worse. For a long time, the quotidian concerns that have been keeping the citizens of Germany awake at night have been accompanied by the steady thrum of an advancing force: boots marching on the streets of Berlin, brown-shirted men barging into bars to throw their weight around. Men who have never had power are now in charge, proud boys determined to take their revenge on those who have lorded it over them for so long. Not any more. Small men are now made big, their uniform giving them power. The street battles that have bedevilled German cities for so long are over. The Brownshirts stand victorious over the defeated Reds. Now is their moment, a time of virile strength, of the loud reclamation of true German values, simple and unsullied by the viruses of internationalism, liberalism and foreign influence. A businessman who for years has been undercut by a more successful rival now has the satisfaction of watching the fellow's company sink; mediocre doctors stuck in the middle ranks of the medical hierarchy now seize their chance to rise on the basis not of talent but of racial purity; liberal intellectuals are no longer permitted to stuff the heads of young boys and girls with degenerate literature. You can throw a Jew off a moving train now and no one will intervene.

It is difficult to comprehend, from the vantage point of the future, the state of paralysed inertia in which vast numbers of German citizens existed in 1933. Unable to predict what is going to happen next, all human beings are apt to grasp at what they consider to be the solid foundations of their existence: their home, their job, their routines, their children's schools, their club, their favourite park. Many Germans supported or adapted to the new regime, suppressed their reservations about its violence and mendacity, or swallowed its lies until they were confronted by evidence too compelling to ignore. But as the pressure builds, eventually a point is reached when it can be contained no longer. The explosion takes everybody by surprise, and yet in hindsight seems inevitable. History tells you that they should have seen it coming. Some will tell you that they did. The writing, for those who cared to read it, had long been on the wall.

So one must ask: what does it take to convince a previously comfortable citizen of Germany that the situation is so bad they must exchange everything they know and love for an uncertain future in a foreign country that, almost certainly, does not want them?

Thin Ice

The novelist Anna Seghers is working in her family flat in the leafy Berlin suburb of Charlottenberg when the police come to question her. Her Hungarian husband, László Radványi, is in Switzerland, her daughter Ruth has been sent to stay with her grandparents in Mainz to avoid infection from her older brother, seven-year-old Peter, who is in bed with scarlet fever. The flat is quiet; the child is sleeping. Anna has time to reflect on the events of recent days: this is February 1933; every Berlin newspaper carries the news of Hitler's appointment as Chancellor.

The knock at the door breaks the silence but it comes as no surprise. The policeman, hovering on the threshold, sees before him a small, attractive woman with thick hair tied in a heavy knot at the nape of her neck. Her gaze is bright and somewhat unnerving. He is about to walk in to question her when she explains, politely, that there is a sick child inside. The police officer hesitates. It's scarlet fever, Anna adds. The officer is a family man; he too has children. With a mumbled excuse he beats a hasty retreat and Anna is temporarily reprieved, much to the disappointment of her neighbour, whose son is a Brownshirt and who has been keeping a sharp watch through the spy hole in her door in the hope of seeing the young woman who keeps such dangerous company hauled away in handcuffs.

Anna believes the time to panic has not yet come. The political situation is worsening but normal life still seems possible, even desirable. The family doctor advises Anna that Peter needs time to recuperate and recommends a children's convalescent home in the Black Forest. There will be snow in the Black Forest in February, fresh air and hearty food. László is still in Switzerland. Why not? Here is a chance for Anna to take a rare break from her writing, to spend some time with her child away from Berlin. So off they go, travelling south by train. On the journey she tells Peter that she will stay with him for a few days. What a joy for the young boy to have his mother all to himself!

As soon as they arrive, Anna takes Peter to a nearby ice rink to teach him how to skate. The winter scene is magical: tall conifers towering above them, a sky of cerulean blue, the ground covered in snow. Skaters glide across the ice, their feet swishing in time to the music that emerges from a loudspeaker – surely a Strauss waltz? The cold is exhilarating; Peter's cheeks are pink. If this is convalescence, then maybe being ill is not so bad.

How long does it last, this rare moment for mother and son, before the urgent bulletin interrupts the musical programme? One has to hope, for Peter's sake, that they managed an hour at least before the announcer conveys the shattering news.

The holiday is over before it has begun. Anna hurriedly deposits Peter back at the convalescent home, explaining that she must return urgently to Berlin. She leaves him with a promise that she will fetch him as soon as possible and departs on the night train.

Conflagration

At around 9 p.m. on the night of 27 February 1933, just three weeks after the appointment of Adolf Hitler as Chancellor of Germany, a passer-by walking near the Reichstag hears the sound of breaking glass. Looking over toward the deserted building he sees flames lighting up the inside. They leap up fiercely, breaking through the glass cupola to release plumes of black smoke which rise high into the sky. Behind the classical pillars of the front entrance a wall of orange illuminates the windows. The fire brigade and police arrive in haste, followed hotfoot by the politicians: the Prussian Interior Minister and President of the Reichstag, Hermann Göring, rushes to the scene, eager to seize this apparently heaven-sent opportunity. If this is no accidental fire, then it is arson. If arson, then someone is to blame. And Göring knows exactly who that will be.

Soon a crowd has gathered to watch the firemen battle to bring the blaze under control. Onlookers watch in horrified fascination as the great neo-Baroque building, the symbol of their democracy, burns. Constructed in the late nineteenth century shortly after the unification of Germany, the Reichstag was the seat of imperial, and then democratic, power. For the past twenty years an endless stream of coalition governments has been meeting there in an attempt to keep the youthful Weimar Republic alive. Above the main entrance is the famous inscription: *Dem Deutschen Volke* – To the German People. While the firemen eventually succeed in taming the flames it is too late to save the debating chamber or the cupola.

A young man is arrested at the scene, panting and sweaty, a flaming torch in one hand. Having entered the building at 9 p.m., by 9.25 he is in police custody. Marinus van der Lubbe is an unemployed bricklayer, an anarchist and former Communist whose eyesight was severely damaged in a work-related accident some years before. Van der Lubbe freely admits to his crime, informing the police that he came to Berlin to make a protest against the world capitalist system which oppresses workers. In the previous few days he has attempted, unsuccessfully, to set fire to three other Berlin buildings. He also claims, adamantly, that he acted alone.

Göring immediately telephones Hitler, who is dining with Joseph Goebbels, to inform the Führer that the Reichstag is on fire as a result of a Communist plot. Hitler, stunned by his good fortune, is said to have remarked, 'Now I have them.' He has long dreamed of provoking the Communists into an act so violent that it will allow him to crush them once and for all, while being hailed as the man who brings order to troubled Germany. Here is his dream made real.

Hitler and Goebbels speed to the scene 'at sixty miles an hour'. After 'clambering over fire hoses' to reach the grand lobby of the

Reichstag, they are met by Göring, who declares: 'This is the beginning of the Communist uprising. Now they are going to strike. Not a minute must be lost!' Göring's associate, Rudolf Diels, later the first Gestapo chief, observes the three men standing together, their faces red from the reflected flames, sweat gleaming on their skin from the heat of the fire. Hitler begins to scream 'in an utterly uncontrolled manner such as I had never before witnessed in him: "Now there can be no mercy. Whoever gets in our way will be cut down. The German people will not put up with leniency. Every Communist functionary will be shot wherever we find him. The Communist deputies must be hanged this very night. Everyone in alliance with the Communists is to be arrested. We are not going to spare the Social Democrats and members of the Reichsbanner either!"'

These are not idle words. By the end of the night of 27–28 February 1933 nearly four thousand KPD (German Communist Party) functionaries have been arrested, along with a random selection of intellectuals, lawyers and doctors whom the Nazis happen to particularly dislike, including Erich Mühsam, Egon Erwin Kisch and Carl von Ossietzky. The official version of events has already been perfected: the burning of the Reichstag is supposed to signal the beginning of a Communist uprising, the first in a series of 'acts of terrorism' planned against the German state and its people with the aim of unleashing civil war.

As word travels around Berlin the implications begin to dawn on those with most to fear from the new regime.

On the Run

As soon as she arrives back in Berlin Anna Seghers goes directly to their apartment to pack up a few belongings, but her zealous neighbour is on the watch again and calls the police. This time the woman is rewarded for her vigilance. The police arrive and, after a search of the flat, Anna is arrested. At the station she is interrogated about her political activities, her Communist connections, her radical

Hungarian husband, László Radványi, who teaches at the Workers University of Berlin. After hours of questioning Anna finally manages to convince the officers that, since she is married to a Hungarian and has Hungarian citizenship, they have no right to keep her. Luckily it is the regular police she is dealing with, not the SA.[†] They agree that she may go home, on condition that she remain there in case they need to call her again. Anna is no fool: as soon as she gets back she grabs a few personal items and escapes via the back garden at night. After a few days in hiding with friends she makes her way to Zurich, where she meets up with László. The immediate and urgent priority is to find a place of safety and then to fetch the children. Where to go? And how to get there without being caught?

A Lonely Place

Gustav Regler is a journalist, so naturally when he hears the news of the Reichstag fire on the radio he hurries immediately to be on the spot. It is morning, the fire engines have gone, the politicians have made their speeches. A cluster of people stand staring at the cupola, from which smoke is still rising. A man reads aloud from the morning paper. According to an official account, a Bulgarian set fire to the building, a Dutchman has been caught, and a German deputy arrested. Or perhaps, thinks Regler, a carrier-pigeon dropped a lighted torch on the roof, or it was a bat, or a Jewish buzzard!

As Berlin descends into chaos Regler wanders the streets in a futile search for the city he once knew and loved so much. A mood of hysteria appears to have gripped the German people. When he calls on an acquaintance, a doctor with whom he has always been on the best of terms, Regler finds the man drunk, declaring that the Communists are to blame for everything. The man launches himself at Regler – who is a member of the KPD – and attempts to strangle him with his

† The *Sturmabteilung*, a Nazi paramilitary organization known as Brownshirts because of their uniform.

leather belt. Later, Regler bumps into a fellow writer, who prevents him from entering a nearby café: 'You aren't going in there, are you? They comb the place three times a day!'

Regler scoffs at this exaggeration, but his friend leads him down the Tauentzienstrasse, informing Regler that the block of flats in the Fehrbelliner Platz, where he lives, has that very morning been surrounded and besieged by the new police. Dozens of their friends have been arrested. Regler's own apartment has been looted, along with others.

'"My books!" I exclaimed, more shaken by this than by anything else.'

The city, once full of comrades, is now a lonely place. After a sleepless night in a friend's attic, the following morning Regler hurries to the train station, where he had previously taken the precaution of leaving a trunk in a locker, just in case. He collects the trunk and heads to his girlfriend Marie Louise's home village in the countryside, hoping to find some respite from the madness. Instead, he is promptly denounced to the police by one of the previously friendly villagers. He is out of German options. It is time to leave. He takes the first available train to his home town of Merzig in the Saar, at that time still independent from the Reich.

Regler arrives at his father's house in the middle of the night. He's thirty-five, still agile. He climbs over the garden fence and knocks at the study window, where a light still shines.

'He seemed not at all surprised to see me, and there was something wonderfully heartening in his calmness. He sat down at his desk again.

'"I have another ten minutes' work to do," he said and looked steadfastly at me.

'I mustn't seem frightened, I thought, and I stared at the familiar objects on his table to steady myself. He pointed to a key lying beside the metal ink-pot.

'"Go and fetch a bottle or two, and put them to cool."

'As we raised our glasses for the first time he said:

'"You'll survive him."'

In the morning, Regler explains to his father that he has come up with a plan to try to expose the Reichstag Fire as a lie: if he can obtain the original blueprints to the building from the National Library in Strasbourg he can prove that it is not the Communists who are responsible for the conflagration but the Nazis themselves, using their inside knowledge of the building's layout to allow the arsonists to enter. He asks his father for advice: should he go ahead?

' "You want to try and prove that they're the ones who set fire to the Reichstag. It may sound stupid and pointless. But nothing is pointless that helps expose great liars and deceivers. We must never give up, even if we're no more than a finger plugging a single hole in the dam."

' "So I should go to Strasbourg?"

' "Certainly, if that's where you can find the plans of the Reichstag to support your theory."

' "But it will mean going into exile," I said.

'My father smiled.

' "I'm fifty-five years old. I've been living in exile all my life." ' '

The Writing on the Wall

The powers seized by the new German Chancellor in the wake of the Reichstag fire allow no doubt. Hitler convinces the elderly President Hindenburg that the danger to public order is so grave that Article 48 of the Weimar Constitution must be invoked for the safety of the German people. The decree, signed into law by Hindenburg with immediate effect, grants extensive powers to the state and revokes all civil liberties. No longer is it possible for those who have opposed the Nazi regime, or whose work falls foul of its critical eye, to convince themselves that somehow it will be possible for them to remain in Germany. No. The writing is written in the flames of the Reichstag, an absolute warning that allows for no ambiguity: PACK YOUR BAGS AND GET OUT NOW!

And so begins a movement, a trickle that will become a stream, that will in turn become a river, a flow of increasingly desperate human beings crossing borders, seeking shelter in the nearest safe haven that will let them in.

Most immediately in danger are those leading figures of the Weimar Republic who have made no secret of their contempt for National Socialism and its fanatical leader, whose prominent position places them in direct and open opposition to the new regime. By the end of March the leaders of the German Social Democratic Party, the SPD (now known as SOPADE – *Sozialdemokratische Partei Deutschlands im Exil*), are in exile in Prague, and nearly all the senior figures in the KPD have left Germany. Its leader, Ernst Thälmann, is being held in solitary confinement, later to perish in Buchenwald. The publishing operations of the Communist master propagandist Willi Münzenberg – nicknamed the 'Red Tsar' or, sometimes, the 'Red Millionaire' for his luxurious lifestyle – have been suppressed, his staff arrested. Münzenberg himself has managed to escape with his partner, Babette Gross, and his faithful chauffeur, Emil Berger, making a dramatic dash from Frankfurt to Saarbrücken in Münzenberg's enormous black Lincoln, before abandoning the car when they are smuggled across the border into France at night.

It is not just political activists who are targeted but writers, philosophers, scientists, journalists, artists, actors, directors – anyone who has not hidden their contempt for Hitler and his goose-stepping acolytes: writers of critical polemics, creators of 'degenerate' art, believers in alternative models of social and political action. For many of those contemplating flight there is an additional danger: they are Jewish.

The roll call of those forced out of Nazi Germany in those early days reads like the guest list for a particularly distinguished university conference. Among them are names both familiar and forgotten, the stars of Weimar's intellectual and political firmament: Bertolt Brecht, Lion Feuchtwanger, Heinrich Mann, Thomas Mann, Golo Mann, Walter Benjamin, Alfred Kerr, Anna Seghers, Alfred Döblin, Bodo Uhse, Gustav Regler, Hannah Arendt, Walter Fabian, Ernst Erich Noth, Ludwig Marcuse, Annette Kolb, René Schickele, Hermann Kesten, Alfred Kantorowicz . . . Austrians, too, including Joseph Roth, Manès Sperber, Franz Werfel, Alma Mahler-Werfel, Stefan Zweig.

For those who insist on hesitating, the news that on the night of 27–28 February 1933 the pacifist poet, anarchist, writer and satirical performer Erich Mühsam has been arrested while trying to escape is sufficient to concentrate their minds.

Federal elections on 5 March enable the Nazis to form a government – just – in coalition with the German National People's Party (DNVP). On 16 March, the first refugees from Germany arrive in Paris. On 22 March, the Nazis open the first concentration camp at Dachau. The following day, the Reichstag passes the Enabling Act, which assigns exclusive legislative power to Hitler and his ministers, bypassing the President and the Reichstag. Within months, the Nazis ban all other political parties. Anti-Semitic measures follow, one after the other, excluding Jews from public life.

This is what things have come to.

Blueprints

In Strasbourg, Gustav Regler discovers that the Reichstag blueprints dating from Wilhelm II's time are indeed held in the National Library but are not available to the public. Posing as an architectural researcher preparing a book, Regler asks the library photographer to make reproductions of dozens of architectural drawings unconnected to what he is really looking for. Eventually convinced that Regler is a genuine researcher, and softened by the offer of a generous tip, the librarian agrees to let the journalist have copies of the original Reichstag blueprints. At this point, Regler runs out of funds. A friend suggests that he use her telephone to call Willi Münzenberg in Paris. Regler knows the Red Tsar only by reputation, but his friend insists that Willi is the only man to call.

Münzenberg understands at once the significance of what Regler is proposing. Since arriving in France in early March 1933 he has established contact with the French Communist Party, obtained political asylum for himself and Babette, and moved into the first of many addresses in Paris, at 19 Quai Voltaire in the 7th *arrondissement*, right next to the Seine. Münzenberg explains that, far from giving up his publishing enterprises, he is planning to devote his time in exile to a campaign to alert the world to the Nazi terror. First on his list is the publication of a 'Brown Book' to expose the Reichstag fire as a propaganda plot. Regler can now consider himself engaged forthwith as a contributor.

'Don't worry about money,' he says. 'Just bring me those photographs!'

The money arrives the following day. Regler pays the library photographer and hastens to catch the first train to Paris.

'I did not examine the photographs until I was on the train and locked in the lavatory. They were exactly what we wanted. The ground-plan of the Reichstag cellars showed the passage running to the presidential residence, where Göring was now installed. The secret entrance used by the arsonists had been found!'

A Fir Cone and a Pfennig

When Anna Seghers and László Radványi are finally able to send for their children they are staying temporarily in Strasbourg with a friend, Franz, before making the onward journey to Paris. Anna's mother, Hedwig, fetches Peter, who has remained in the convalescent home long after his illness has passed. He has been happy enough, enjoying the fresh air and the freedom of his rural surroundings. But for the first time in his short life he has heard the word 'Jew' pronounced by a roommate with a singular intonation. Hedwig accompanies Peter and Ruth to Strasbourg, where the handover is to take place. The children throw themselves into their parents' arms, thrilled to be reunited with Tschibi and Rodi, their nicknames for Anna and László. Hedwig Reiling waves goodbye to her daughter and her two beloved grandchildren, then crosses back over the river to make the melancholy journey home to Mainz. She will never see them again.

After the children have gone to bed, Anna is talking softly to Franz as she tidies their clothes. Emptying her son's trouser pockets, she pulls out her hand and opens it to find, in her palm, a few fragments of dried grass, a pfennig, a transport ticket, and a fir cone. Here is half of Germany, she thinks, in a child's pocket.

A Temporary Stay

It's only an excursion, the time to let the storm pass, three or four months at the most: then we'll be done with the Nazis [. . .] with a small suitcase in hand, I left alone.

Alfred Döblin

When people are forced to flee their homes they generally do not go far, not at first. They move to neighbouring countries, places where contacts back home can be easily maintained, from which the return journey can be made with ease.

Many of the first wave of anti-Nazi refugees fled to Czechoslovakia, Holland, Switzerland, Belgium. A handful travelled north – Bertolt Brecht received an invitation to stay on a small island in Denmark and remained there until the war – but the majority chose to escape to France, that bastion of *liberté*, *égalité* and *fraternité*, the country that, in the nineteenth century, welcomed Polish patriots escaping Russian imperial oppression and, in the twentieth, hosted Russian aristocrats fleeing the Bolshevik revolution.

A small number of established artists, those with the means to survive independently, travelled not to Paris but south, to the French Riviera. Heinrich Mann settled in Nice while others, including best-selling novelist Lion Feuchtwanger, headed for the pleasant seaside town of Sanary-sur-Mer near Toulon, an artists' colony where Aldous Huxley had recently written his great dystopian novel *Brave New World*. Here they formed a little German outpost where they continued their intellectual lives from the comfort of spacious villas rented at knockdown prices, enjoying the inexpensive pleasures of excellent

seafood and good wine, taking their aperitifs by the seashore and holding parties where they jostled for intellectual superiority and showed
off to one another. It wasn't home, but if you are going to have to live
in exile somewhere, the south of France is not a bad place to do it.

Most of the refugees did not have the luxury of international
book sales to keep their bank balances afloat. In the French capital
there was at least a greater chance of finding work, as well as the
solace of inspiring architecture and a vibrant intellectual life. Many
Germans were already familiar with the city, its cultural treasures,
its museums and cafés, its atmosphere, its light. Paris was, they felt,
perhaps the only city in Europe that could rival Berlin.

At the border the performances become more elaborate, a Stanislav-
sky exercise in playing 'relaxed unconcern' as passports are handed
to border officials and suitcases opened for customs officers. Hats
are pulled down over eyes, books studied with intense attention, the
same line read again and again. It is not until the moment when the
French conductor opens the door to request their tickets in a voice
of ordinary, everyday cheerfulness that there is a sudden, collective exhalation of breath. Everyone starts to talk loudly, confessing
their fears and sufferings since Hitler came to power. Then, as they
approach the subject not of the past but of their future, they begin
to speculate: how long is this going to last?

Well, how many Weimar coalitions have come and gone in recent
years? How many elections have been called? Von Papen lasted six
months, von Schleicher only eight weeks. Why would Hitler's government be any more enduring? The Nazis have made many promises
to the German electorate that they will not be able to keep. They will
certainly not be able to control the economy. It follows that this must
only be a brief episode in the history of Germany. The madness will
surely pass, the German people will come to their senses, the rational
voices in the cabinet will prevail, they will rein Hitler in.

A few months, then? Perhaps a year at most?

Until then, the freshly minted refugees promise themselves that
they will take advantage of this short break before normal service

is resumed. After all, they are heading to places they have visited before as tourists or students, or as august lecturers attending conferences. Before them are surely many happy weeks exploring the delights offered by one of the great cities of Europe.

And thus their emigration begins in holiday mood, as the fear that has been steadily oppressing them gradually lifts and hopes rise, like clouds of steam, on a gust of optimism. Perhaps, after all, a temporary exile will not be so bad.

Crossing the Border

At the French border a customs official enters the compartment, accompanied by a plain-clothed Gestapo officer and an SS man. They search Gisela's suitcase, find her camera, order her to open it. The plain-clothed officer inspects it carefully, returns it to her. Is he going to search her? No. He leaves, followed by the others.

As the train moves off Gisela sees, through the window, a man and a woman being taken off by the police. Her companion, now very much awake, is watching her. He has taken off his hat and his eyes, set in a crinkled face, observe the young woman with compassion.

'You don't have to be scared any more,' he says, smiling. 'The border is behind us.'

Her reply is defensive: 'I'm not scared, why should I be scared?'

At the same moment she thinks: *Will I ever see my friends again?*

That night her group were supposed to meet outside the local cinema. Was it possible that someone had denounced them? If so, then who was the traitor? The idea was unthinkable.

'And me, seated in a train which was taking me toward an unknown destination, how would I survive in Paris? What would my parents say when they learned of my departure? They would understand nothing of my decision. They despised the Nazis, but like so many other bourgeois families who lived peaceful, protected lives, they could not imagine that the new regime would affect their own destiny.'

At dawn the train crosses the suburbs of Paris. It is 6 a.m. when Gisela Freund arrives at the Gare de l'Est. A few days later, she learns that all her student comrades have been arrested.

Welcome to France!

Those who arrived in France earliest were greeted by an outpouring of generosity from people who admired their stand against Hitler. Even the French government took measures to facilitate their arrival: in April 1933 French border officials were allowed to admit German refugees onto French territory without passports; French consuls in Germany were instructed to 'examine in the broadest and most liberal spirit' any visa applications that might be submitted by Jews carrying German passports. But despite the warm words of welcome, the centre-left government of Édouard Daladier had no political incentive to encourage the refugees to settle. It did not play well with the French electorate to make life easy for the new arrivals and the right-wing press soon busied itself railing against these foreigners, these Germans, these Jews who were threatening to take French jobs. Extreme publications such as *L'Action française* or *L'Ami du peuple* wrote of a 'Judeo-Masonic' invasion and 'a rush of Judeo-Social-Germans', while mainstream publications like *Le Temps* spoke in critical terms of 'truly biblical' scenes at the Gare de l'Est, referring to an 'exodus' from Germany, and *Le Figaro* described immigrants bringing their quarrels to the streets of France and endangering the safety of French citizens.

The French government accordingly opted to fudge the issue, combining rhetorical openness with practical hostility: in theory, the German refugees were welcome; in practice, the hurdles they needed to overcome to survive were many and complex, and grew more so as time went on and the refugees kept coming.

Many of those who fled to France either had no passport or – in their haste – did not check its validity. Those who travelled with perfectly legitimate papers soon discovered that, once their passport expired, the Nazi government refused to renew it. Under the Nazi regime, any German citizen who failed to show loyalty to the state, or who refused to return to Germany when ordered to do so, could be deprived of their nationality. Since the Gestapo were known to arrest returning emigrants and throw them into concentration camps, few were willing to return, leaving thousands of former German citizens effectively stateless.

What the French government wants, encourages and hopes, is that the Germans' stay will only be temporary, a sentiment shared by the exiles themselves. Everybody wants this to be a passing phase rather than a permanent state of affairs. Meanwhile, one has to eat.

Numbers

In 1933 alone, 60,000–65,000 people fled Germany.

Of these, France accepted approximately 25,000 refugees, 85% of whom were Jewish.

Almost 90% of German citizens reaching France were male, most of them under the age of forty.

Of the 11% who were female, only 3% were married.

Although the number of refugees from Germany was relatively small, France already had a foreign population of approximately 3 million in 1931 (7% of its total population), a result of having recruited thousands of foreign workers in the 1920s to compensate for lives lost in the Great War.

Paris, Rive Gauche

All cities possess within them a series of mini-communities, village-like districts with a distinct identity. Paris is divided into *arrondissements* or *quartiers*, each with its own specific flavour. In the late nineteenth century the place to be for any aspiring artist or dreamer was Montmartre, that vertiginous quarter of tiny alleyways and steep steps dominated by the great white curves of Sacré Cœur. To stand and look out over Paris from that vantage point is to enjoy the grand scale of the city, the contrast between the serpentine curve of the Seine and the elegant lines of Haussmann's boulevards which render central Paris so immediately photogenic. It is here that fifteen-year-old Eva Tichauer comes on her first night in Paris.

The Tichauer family are lucky: as political refugees they have received visas that allow them to stay in France legally. Theodor Tichauer is a prominent social democrat and lawyer; his wife, Erna, works with him, running his office; both are Freemasons, another group in Hitler's sights. Eva is their oldest child; her younger brother Felix suffers from weak lungs. When in April 1933 the Nazi government issued a decree dismissing Jews from state employment, Eva's parents' first reaction was to get as far away from Berlin as possible, immediately. They were on their way to the train station when Eva's aunt came after them. She reminded Theodor that he was a decorated war veteran, a holder of the Iron Cross. You are not Communists, she insists. Things will calm down. So they stayed on. But when, a couple of months later, amid mounting restrictions on Jewish participation in public life, Theodor and Erna were both debarred from legal practice, they decided to ignore the optimistic aunt and leave Germany immediately.

When they arrive at the Gare de l'Est on 27 July the family are met by a friend, Greta, who takes them to a hotel on rue du Delta where she has booked them a room. Before they can even unpack, Greta tells them that she wants to take them out to show them something. It is late, almost midnight, but she insists. It's not far, she says. A fifteen-minute walk at most.

Greta leads the family up a street, past a park, toward some narrow steps. Up they go, up and up, it never seems to end. Felix begins to wheeze, but Greta is excited and doesn't turn back. When they finally emerge onto the broad terrace the family glance, first, at the bone-white curves of Sacré Coeur rising above them. Yes, yes, all very beautiful, but why—? Greta points triumphantly in the other direction. Ah, now they get it! My goodness, look at that!

For there is the whole of Paris, laid out beneath them in all its elegant beauty. Eva is entranced. This image becomes the first memory of her new existence: the stunning sight of the capital city at midnight, a Citroën advertisement brightly lit up on the Eiffel Tower. A symbol of her future.

'I was so dazzled. I have often tried to retrace my steps and find that emotion again but I could never recapture it.'

By the twentieth century the bohemian artists had left Montmartre and moved on, as they always do, in search of cheaper accommodation and studio space, leaving the tourists to gawp at what they have left behind. The place to be in Paris in the 1920s and 30s if you were poor, foreign, intellectual, artistically inclined or a combination of all the above, was on the Left Bank, the *Rive Gauche*, in the Latin Quarter and Montparnasse. The Left Bank is both the intellectual heart of Paris, teeming with students – here we find the Sorbonne, Sciences Po, the École Normale Supérieure – and the centre of political decision-making. The President may reside at the Elysée Palace on the *Rive Droite* but the Senate and the Assemblée nationale are on the other side of the Seine, as well as the Hôtel Matignon, the official residence of the French Prime Minister.

It is to this area that the majority of the German refugees come, carrying their suitcases and whatever else they were able to save in the haste of their departure, dozens of exhausted, grey-faced people who step down onto the platform of the Gare de l'Est like guests unsure if they are at the right party, in the right clothes, at the right time. Those with contacts – friends, family, earlier arrivals – might hope to be met at the station with a smile and, importantly, an address, some indication of where they are going to unpack their suitcase and make their temporary home. But the majority arrive in Paris without the comfort of companions, and are soon forced to learn the meaning of that crucial French verb, *se débrouiller*: they must somehow manage, cope, get by *tout seul* – alone.

Hôtel garni

Since they are, for the most part, desperately short of funds, few of the exiles can afford to rent an apartment. So it is a room they must seek, usually in a down-at-heel, no-star *hôtel garni*, a hotel supplying furnished rooms for semi-permanent occupation. Here they must unpack their bags and sit on an ancient bed to contemplate the reality of what has happened. Gone are the comforts and familiarity of home; gone is work, money, reputation, language, friends. Instead, this hotel room, these four walls.

The twenty-eight-year-old Austrian writer and psychologist Manès Sperber, who fled Berlin after being imprisoned by the Nazis for his Communist activities, lives for a while in a room at the Hôtel des Sports at 69 rue Cardinal Lemoine in the student-filled 5th *arrondissement*, just around the corner from the ruins of an ancient Roman amphitheatre:

'Everything in it was of modest ugliness: a bed, a night table, three chairs, an old easy chair, an armoire that did not close properly, and an oblong mirror that maliciously made everyone who looked in it homelier than he was. The wallpaper conveyed the lushness of tropical plants with obtrusive vividness. Its appearance gave even the most peaceful occupant an urgent desire to shoot holes into those walls with a machine gun. No one did, however, for you can't kill ugliness.'

Exile Time

I was now in Paris, Rue Montaigne, but above all in Germany.
Ludwig Marcuse

To live in exile is as much a state of mind as it is a physical reality. Yet the practicalities of exile are everything: the possession of the means with which to buy food and pay rent; the right to work; obtaining the correct paperwork. Without papers, there is no work, no food to put on the table. Without papers, one has no identity.

The Weimar intellectuals who failed to prevent the rise of fascism in their home country are forced to reckon with themselves in the humiliation of exile. Unable to earn a living, abandoned to an incomprehensible bureaucratic system, many exiled Germans are left reliant on a variety of ill-funded, well-meaning aid committees. While the most famous can expect to find support, protection and money anywhere – what country would refuse to welcome Albert Einstein or Thomas Mann? – the majority are condemned to live each day in growing solitude, anonymity and humiliation. Men who in a recent life were intellectuals, professors, scientists, publishers, must now line up at counters to obtain food coupons, cash handouts, information, advice. They must show up, time and again, at the Préfecture de Police and plead with a bored official to have their papers stamped. Their clothes wear out, their shoes wear thin. In January 1934, the Ligue des droits de l'Homme, collecting clothes for German refugees, cites the case of a well-known writer who has been unable to go out for several weeks because his only suit is in tatters. 'Think', the appeal concludes, 'of those who last year had a comfortable home and who today are experiencing the worst misery in exile.'

Time passes, exile time, simultaneously too long and too short. The sun rises and sets over this beautiful city as the exiles walk the streets of Paris, unwilling *flâneurs* with too much time on their hands between appointments at the Préfecture or visits to the aid committees. No one needs them, so they wander, trying to convince themselves that they are enjoying the beauty of Parisian architecture. They visit churches, galleries, other places that offer the solace of art for free; they turn up for cheap afternoon matinees in the local cinema; they walk along the banks of the Seine, sun themselves in the local parks.

Most of all, they while away the hours in cafés on boulevard de Montparnasse: the Dôme, the Coupole, the Select, or the lesser-known Capoulade on the corner of boulevard Saint-Michel, much

Anna Seghers, 1934, by Fred Stein

favoured by members of the SAPD.[†] On the terrace of a café an emigrant can feel at home. He (it is usually a he) can spend hours nursing a single coffee, untroubled by the waiter, recreating the café life he has left behind in Berlin. Some sit in solitude, avoiding their companions in misfortune; others sit together, endlessly chewing over events back home, searching for clues that might foreshadow the coming collapse of the regime. The café is a proxy living room, a place where news is exchanged and arguments exercised, an informal job exchange where the latest employment possibilities are advertised: morgue attendant, typist, bookkeeper, hotel porter, errand boy. It is also a democratic forum, a public space. It is in the basement of the Mephisto that the exiled German Writers' Union meets; Leopold Schwarzchild discusses his newspaper

[†] The Socialist Workers Party of Germany, an offshoot of the SPD.

Das Neue Tage-Buch with his editors in the Weber; Willi Münzenberg's publishing house, Éditions du Carrefour, is on boulevard Saint-Germain, while Anna Seghers is often to be spotted working in one of the cafés that line the street. Seghers is lucky: she lives outside the city centre, in a peaceful apartment near a forest where her children can go to school and enjoy a normal life. Sometimes she works at her typewriter in the flat, sometimes outside in the garden, but on occasion she likes to escape to the city, taking the suburban train from Meudon into Montparnasse. She likes the hubbub of a busy café, so long as the conversations have nothing to do with her. It provides a sort of windbreak, a wall of noise that allows her to think.

On their long walks around the city, as the exiles pass through the Jardin de Luxembourg and stop to admire the toy boats sailed by children on the lake or watch a game of outdoor chess, it is hard not to be reminded of everything they have left behind. The beauty of Paris brings with it a sense of melancholy, because they are not a part of this busy life they are observing. It is not their children who are playing by the water, not their game of chess. They are outsiders looking in, kept apart by language, culture, poverty.

And always, around them, the resentment of the host nation: the dislike of foreigners in a city filled to bursting with immigrants. To speak German on the street in France in 1933 is to invoke dislike, contempt, hostility. *Ah, les sales Boches . . . Dirty Krauts.* The last war is fresh in the minds of the French. And to master French is not within everyone's capability. So, then, the existential question: who am I? If the German language has been co-opted by bullies and monsters, in what language are the exiles then to write, speak, think?

After a false start at a local lycée, where Peter is bullied as a *'sale Boche'*, Anna comes across a newly opened school a couple of streets away from their apartment in Bellevue-Meudon which follows a modern, liberal curriculum. Soon, both Peter and Ruth are settled happily and speaking fluent French. At some point in the coming years Peter becomes Pierre (we do not know precisely when). This is the advantage of youth: the ability to adapt and assimilate, to leave behind one's old identity and forge a new one. Anna's French is good, but she has an accent and people can tell she is foreign; László's Hungarian accent is even more pronounced. When the family go out together the children refuse to speak German in public. Pierre is embarrassed: 'You have to remember the atmosphere at the time,' he later recalls. 'The French had hated the "Krauts" ever since 1914, even 1870. Of course, Hitler didn't help matters. Officially, I was a Hungarian born in Berlin. In class I used to say I was born "in Charlottenburg" because I realized how frightening the word "Berlin" was.'

Hotel Lutetia

On their wanderings the exiles might find themselves heading vaguely toward the Seine, past the church of Saint-Sulpice and onto boulevard Saint-Germain. Or a different route, on another day, following rue Cherche-Midi, past the prison, then up boulevard Raspail toward the Sèvres–Babylone crossroads. Here there is one hotel that stands out, a grand transatlantic liner of a place far removed from the shabby establishments where they must make their home.

> *Hôtel Lutetia*
> *Le confort parfait*
> *Une bonne cuisine*
> *Une excellente cave*
> *A des prix raisonnables*

The Hotel Lutetia is unique. The other hotels of a similar class – the Crillon, the George V, the Ritz, the Meurice – are all located on the Right Bank, many of them housed in historical buildings that once belonged to aristocrats. The Lutetia symbolizes something slightly different: attainable luxury, its clientele pulled mainly from the French provincial bourgeoisie. Opened in 1910, the Lutetia was conceived as the companion piece to Le Bon Marché, the city's very first department store, a temple of commerce originally founded by

Aristide and Margeurite Boucicaut in the 1850s, which introduced the novel concept of selling hundreds of different goods at fixed prices under a single roof. The Boucicauts started small, first buying a little shop on the corner of rue de Sèvres and rue du Bac, then gradually building it up until, in 1869, they decided to construct a new, grand, purpose-built store. When work on Le Bon Marché was finally completed in 1905, the Boucicauts were no longer alive, but Margeurite had bequeathed her large fortune to her employees and, in 1907, a group of store directors gazed across the little square that now bears their benefactors' name and spotted an opportunity: the Gare d'Orsay, constructed for the 1900 Paris World Fair, was bringing thousands of visitors into Paris and disgorging them directly onto the Left Bank. Why not create a hotel where their future customers could stay while visiting the city?

They were lavish in their ambitions: the hotel was decked out with crystal chandeliers, mosaics, frescoes, parquet floors. There were sound-proofed bedrooms with leather-padded doors, telephones connected to the maître d' and bells with which to summon the valet or the chambermaid. Of the two hundred bedrooms, ninety included a bathroom with hot and cold running water. There was a restaurant, a reading room, a smoking room, a billiards room and an American bar in the basement. A tea shop was built with a separate entrance on the Sèvres–Babylone crossroads, with a patisserie and an ice-cream shop, perfectly conceived for customers of Le Bon Marché to rest after a hard day's shopping. In 1912 an extension to the hotel was added along boulevard Raspail, with ten grand salons constructed to accommodate the growing number of banquets, balls and other celebrations taking place at the hotel.

In style the Lutetia marks a bridge between Art Nouveau and Art Deco, with its undulating façade and shell-like canopies that line the street. Vine motifs overhang the windows; greedy cherubs cling vertiginously as they stretch out chubby hands to reach ripe grapes. The name of the hotel is a reference to the ancient origins of the city first known as Lutetia, its inhabitants the Gallic tribe of the Parisii, later conquered by the Romans. Many traces of the Roman occupation are to be found in the streets of the Left Bank, close to the hotel. The hotel adopted not only the name of the city but its coat of arms, depicting a ship, and its motto: *Fluctuat nec mergitur* – 'Tossed by the waves but does not sink'. The building's maritime theme continues in homage to the early twentieth-century fashion for transatlantic ocean travel: the hotel's interior, all dark wood and brass fittings, was designed to feel like a grand ocean liner, the building's prow jutting out from the corner of boulevard Raspail and rue de Sèvres to offer a viewpoint overlooking the crossroads, with Le Bon Marché temptingly visible on the other side of the square.

Passing the canopied entrance on boulevard Raspail, the reluctant *flâneur* might catch sight of a uniformed concierge hailing a cab, or the hotel's car drawing up to deposit a client just arrived from the station. A swish of a fur coat, an elegant ankle . . . *This way, please, how delightful to see you again.* How tempting it would be to step through those doors. Hotels are open to everyone, after all, just like department stores. Why not?

From the outset the core of the Lutetia's clientele was mainly French, a mixture of provincial businessmen and artists, politicians, thinkers and writers drawn from the surrounding area. French intellectuals like to gather here to discuss their latest works. A young French officer named Charles de Gaulle spent the night here with his bride, Yvonne, en route for their honeymoon in Italy. Ernest Hemingway hung out in the basement bar in the 1920s. James Joyce – a resident of Paris for nearly twenty years – is still a regular.

Banquets and balls are a feature of the hotel's reputation: it is here that Parisian families come to mark christenings, birthdays, anniversaries, marriages. There are talks given by eminent dignitaries, gatherings of international visitors, dance competitions, annual jollies dedicated to social and civic solidarity: the Glovemakers' Ball; a banquet of the Paris Esperantist group; the annual ball of the Friendly Society of Engineers of the Higher Institute of Electricity; the ball of the Paris group of former students of the Cluse National School of Watchmakers, Precision Instruments and

Electrical Items (starts at 10 p.m. sharp); meetings of the war blind and their families. And so on.

So why not step inside? It is not as if a grand hotel is a novelty for the liberal intellectuals of Weimar Germany. In Berlin they drank in the bar of the Eden or the Adlon, rubbing shoulders with film stars and international guests. They stayed in smart hotels on holidays abroad or when attending conferences as honoured guests.

For the great Austrian writer and 'hotel patriot' Joseph Roth, arriving at a hotel was a form of homecoming. He loved the things that others dislike: the impersonal quality of the room, the cheap wallpaper, the spotless basin, the gleaming taps, the telephone directory. When he left Berlin on the evening of 30 January 1933 – he did not tarry, he got out the moment Hitler was appointed Chancellor ('Be under no illusion,' he wrote to his friend Stefan Zweig. 'Hell reigns.') – he returned to a familiar hotel in Paris, the Foyot in the 6th *arrondissement*, just on the northern edge of the Jardin de Luxembourg. There he remained until it was demolished in 1937, thereafter embedding himself in the Hôtel de la Poste opposite, where for a while the Hungarian writer Arthur Koestler lived, as did Gustav Regler with his girlfriend, Marie-Louise. Roth spent most of his time seated at a table in the Café le Tournon writing constantly, talking with friends and colleagues about the old days (the café was popular among Austrian émigrés), but mainly drinking himself to death, a feat he eventually managed in May 1939.

It is only now, in the poverty and want of exile, that these Germans who are neither tourists nor residents lose the courage that comes with knowing that you have money in your pocket and can speak the language in which the concierge will greet you. Poverty is a novel state for this first wave of refugees, for these are the stars of Weimar's intellectual, artistic and political firmament. To be conscious of the state of your shoes, your threadbare coat, your hat or shirt is an unfamiliar humiliation. To know that your accent may be received with hostility, your attempts at French greeted with barely concealed impatience, these are also novel sensations. To enter a smart hotel without an invitation one has to have a certain confidence, not be distracted by hunger, wondering if the bell boy can hear your stomach rumbling.

So for the moment the Hotel Lutetia is just a name, a building an exile might pass on his way to a cheap café, a grand reminder of better days. Perhaps he might encounter one of his French colleagues – André Gide, perhaps, stepping out onto the street, book in hand. Every day the author walks from his home on rue Vaneau in the 7th *arrondissement* to the office of the literary journal *La Nouvelle Revue française* on rue Sébastien-Bottin, regularly stopping at the Lutetia en route. A few words of conversation in front of the hotel entrance, a hungry German writer on one side of the invisible barrier, a well-fed, well-meaning Frenchman on the other.

Most of the exiles will not pass its threshold until 1935.

Sundays with the Family

The Radványi family routine on Sundays is to eat an early lunch together, then Anna and László take a long walk alone, usually heading in the direction of the Ermitage de Villebon where they drink coffee or tea in a pleasant spot near a large cedar tree. It is their chance to spend some time together discussing their work, their children, their concerns. While Anna writes, László teaches, organizing and directing the 'Free German College' under the pseudonym Johann-Lorenz Schmidt. The college brings together anti-fascist German scientists and organizes courses on social and natural science topics for German students living in Paris. At around 4 p.m., invited friends show up at the Bellevue flat. The children are tasked with keeping them occupied if their parents have not yet returned from their walk.

For many of their friends, the Radványi family home represents a kind of haven, a momentary escape from their lives in Paris. To be in Bellevue is to sit in a peaceful, tastefully furnished apartment in a leafy suburb, eat fresh food cooked by Anna, enjoy conversation, the presence of children, music, a garden where they play boules. It is to pretend, just for an afternoon, that life is as it once was – comfortable, easy, pleasant, peaceful. Manès Sperber was a regular guest: 'The return to the city, to a room that was usually not made up on Sunday and then appeared even more miserable, was scheduled as late as possible.'

Gisela / Gisèle

Gisela Freund arrives in Paris with a suitcase, her Leica and not a penny to her name. Unlike her older compatriots, she is not overly concerned by her precarious situation: she is twenty-four years old and finally feels free of the oppression that has been slowly suffocating her in Germany. For her, France offers possibilities. She is young; she isn't interested in the past but in the future, her future. At some point in the next few years Gisela becomes Gisèle. It is not clear when the change occurs but it marks her intent: she does not wish to stand out as a foreigner. It helps that she speaks excellent French.

Gisèle's first home in Paris is a small student hotel on rue Saint-Julien le Pauvre in the 5th *arrondissement* next to the Seine. The streets around it are teeming with students, workers, stray dogs and cats, the air filled with the smell of grease from a chip shop nearby. At the corner of rue Lagrange and rue du Fouarre is a little café-bar where tramps can spend the night when it is too cold under the bridges. They sleep standing up, leaning against a rope that the owner charges them twenty centimes to use. Gisèle's room is indistinguishable from hundreds of others in the Latin Quarter, worn out by generations of students. The walls are covered in greenish paper, decorated with faded red tulips. An iron bed, a table and an ancient armchair complete the furnishings. The budding photographer uses the bathroom as a darkroom, placing her trays on a board above the washbasin and the enlarger on the bidet. The area is run down, her room is scruffy, but oh, the view! From her window she can see Notre-Dame.

With a self-confidence and a sense of purpose that is to define her throughout her life, Gisèle promptly sets to work to ensure her own survival: she needs to perfect her French, complete her doctoral dissertation, and find some work to pay the bills. Her first step is to enrol at the Sorbonne, taking her books to the Sainte-Geneviève library where she tries to study, but the noise of all the students constantly coming and going makes it impossible to concentrate. In search of quiet, Gisèle discovers the Bibliothèque nationale on rue de Richelieu across the Seine, which lies in the heart of Paris's smallest district, the 2nd *arrondissement*, known as Bourse after the Stock Exchange which is situated here.

Libraries are democratic places: here, beneath the great glass dome, in the familiar atmosphere of dusty silence, exiled intellectuals can sit undisturbed for hours, convincing themselves that they are still being productive in this peaceful temple, where books are not burned but preserved for posterity. The library is also the place where exiles can forget the things they have left behind: their own dear libraries, their archives, their work.

It is to the Bibliothèque nationale that the exiled Hungarian-born writer Arthur Koestler comes to write during a period when he and his new wife, Dorothy, are sharing a tiny room in the Hotel de la Paix, a rundown establishment on the Île Saint-Louis with terrible plumbing and a beautiful view of the Seine. And it is here, among the book stacks and the index cards, that Gisèle spots one of Germany's most unique and eccentric scholars, that rare, shy creature, Walter Benjamin.

The flâneur

Walter Benjamin loves Paris, has loved Paris ever since he first became entranced by its cafés and arcades, its broad boulevards

Walter Benjamin at the Bibliothèque nationale, 1937, by Gisèle Freund

lined with houses. Paris is the city where Benjamin has always felt most at home, the city of *flâneurs* – urban strollers, idlers, browsers – a concept born in nineteenth-century France and introduced to German audiences by Benjamin's close friend Franz Hessel, with whom Benjamin – back in the better days – translated Proust. And Paris forms the subject of Benjamin's monumental, unfinished project *Passagenarbeit* (*The Arcades Project*), which absorbs and obsesses him while the old world disintegrates around him.

In truth, the Paris that so captivates Benjamin is not the city he inhabits today, where – after fleeing Germany – he lives in penury in cheap hotels, surviving on intermittent payments from his colleague, Max Horkheimer, for articles published in the magazine of the Institute for Social Research, once based in Frankfurt, then Geneva, now New York. Later, he finds a room on rue Dombasle in the 15th *arrondissement* which he sublets from a friend. For a while Arthur Koestler lives in the same building.

Benjamin is an outsider among outsiders, a man simultaneously ahead of his time and consumed by the past. He finds no solace in the crowds of exiles, preferring instead the company of books in his beloved Bibliothèque, where, before the catastrophe, he spent so many happy hours. Where, now, he takes refuge from the endless struggle to survive, walking every day to sit in the reading room. He writes constantly about anything that piques his curiosity, his tiny handwriting creeping round the edges of papers and postcards, inside books. It is at the Bibliothèque nationale that he completes *Paris, Capital of the Nineteenth Century* and *The Work of Art in the Age of Mechanical Reproduction*, which will later – far later, long after his death – become a seminal text of cultural theory.

When Gisèle spots Benjamin in the library she does not hesitate to greet him. She knows him by sight from her student days in Frankfurt, where she attended lectures at the Institute for Social Research and her teachers included Horkheimer and Theodor Adorno. Soon, she and Benjamin are meeting regularly. They make an unlikely pair: she – young, attractive, confident; he – stout, serious, intensely shy, with his thick greying hair and owlish glasses. She is instinctively at ease in any environment, he is stiff and awkward, with an aura of an old-fashioned German formality. But they hit it off and are soon firm friends.

Sometimes they go for a stroll in the corridor, or cross rue de Richelieu to sit on a bench in the Square Louvois, where Benjamin smokes his pipe while they discuss politics or contemporary literature. Often they leave the library together at closing time and walk across the Tuileries and along the quay beside the Seine, where Benjamin always stops at the bookstalls. Twice a week they meet on the first floor of a café on boulevard Saint-Germain to play chess, a single black coffee lasting them through the game. Benjamin, it turns out, is a bad loser. Freund has begun taking portrait photographs of the people she meets. She snatches a picture of Benjamin in his natural habitat.

Studio Stein

Starting at the bottom comes naturally to the young; living cheaply comes more easily to people who are fresh from student life. And they have that indefinable extra ingredient that comes with youth: call it optimism, blind hope, naivety. Whatever it is, it allows people like Gisèle Freund, and another pair of German exiles, Fred and Lilo Stein, to hustle their way into a profession that is – helpfully – in its infancy: photojournalism.

Like Gisèle Freund, Fred Stein is twenty-four years old when he flees Germany with his new wife, Lilo, under the pretext of going on their honeymoon. Only three weeks away from fully qualifying as a lawyer in Dresden, he was forced to stop for 'racial and national unreliability' and then to flee for his political activity as a member of the SAPD. He knows that law is out of the question in France, but – like Gisèle – Fred has a great advantage over his more established compatriots: he has no long career to regret or leave behind.

With no technical knowledge, possessing only a little Leica camera which they bought for themselves as a wedding present, and a small enlarger which they acquire in Paris, Fred and Lilo boldly announce the existence of 'Studio Stein'. They place a couple of photographs in the showcase outside their building and start looking for customers, scanning the papers and local advertisements for weddings and other events, turning up at the local hall, where they set up their 'studio' in a corner with a hand-made sign, hand out free sample portraits and wait for customers. They return home in the early hours of the morning, dead tired, but with a little money in their pockets. Fred once saw his career in law, but in photography he accidentally finds his vocation. It is a precarious existence, but it delights and fulfils him.

Although they do not know one another, over the coming years the paths followed by Fred Stein and Gisèle Freund will sometimes intersect as they both discover a talent for taking portraits. But where

Gisèle is drawn to the French literary scene, Fred's background as a political activist keeps him rooted in the German émigré community. Where Gisèle takes portraits of the rising stars of France's literary firmament, Fred documents the leading intellectual 'personalities' of German exile – free of charge, of course – whom he encounters at the meetings of the various organizations which spring up in Paris after 1933: Heinrich Mann, Anna Seghers, Alfred Kantorowicz, Lion Feuchtwanger, Gustav Regler, and dozens more. Fred takes portraits of them all.

Work

Yes, it is much easier for the young. Despite having all the correct paperwork, both Eva Tichauer's parents struggle to find employment. Like Fred Stein, Theodor soon discovers that for a foreigner to practise law in 1930s France a series of seemingly impossible conditions must be met: one needs money, and papers, fresh qualifications, influence, connections. Despite all his experience as a lawyer in Germany, Theodor has none of these. He does his best, trying his hand at a series of manual jobs, for which he has no talent, and business ventures which swiftly fail. He is an intellectual, a man who trained for years to be skilled in one particular profession. He is unable to adapt. Erna, fluent in several languages, manages to pick up a few piecemeal jobs as a translator.

Determined that their fifteen-year-old daughter should assimilate where they cannot, Theodor and Erna decide to place Eva as an au pair with a French-speaking family while she goes to school so that she will learn to speak the language properly and be able to complete her education in France. She wants to study medicine, an ambition of which her parents thoroughly approve. It is hard for Eva to be separated from her family, but the decision proves prescient: it is Eva's French education that will later save her life.

*

While prominent writers like Heinrich Mann, Lion Feuchtwanger and Anna Seghers have income from abroad that permits them to survive, the options for the majority of writers and journalists among the German exiles are few. Émigré publications pay little; their circulation is tiny. Some can contribute to the French press, but many do not have sufficient command of the language; they certainly cannot afford to pay a translator. And so writers whose livelihoods were built on their mastery of the German language now find themselves without a voice, their inability to speak French rendering them unemployable. It silences some completely, unable to write from sheer despair. Some give way to the darkness, commit suicide in hotel rooms, drink themselves to an early grave. Others go on writing, in German or bad French, about the loss of their homeland, the failure of their politics. They write and write. There is even a name for their output: *exilliteratur* – the literature of exile. They scribble away in their hotel rooms, penning novels and essays that nobody will read, in a language that no longer belongs to them, unable to make the transition to a language in which they will never be fluent. At their backs all the time is the spectre not of intellectual despair, but of hunger and destitution.

'In my hotel the typewriters crackle. Writers at work. They are trying to "give meaning to time",' writes the poet, critic and novelist Hans Sahl. 'On the first floor is R., who is writing a play about the persecution of Christians under Nero. On the second floor, the poet S. is trying to wring some fiery stanzas for freedom out of his starving existence. D. and T. live in a room with a double bed and are working together on a theoretical paper on the role of women's work in the age of Marx and Engels. W. can no longer write, and is content to pen letters to a relative in America, which he later tears up, asking them to understand his situation and to send him money for the crossing. On the third floor, right next to the tap, is Dr Blanc, who suffers from his unhappy love of classless society and is working night and day on an apologia for the Communist Party, in which he tries to prove that the gossip against him is totally unfounded.'

Cognac on an Empty Stomach

Winter makes everything worse. Hunger pursues the exiles every-where, a gnawing need to eat that is never fully satisfied. And yet, among the well-meaning French intellectuals who are constantly signing petitions and expressing their support, there is little compre-hension of the utter destitution in which so many of their German colleagues exist.

One day as he sits shivering in his unheated hotel room, Manès Sperber receives an invitation from André Malraux to come over after lunch and meet André Gide. At this time, Gide and Malraux are the twin poles of attraction in Parisian literary life for the émigrés: young, charismatic Malraux is at the peak of his fame and deeply concerned by events in Germany, his apartment on rue du Bac a regular meeting-place for the exiles. André Gide is a literary giant who gives generously to assist the refugees.

In his eagerness, Sperber arrives early at Malraux's apartment to find the three Frenchmen – Malraux, Gide and Paul Nizan – still eating. Malraux asks Sperber if he would like a cognac. Hoping it will warm him up, Sperber accepts the offer gladly and quickly empties the glass, then sits down on a couch next to Gide, who immediately strikes up a conversation. This is Sperber's first private meeting with the famous French author whose tall figure, with his sloping shoulders, close-cut hair and penetrating grey eyes lend him the air of a monk. Gide speaks deliberately, weighing each word as if laying out a legal case. The conversation – which concerns the private diaries of the artist Eugène Delacroix – is far from riveting.

'Well, then it happened. I gave a start and noticed that Gide was somewhat impatiently repeating, probably for the second or third time, a question that had nothing to do with the painter. I realised that I had nodded off, put to sleep by the warmth and the cognac I had drunk on an empty stomach. I answered quickly, with both embarrassment and amusement. In those days it was inconceivable that anyone could fall asleep in André Gide's company [. . .] I had a hard time wiping the stupid, embarrassed smile from my lips, for I realised too clearly that this tiny, barely perceptible incident was paradigmatic of the situation of an émigré intellectual and also of that of an impoverished person who is the more infrequently invited for meals the more urgently he needs them.'

At the meetings of the exiled German Writers' Union, which gathers on Monday evenings in the Café Mephisto on boulevard Saint-Germain, supportive French writers join their German peers. Among established French stars such as Gide, André Malraux or Louis Aragon, Anna Seghers is often the only woman present, younger and lesser known. They pay little attention to her, although she is a member of the board. She observes that often after meetings the French writers repair to a good restaurant for a meal, seemingly oblivious to their German colleagues, left behind carefully counting their francs to see whether they can afford the *prix fixe* menu.

Fire in the Belly

There is one thing that keeps the exiles going, one passion that drives them forward and helps them forget about their empty stomachs. The fire that refuses to be extinguished is their urgent desire to alert the world to the dangers of fascism, to warn others not to fail as they have done. There are two men in France who work tirelessly to conjure life from the moribund body of Weimar politics. They are as different from one another as Gisèle Freund and Walter Benjamin: one, an elderly writer with a penchant for fine wine and good food who lives in the South of France; the other, a squat proletarian whose powerful shoulders give the impression that bumping against him would be like 'colliding with a steam-roller', a force of nature as irresistible as a river that has burst its banks, a man who sweeps everyone along in his wake.

It is these men who will eventually lead the German exiles across the threshold of the Hotel Lutetia and bring them inside.

The Red Tsar

When Gustav Regler arrives in Paris in the spring of 1933, the first thing he does is present himself, blueprints in hand, at the office of the famous propagandist and former Communist MP, Willi Münzenberg. Gaining access to the apartment on rue du Faubourg Saint-Honoré is not easy: Münzenberg has a price on his head back in Germany, and his employees have been instructed not to admit anyone they do not know personally. Since their arrival in Paris, Willi and Babette have been under surveillance by French police, both as a precaution and a measure of protection (French police note the existence of a Nazi plot to kidnap Münzenberg as early as July 1933). Münzenberg is used to being careful: he makes sure that preparations for his new venture do not take place in his own flat, instead renting an apartment in the smart 8th *arrondissement* to use as an office.

As Regler explains his mission to the suspicious young man who answers the door, adding that – he thinks – he is now actually employed by Münzenberg, Willi himself arrives and all is made clear. Regler is warmly welcomed and introduced to the team. Münzenberg's inner circle consists of five people who escaped to France with him: Babette Gross, Otto Katz, and the 'Three Musketeers': secretaries Hans Schulz and Jopp Fuellenberg, and driver Emil Berger. Inside, the living room is strewn with books and newspapers, the air filled with smoke. The atmosphere is energetic, feverish even. Regler may not yet realize it, but he has arrived at the epicentre of German anti-fascist activity in France, a hub of constant activity in profound contrast to the torpor that afflicts so many of his exiled compatriots. Among the staff are faces Regler knows well: the journalist Kurt Kesten, the writer and critic Alfred Kantorowicz, and Arthur Koestler, with his odd, otter face, a cigarette dangling from his lips. And at the heart of this operation is a man whose energy passes like an electric current to everyone around him.

Willi Münzenberg is a rare maverick in the tightly controlled Communist world. Through the wide-ranging activities of the International

Workers' Aid Trust (IWA or IAH) in Berlin, nicknamed 'the Münzenberg Trust' and encompassing newspapers, periodicals, associations, committees, film and stage productions, Willi has succeeded in reaching an international audience that the official Party press can only dream of. His unique gift as a propagandist – his genius, even – is his ability to persuade 'fellow travellers' – liberal sympathizers, progressive intellectuals and public figures – to lend their names to one of his organizations, often without realizing that they are providing a front for a Comintern-funded enterprise.† His success brings him extraordinary freedom: he answers directly to the Comintern in Moscow rather than to any local Communist party, a fact that incurs the jealousy of Germany's pious KPD leaders, notably Walter Ulbricht and Wilhelm Pieck, who loathe him with a passion. His early friendship with Lenin adds to his aura of untouchable power.

Münzenberg's style of working is frenetic, abrasive, unremitting. On his daily visits to the apartment he saunters into the room 'with all the casualness of a tank bursting through a wall' to issue orders at breakneck speed:

'"Write to Feuchtwanger," he would dictate to his secretary – tall, lame, self-effacing young Hans Schulz, who was known to work until three or four o'clock in the morning to get the ideas that incessantly spouted from Willi's fertile brain into shape – "Tell him articles received and so on. Ask him to do a pamphlet for us, ten thousand copies to be smuggled into Germany, upholding cultural heritage and so on, tradition of Goethe and so on, leave the rest to him, love and kisses."'

Yet his young collaborators – nicknamed *Münzenberg-Leute* ('Münzenberg People') – are devoted to their charismatic boss.

Babette is the physical opposite of Willi: tall, patrician, born into a wealthy middle-class family whose bourgeois values she and her sister Grete have heartily rejected, Babette's first marriage, to the

---

† The Comintern, or the Communist International, was an international association of national Communist parties founded by Lenin in 1919 to promote world revolution.

writer Fritz Gross, ended when Fritz was foolish enough to introduce her to Münzenberg. She and Fritz have a son, Peter, who
remains in Germany with Fritz's parents. Babette and Willi have
never bothered with anything as bourgeois as a wedding ceremony,
but they share everything – life, work, commitment – and consider
themselves married. Babette, who speaks fluent French, runs the
financial affairs of his publishing enterprises and handles all their
French contacts. She is also the only member of their circle, aside
from Emil, who can drive the green French-made Ford saloon that
they have purchased to replace the black Lincoln.

Regler arrives just as preparations are reaching a peak for Münzenberg's new project.

The Counter-Trial

Shortly after Marinus van der Lubbe was arrested for starting the
Reichstag Fire, the Nazis decided that it was inconceivable he could
have acted alone and promptly arrested three Bulgarian Communists
who happened to be in Berlin at the time, including Georgi Dimitrov, soon to become head of the Comintern. They then arrested
the chairman of the German Communist Party in the Reichstag,
Ernst Torgler, and charged all four men with being the masterminds
behind the fire.

Before the Nazis can even begin their trial, Willi Münzenberg
upstages them by organizing a mock counter-trial in London and
publishing *The Brown Book on the Reichstag Fire and Hitler Terror*. Put
together with amazing rapidity by Münzenberg's team in Paris, the
publication is intended to produce a major explosion, for the *Brown
Book* contains numerous accounts of Nazi brutality, backed up by
photographs, as well as ninety pages of documentation purport-
ing to show that a team of Nazi-sponsored arsonists entered the
Reichstag through a secret tunnel from Göring's official residence,
set light to the building, then returned through the tunnel to safety,
leaving the hapless van der Lubbe to take the blame. The entire

operation, argues the book, was conceived by the Nazis to create an event of sufficient dramatic impact to justify the suppression of their political opponents.

The Reichstag 'counter-trial' is held at the meeting hall of the British Law Society in London in September 1933 with the international press in full attendance. Münzenberg, who has made several trips to London to organize the event, has persuaded Sir Stafford Cripps to preside over it, along with H. G. Wells and the well-known Labour MP 'Red' Ellen Wilkinson. Over five days, thirty experts and witnesses are called. The verdict, handed down on 20 September and published in fifteen languages, concludes that there is no connection between the KPD and the Reichstag fire and that, in all likelihood, the fire had been lit under the direction of Nazi leaders.

By the time the actual trial itself begins, Münzenberg's propaganda has so effectively convinced the public of the innocence of the four accused Communists that the Leipzig court, under pressure from international public opinion, declares them not guilty. Van der Lubbe himself, having confessed to the crime, cannot be saved and is sentenced to death.

As Arthur Koestler later notes, in reality nobody in Münzenberg's extraordinary enterprise had the faintest idea of the concrete circumstances of the fire. 'We had to rely on guesswork, on bluffing, and on the intuitive knowledge of the methods and minds of our opposite numbers in totalitarian conspiracy.' If the world believed that the pantomime being played out before them was a struggle between truth and falsehood, the reality was somewhat muddier: both parties were lying, and both were afraid that the other knew more than they really did. For Koestler, at this stage a fledgling writer and an active member of the Communist Party, the experience of witnessing the trial and counter-trial taught him a valuable lesson in the nature of politics: 'That in the field of propaganda the half-truth was a weapon superior to the truth, and that to be on the defensive is to be defeated. It taught me above all that in this field a democracy must always be at a disadvantage against a totalitarian opponent.'

★

Over the next four years of his exile in Paris, Münzenberg will create and finance a dizzying array of committees, conventions, leagues and congresses on behalf of the Comintern. He seizes his first opportunity just a couple of months after his arrival in Paris, when on 10 May 1933 Nazis begin burning books in solemn ceremonies, each book denounced with a *Feuerspruch* – a 'fire speech' – and serenaded by the martial music of an SA band. Münzenberg immediately marshals dozens of international notables into a front called the 'World Committee for the Relief of the Victims of German Fascism' to protest against the suppression of intellectual freedom in Germany. After this comes the Committee Against Imperialist War and Fascism, the Congress of Anti-Fascist Workers, the Congress of Women Against War and Fascism, the Home for Refugee Children, the German Freedom Library, the Writers' Congress in Defence of Culture, the Committee for War Relief for Republican Spain, the Committee of Inquiry into Alleged Breaches of Non-Intervention Agreement in Spain, and so on. The aim of these organizations is always the same: to create publicity and raise funds for the anti-fascist cause, persuading prominent intellectuals to act as their public face.

Münzenberg's partner in many of these initiatives is a man who considers it his solemn duty to the German people to occupy the exhausting, often uncomfortable, position of figurehead of the exiled anti-fascist movement: the writer Heinrich Mann.

Mann

Heinrich Mann writes constantly – letters, speeches, articles – at home or in cafés, in hotels, bistros and railway-station waiting rooms. Mainly, though, he is working on his historical novel about the French king Henri IV. At his regular table at the Café Monnot in Nice the waiter knows him as Monsieur Henri. His partner, Nelly, types up everything, reads the newspapers, listens to the radio. They host guests, eat and drink well, enjoy the warm Mediterranean climate (but not the mosquitoes). Nelly keeps the windows open to encourage birds to fly in and out, setting out food for them. They do not appear to disturb the writer at work.

At sixty-three, Heinrich Mann is one of the oldest of the exiles, and one of the first to be stripped of his German citizenship. He has no papers so he cannot travel abroad, but his work in France keeps him endlessly occupied and he insists on making the long journey by train from Nice to Paris when there are meetings to attend, staying sometimes at the Hotel du Louvre, then, later, at the Hotel Lutetia. Unlike his brother Thomas, in exile in Switzerland and reticent about making overt political statements, Heinrich Mann has allowed himself to become the public face of a host of exiled opposition organizations: in October 1933 he is elected honorary president of the *Schutzverband Deutscher Schriftsteller*, the exiled German Writers' Union; in April 1934 he accepts the presidency of the exiled German PEN. On 10 May 1934, the first anniversary of the orgy of book burning that swept across Nazi Germany, he is to be found in Paris opening another of Willi Münzenberg's initiatives, the *Deutsche Freiheitsbibliothek,* the German Freedom Library. Situated in a corner of Montparnasse, at 65 boulevard Arago, the library gathers together in a few small rooms more than 20,000 books and pamphlets banned by Hitler, much of it material accumulated during the preparation of the *Brown Book*. Alfred Kantorowicz is its director.

For months Heinrich Mann dutifully turns up to all these manifestations of anti-fascist sentiment, but in truth he is frustrated: what is the point of all these worthy initiatives if nothing concrete is being done to defeat Hitler? There should be some kind of action. Mann looks at the French left and sees there signs of something he dearly wishes their German equivalents would emulate: co-operation. Grave events have shaken French society in recent months, pushing French Communists and Socialists to work together.

Stavisky

Despite their isolation the exiles do not live apart from the political ferment of the period but alongside it, witnessing and participating in the struggle between right and left that is convulsing Europe. In February 1934 violence erupts in Paris as far-right groups take to the streets in protest against the government in the aftermath of the Stavisky affair, a financial scandal involving a Ukrainian-born Jew, Alexandre Stavisky, which reaches to the very top of government.

In the febrile atmosphere that follows the riots, many immigrants are subjected to verbal attacks. Virulently anti-Semitic campaigns are run in some sections of the press underlining the fact that Stavisky is a foreign-born Jew. Proto-fascist leagues and their supporters use the excuse of government corruption not just to foment a climate of xenophobia, but to pressure the series of short-lived governments that come and go over the following months into adopting hardline anti-immigrant policies. When a Bulgarian revolutionary assassinates King Alexander of Yugoslavia and the French Foreign Minister Louis Barthou during an official visit to Marseilles in October 1934 a fresh wave of xenophobia is unleashed. The government subsequently introduces legislation denying foreigners residence permits if they do not have a work permit. Anyone who does not have a residence permit can be expelled. From now on, France is to serve only as a transit country.

Left-wing politicians intervene in parliament in defence of immigrants, the Socialist leader Léon Blum speaking up on behalf of the German exiles in particular: 'Among the men who leave their country rather than join a government that oppresses their thinking,' he tells the Minister of the Interior, 'the most deserving, the most heroic, those to whom you should reserve the most benevolent hospitality, are precisely those who have crossed the border alone, naked, without resources.' In his response, Home Secretary Marcel Régnier speaks of undesirable elements 'who not only clog up our towns and countryside, but compete with French workers, aggravating unemployment'.

But out of bad things better things can emerge: in response to the riots, trade unions organize a general strike and mass demonstrations against what they see as an attempted fascist coup. A Committee of Vigilance is formed by a group of prominent French intellectuals, including Louis Aragon, Henri Barbusse, Paul Eluard, André Gide and André Malraux.

Across Europe there is a growing realization among politicians of the left that the time has come to rise above their differences to form a united front against the growing threat of fascism. Contrary to the hopes of the fleeing exiles, Hitler's regime has failed to collapse. Instead, it grows stronger and bolder with every month that passes. When, in June 1934, hundreds of members of the SA are murdered by the SS on Hitler's orders, the exiles celebrate, believing that the 'Night of the Long Knives' signals the imminent disintegration of the Nazi regime. Far from it. In early August, Gustav Regler is at the printers engaged in correcting the proofs of an article foretelling the downfall of the new Reich when he hears the news that, following the death of the elderly President Hindenburg, Hitler has issued a decree declaring that the offices of President and Chancellor are to be unified. He will now be known as Germany's *Führer*, its supreme leader. All members of the armed forces will be required to swear an oath of loyalty to him.

No, the Nazi regime has not fallen. Instead, Hitler has consolidated his power so swiftly and completely that the citizens who elected him Chancellor of Germany have barely realized that he is now their dictator.

For Heinrich Mann it is obvious: it was the fragmentation of the opposition to Hitler that allowed the Nazis to triumph. When are the party apparatchiks going to get the message, bury their differences and work together for the common good?

Or is this just a pipe dream?

★

Meanwhile, German immigrants are arriving in France at a rate of hundreds, sometimes thousands, per month. These are no longer the prominent intellectuals and political leaders who fled in the first wave, but increasingly desperate individuals and families, the majority Jewish, many without any means of survival. When, in January 1935, the people of the coal-mining region of the Saar basin are asked to decide in a referendum whether to continue under the administration of the League of Nations, become part of France, or reunite with Germany, they vote resoundingly in favour of joining the Reich.[†] The following day several thousand new refugees arrive in France, both native Saarlanders and Germans who fled there to escape Nazi persecution. The vast majority are destitute.

With each successive wave of emigration, the demographic changes, and the French welcome cools accordingly. Under the new laws immigrants are shunted from one office to another, trapped in a vicious circle: no identity card without a job. No job without an identity card. Sooner or later, everyone ends up committing an offence, whether knowingly or not. First off comes the blue paper: *refoulement* (being sent back). Next is the pink one: *expulsion*.

At the annual dinner of the British Legion, held at the Hotel Lutetia on Friday, 25 November 1934, the assembled guests break into a lusty rendition of a traditional children's song:

> The more we are together,
> together, together
> The more we are together
> the happier we'll be,
> For your friends are my friends,
> And my friends are your friends,
> So the more we are together,
> The happier we'll be.

[†] Formerly part of Prussia and Bavaria, the Saar region was occupied by the British and French after the 1914–18 war under a fifteen-year League of Nations mandate.

Adrienne

Gisèle Freund has finally finished her doctoral thesis but cannot afford to have it printed, as required by the rules of the Sorbonne, which means she has to postpone defending it. One chilly morning in March 1935, she is strolling down rue de l'Odéon when her eye is drawn to a cat, asleep in a Louis XV armchair in the window of an antique shop. A little further on she notices a bookshop, painted grey. Above the door is a sign:

LA MAISON DES AMIS DES LIVRES
READING SOCIETY
BOOKSHOP
A. MONNIER

Out at the front hangs a little box filled with books for sale. She stops to rummage through it. Finding a volume whose title and price appeal, Gisèle enters the shop. In the centre of the room is a long table where several customers are leafing through the latest publications. Portraits of writers hang on the walls between the book-lined shelves. Seated at a work table facing the entrance is a small, plump woman of around forty with short-cropped chestnut hair. She wears a grey waistcoat over a woollen jumper and a long, pleated peasant skirt. Behind her, in the corner, is a small black stove. The woman raises her head and gives Gisèle an encouraging smile. Her greenish-brown eyes reflect a sharp intelligence; her whole being emanates an air of absolute serenity. This is the owner, Adrienne Monnier, poet, writer, feminist and publisher, something of a legend in Parisian literary circles. Monnier's *Maison des Amis des Livres* (The House of Book Lovers) is not just a bookshop but a lending library, a publishing house, and a gallery space. Since the 1920s she and Sylvia Beach, who runs the equally famous English-language bookshop, Shakespeare & Company, across the road, have created twin literary hubs where anyone who aspires to be anyone in the French or English avant-garde will find a warm welcome and a courageous publisher. James Joyce, T. S. Eliot, André Breton, Samuel Beckett, Paul Eluard, André Gide – all meet here, attracted by the warm welcome, the generous hospitality offered by Monnier (a keen cook), and the knowledge that here are two women unafraid to publish works that other publishers have shunned. It was Sylvia Beach who brought James Joyce's *Ulysses* into the world, Adrienne Monnier who published the French translation.

Adrienne and Gisèle strike up a conversation. It doesn't take long for Adrienne to learn that the young woman is a student and an anti-Nazi exile who knows very little about French literature but speaks excellent French and fluent English. Adrienne encourages her to take out a subscription to the lending library, promises to advise her on what to read, and offers to take her across the street to meet Sylvia. Soon, Gisèle is a regular visitor to rue de l'Odéon, often joined by Walter Benjamin, whom Monnier greatly likes and admires. Adrienne becomes Gisèle's mentor, her protector and, for a while, her partner, transforming the young photographer's prospects by introducing her to the French literary world. One of Gisèle's first portrait photographs is of André Malraux, who then invites her to cover the first International Congress of Writers for the Defence of Culture, due to take place in June.

Gisèle's new life is finally beginning to take shape when she pays a reluctant visit to the German consulate because her passport has expired. Instead of stamping the passport, the official tears it up.

'You are no longer a German citizen,' he says.

The 'Internationale'

There is a new energy in the air in Paris, a sense of possibility, even hope, that the dark forces of fascism can be pushed back by the combined efforts of a united opposition. When Willi Münzenberg decides to organize the first Congress for the Defence of Culture, held in June 1935, he manages to persuade two hundred writers from thirty-seven countries to attend: a veritable who's who of liberal and leftist thought, representing a wide range of political and social standpoints. They gather in the enormous Mutualité assembly hall in the 15th *arrondissement* to listen as Heinrich Mann delivers the keynote address, received with rapturous applause by the audience in the packed and sweaty auditorium. Henri Barbusse, André Malraux, Louis Aragon, Ilya Ehrenburg, Mikhail Koltsov, Boris Pasternak, Bertolt Brecht are in attendance; E. M. Forster and Aldous Huxley represent the UK. Walter Benjamin hovers on the fringes of this illustrious gathering. He has not been invited to speak, but he attends the lectures and discussions, mainly so that he can have the pleasure of spending time with his friend Brecht, visiting from Denmark.

The great triumph of the Congress is the moment when André Gide proclaims his allegiance to Communism, delivering a speech that causes a sensation, for here is one of Europe's most prominent intellectuals openly engaging with the Communist cause. Louis Aragon, filled with pride at the success of this conversion (for which he takes the credit) is among the many admirers surrounding the writer. More dramatic still is the appearance of a masked anti-Nazi activist who has managed to escape Germany to deliver his speech, at great personal risk. With him, he brings proof that there exists a clandestine literature in Germany and holds out the hope that a 'genuine opposition to the Nazis is possible'.

The audience is intoxicated. Documenting the excitement are Gisèle Freund and Fred Stein. They hold up their cameras, slyly capturing the faces of the speakers. Freund observes 'Henri Barbusse, his features already blighted by illness; Aldous Huxley, half blind behind his thick glasses; Bertolt Brecht, with his shy smile and his head shaved like a prisoner's; Ilya Ehrenburg, with his lion's mane; Heinrich Mann, who looks like a quiet bourgeois.'

Anna Seghers makes an earnest speech. Lion Feuchtwanger, up from Sanary-sur-Mer, is delighted when the Soviet journalist Mikhail Koltsov offers him an official visit to Moscow. Gustav Regler, meanwhile, is so carried away by the heady atmosphere that when it is his turn to address the audience he forgets his carefully composed speech, and instead pulls two anti-Nazi leaflets out of his pocket and waves them in the air, challenging the Gestapo agent – whom he is convinced is seated somewhere in the audience – to come up and look at them.

'I want to say a word to that spectral figure from the secret police who follows us around as a shadow follows the sun. I want to say this to him: "You have killed Mühsam! You are holding Ossietsky! But you cannot silence our voice! You will never extinguish our love for the people, or the flame of our passion for truth!"'

To Regler's astonishment, at this moment the whole assembly rises to its feet and, as one, begins to sing. Regler is called off-stage by the Communist poet Johannes R. Becher.

' "You must be mad!"

' "Can't you hear what they're singing?" I asked in a voice that trembled with emotion.

' "That's just it!" he said, having to shout now against the mighty chorus that arose. "The Internationale! You've ruined everything – you've given us away! This congress can't pretend to be neutral any longer. God almighty! You'll be turned out of the Party!"'

Regler fails to comprehend the meaning of this warning. He looks at Gide, Barbusse and all the others on the platform who have stood up and are joining in.

' "It will be heard across the Rhine," I said, breathless.

' "You're a saboteur," said Becher.'

Four days later, at the meeting of his Communist Party cell, Regler is taken to task by the Party representative, who informs the writer that it is not for any individual comrade to decide when the 'Internationale' shall or shall not be sung.

'Revolutions,' declares the Party official, 'are not required to be spontaneous.'

The representative then reminds Regler that the Party is in an undercover phase, and that it is counter-revolutionary to break cover. The song is like everything else – a means to an end.

★

Alfred Kantorowicz, a close friend of Regler's, a member of his communist cell and an assiduously bitter diary-writer, observes the tendency of his 'attention-grabbing' fellow writers to steal the limelight. His Party comrades, meanwhile, are 'blatherers, plotters, gossips, office revolutionaries' who devote (precisely) 60 per cent of their energy toward bigging themselves up, 35 per cent toward tarnishing the reputation of others, and only 5 per cent on putting their ideas to use. Anna Seghers, he adds, is 'peculiar', though he is impressed by her, despite her noticeable dislike of him. He concludes that her characters are two-dimensional, and claims she will never be a great writer due to her lack of humanity.

Aldous Huxley returns to Sanary-sur-Mer disgusted by the overtly Communist nature of the event. 'I had hoped for serious, technical discussions – but in fact the thing simply turned out to be a series of public meetings organised by the French Communist writers for their own glorification and the Russians as a piece of Soviet propaganda.' So much for the undercover phase.

The congress is not the only show in town: huge demonstrations are taking place around Paris, culminating on Bastille Day, 14 July, in a mass demonstration celebrating the official birth of the French Popular Front. Half a million men, women and children march arm in arm from place de la Bastille to Porte de Vincennes. They carry flags and banners, placards declaring their commitment to peace and the fight against fascism. With fists raised they sing the 'Marseillaise' and the 'Internationale'. They cry 'Bread and work!' 'Unity will win!' and 'Popular Front'. What a moment of hope for the German exiles to witness this symbolic moment in French history! All is surely not yet lost.

On the same day, a rival march organized by the right-wing Front National marches toward the Tomb of the Unknown Soldier waving the banners of the Croix de Feu. The two groups neither meet nor clash, as rival crowds have done so frequently in recent years, but a short report in a French newspaper reveals the tantalizing information that, just a few days prior to this event, about a hundred young

Germans dressed in brown shirts, with swastikas and wearing back-packs, arrived in a bus, escorted by a police car, and drew up in front of the Lycée Michelet in the Parisian suburb of Vanves. The young men lined up for inspection, saluted their leader with raised arms and then took up quarters in the school. On the same day another group of Germans arrived in coaches for a sojourn at the Hotel Lutetia. The newspaper does not comment on their attire, but they cannot be exiles since exiles do not travel en masse and certainly cannot afford the prices at the best hotel on the Left Bank. There are similar reports of large numbers of Germans in various parts of the Parisian sub-urbs. The author of the article poses the obvious question: is there a connection between the arrival of these foreigners and the demon-strations planned for 14 July? Or are they simply innocent groups of German tourists come to admire Paris in the summer?

Heinrich Mann travels back to the south of France, where he and Nelly move to an apartment in the seaside resort of Bandol for a few weeks' holiday. Mann is exhausted: on top of his political activities, he has just completed the first volume of his historical novel, *Henri IV*. But the burden of leadership weighs heavily on him and even on holiday he cannot fully rest: while he is in Bandol he writes to Willi Münzenberg to say there is no time to lose in their plans to topple the Nazis. The French left are uniting to fight fascism. Something has to be done by us, the German exiles, something more than just fine speeches.

Débrouillez-vous

Gisèle Freund arrives at Adrienne Monnier's flat at 18 rue de l'Odeon in a state of panic. Following her loss of German citizenship she has received an expulsion order and has been given forty-eight hours to pack her things. Adrienne, always calm, immediately offers to let Gisèle stay with her until the whole thing is cleared up. Sylvia – with whom she shares the flat – is away in the United States, and living in a French home will protect her. Nothing more is said. Gisèle accepts the offer and moves in the same day.

At the Préfecture de Police the waiting room is already packed with men, women, children, the air pungent with sweat and tobacco. French police officers try to corral the anxious, desperate foreigners: *Here, take this ticket. Wait your turn. They will call your number.* It is not until three in the afternoon that Gisèle is called to converse with an exhausted-looking clerk. She explains the problem: she has no passport, and now here is this order to quit the country, for reasons unknown – is he able shed any light on the matter? The clerk gazes impassively at the young woman, offers a gallic shrug, 'It is none of my business why they want you out, Mademoiselle.' Then he gives her a week's reprieve and, with the brusque admonition *'Débrouillez-vous'* ('Sort it out yourself'), he calls his next customer.

Thousands of refugees are in the same boat. They are France's 'undesirables'. Every day, anxious former citizens of Germany contact one of the various committees set up to offer aid. 'I have received an expulsion order, with no mention of the reasons why; I've got ten days. But I haven't committed any offence and my papers are in order. What do I do now? Where do I go?' There follow countless visits to the Préfecture de Police, a giant, dirty green building on the Île de la Cité where they are confronted not just with an unfamiliar language but with a total lack of understanding of the nature of their situation.

'Are you a Communist?' a police inspector asks theatre critic Maximilian Scheer.

'I'm a theatre critic,' he replies.

'Then why did you leave Germany?'

'Because they don't just persecute Communists, Sir.'

It is an absurdist nightmare, made worse by the fact that the situation is no better elsewhere: no country wants these refugees. In fact, they compete with each other in the regulations and restrictions they impose to make themselves less desirable to this desperate mass of humankind in search of that intangible thing they call a home.

Walter Benjamin writes to Max Horkheimer: 'My situation is

as difficult as any financial position that does not involve debts can possibly be. [. . .] I have reduced my living expenses enormously, compared to what they were in April when I returned to Paris. I am consequently living as a boarder with some émigrés. Beyond that, I have succeeded in obtaining permission to take my midday meal at a restaurant that has a special arrangement for French intellectuals. In the first place, however, this permission is temporary and, in the second place, I can make use of it only on those days I am not in the library, for the restaurant is very far from there. I will only mention in passing that I ought to renew my *carte d'identité* but do not have the 100 francs this requires. Since it involves a fee of 50 francs, I have also not yet been able to join the *Presse Etrangère*, which I was urged to do for administrative reasons. The paradoxical thing about this situation is that my work has probably never been closer to being publicly useful than it is right now.'

The Popular Front

In July 1935, the sense of urgency that has been pushing European parties of the left to co-operate finally penetrates as far as Moscow, where Georgi Dimitrov makes a formal announcement at the VIIth Congress of the Comintern to confirm what is already happening on the ground, by inviting Communists all over Europe to embrace their erstwhile foes and form a 'People's Front Against Fascism and War'. What a shame it has taken them so long: in Germany the combined vote for the Communist and Social Democratic parties would have easily kept Hitler out of power.

While KPD leaders Walter Ulbricht and Wilhelm Pieck are tasked with opening formal negotiations with the German Social Democratic Party's exiled Executive (SOPADE) in Prague, Willi Münzenberg's mission is to gather together the exiled political communities in Paris: the Communists and social democrats, the SAPD and other prominent opponents of Hitler. He is, in short, to follow where the French have led and lay the ground for a German Popular Front.

An informal circle dubbed the 'Provisional Committee for the Preparation of a German Popular Front' had already been set up the previous month by a group of intellectuals – Heinrich Mann among them – frustrated by the lack of action from the politicians. They have been holding meetings at the Hôtel des Sociétés Savantes on rue Serpente near the Odéon metro station, signing themselves up as a club of writers and academics under the name 'Literary Society'. Münzenberg's first step is to persuade the group to join his new, bigger, better, as yet unnamed, committee. His next is to identify a suitable venue for his grand new venture. Not just a café where a dozen people can cram round a table to shout at one another, but a fitting backdrop for a political project of this ambition – a place where large numbers of delegates can gather. Where better, then, than a hotel; not a modest establishment like the Hôtel des Sociétés Savantes, which speaks of scientists and dusty academics, but a grand setting where they can meet like a proper government-in-exile? And which hotel could be more appropriate than the only luxury establishment on the Left Bank, popular among intellectuals, artists and politicians alike, that glamorous, much-loved Paris institution, the Hotel Lutetia? Dubbed by some the 'Switzerland of Paris' for its willingness to host diverse political groups, the Lutetia is neutral territory on which anyone can meet. So a booking for a conference of exiled German political activists is nothing the discreet staff cannot cope with.

This is the moment when we move in from the outside.

Who is it that Willi charges with making the booking? It won't be him: he doesn't speak French. His secretary, Hans Schulz, perhaps? Or Babette? At the desk, the polite request: *Have you a room free for a meeting of several dozen guests? Perhaps a tour of the available salons? We don't yet know how many will attend or with what frequency, but I can pay the deposit now (courtesy of the Comintern, since you ask).* The President Salon is the biggest and most exotic. Maximum capacity at least 250.

Will you be requiring refreshments, monsieur/madame?

We cannot answer that question, because nobody ever records

what political activists eat and drink at their meetings. One can only reflect that the provision of food would be a surefire way of ensuring enthusiastic attendance among a group of semi-starving exiles.

The Lutetia Committee

It is a mild day in late September 1935 when the inaugural meeting of the Lutetia Committee takes place. In they file, stepping out of the bustle of boulevard Raspail and through the revolving door into the hotel lobby to take in the first sight, beneath their feet, of a mosaic depicting a ship. Above their heads hangs an enormous chandelier. On a bench by the door, three white-gloved errand boys sit poised for action while the head concierge, Roger Harrault (blue redingote, red collar) attends to a guest. Many of those present today are the same hungry exiles whose habitual haunts are the cafés on boulevard du Montparnasse. How often have they passed the Lutetia as they wander along boulevard Raspail, gazed longingly through the window of the tea shop? And now, inside at last. *Which way to the President Salon please? Upstairs, to the right, first floor.* Impassive staff take in the parade of threadbare suits, grey faces, worn-out shoes.

Willi Münzenberg looks on with satisfaction as the delegates enter the enormous banqueting room. Nearly everyone he has invited has shown up: there are four Communist Party representatives, twenty-two Social Democrats, and twenty-five other participants, including several well-known intellectuals in the form of Heinrich Mann, Georg Bernhard, and even Leopold Schwarzschild, editor-in-chief of the successful German émigré weekly *Das Neue Tage-Buch*, a man not known for his Communist sympathies. Heinrich Mann has once again taken the long train journey up to Paris from Nice and is staying at the hotel.

The air grows thick with smoke, the atmosphere a mixture of optimism and mistrust. Münzenberg takes charge, proposing that Heinrich Mann be named as president. This proposition is adopted unanimously, adding to Mann's growing portfolio of presidencies.

A smaller, ten-man Lutetia executive committee is formed, its first aim to promote anti-fascist unity between the two main, previously hostile German opposition parties, the KPD and the SPD, and to work toward the creation of a German Popular Front. Mann is its chairman, of course; Münzenberg is at his side.

Whereas in their former lives the comforts of fine living were taken for granted, now a delegate might take advantage of a break in proceedings to avail himself of the rest rooms to enjoy the simple pleasure of sweet-smelling soap as he runs his hands under hot water and gazes at his face in the mirror, reflecting on how much he has changed, and not for the better, as an attendant passes him a towel to dry his hands. There is the awful thought, passing fleetingly through his head, that had the attendant not been there he might have pocketed the hand towel, or torn off a few sheets of paper to take back to his *hôtel garni*, where small squares of newspaper impaled on a hook must serve.

Heading back toward the smoke-filled room, he might stop for a moment to light a cigarette, his ears automatically attuning to the familiar soundtrack of the lunchtime service: the sound of clanking plates, the murmur of conversation, the pleasant melody of a piano, someone playing a ragtime tune. Everything, everywhere, a reminder of a past that is no longer in reach.

Your stomach rumbles. You're used to ignoring it now. Your trousers have grown loose, the belt tightened by an extra notch or two. The urge, almost impossible to resist, to reach out and grab the fresh rolls from the bread basket while the waiter's back is turned. The tantalizing smell of good coffee. An attractive young woman passes by. She doesn't even see you. The scent of perfume lingers in her wake.

Everywhere, this air of normality. Suddenly you want to scream *Wake up!* But people living normal lives cannot imagine that their normality will ever end in a single, cataclysmic moment of change. A bomb dropping, war declared, a dictator taking power. Everything lost, in a single moment. Another sound: of German being spoken, loudly, voices raised in argument (they are always arguing).

It may attract unwanted attention, even hostility, from guests who turn their heads, annoyed, to identify the source of all the noise. But the Lutetia staff have perfected their neutral gaze. They do not judge, not outwardly at least. They are here to make their guests' lives comfortable, to anticipate their needs and remain invisible. Standing on the edges of the meeting, a tray of coffee ready to be served, how are they to know that they will soon be taking orders from men speaking German in this same hotel?

In truth, the German exiles make little impression on the Lutetia, for the simple reason that they are just one group among hundreds who hire a room for meetings in any given year. They are free to enter, come and go as they please, attend their conferences, sit in the bar if they can afford the drinks, eat in the restaurant if they can afford the food, sleep in the bedrooms if . . . Yes, we know, we know. It is busy here, with the banquets and balls, the press conferences and the annual jamborees. Why should anyone pay more attention to a band of German politicians than to the hundreds of energetically drunk Russian exiles, victims of the Bolshevik revolution, who crowd into the President Salon for their annual New Year's Ball? This is neutral territory, after all; who cares what politics the guests espouse? In March 1936 Nikolai Bukharin, former head of the Comintern, turns up at the head of a small delegation and stays for several weeks. Bukharin is followed everywhere by Stalin's secret police, the NKVD. He is also being watched by the French police, for different reasons. When they receive a tip-off concerning a possible attempt on the famous Bolshevik's life by a group of White Russian exiles, they cordon off the Lutetia for two entire days to safeguard the Soviet delegation.

The Lutetia Crowd

Between 1935 and 1938 the German exiles meet several times at the Lutetia, sometimes the smaller executive group known as the

'Lutetia Circle', sometimes the full conference, the 'Lutetia Committee'. The Nazis disdainfully name them the 'Lutetia crowd' and try to spy on them. Their goal is ambitious: to thrash out a political and social plan, its theoretical framework and the fundamental articles of a new German constitution to be ready to be put in place on the day that Hitler finally falls, which surely must be soon. Heinrich Mann, who places a great deal of importance on style and respect for tradition, feels particularly at home at the Lutetia, always staying in a suite, although one wonders how much time he has to enjoy its comforts between his many meetings. He writes to his brother Thomas: 'You can reach me by letter or telegraph until the 25th in Paris, Hotel Lutetia, Bd. Raspail.'

It is no easy task, this *rapprochement* between old enemies: while the Social Democrats in Paris declare themselves ready to re-establish communications with the Communists, their leaders in Prague still

Heinrich Mann at the Hotel Lutetia, 1935, by Fred Stein

refuse to co-operate. Lion Feuchtwanger, in the capital for a few days, manages to squeeze in a committee meeting amid his busy schedule of amorous liaisons. He finds the whole thing 'un-impressive', and when he lunches with Heinrich Mann the following day he declares Mann to be 'very upset' at the lack of progress. After a further dinner with Mann, Willi Münzenberg and Babette Gross ('boring'), Feuchtwanger decides he cannot face any more earnest political talk and makes an excuse not to meet again.

Meanwhile, in Germany, on 15 September 1935 Hitler introduces the Nuremberg Laws – the Reich Citizenship Law and the Law for the Protection of German Blood and German Honour – which form the basis of the official persecution of Jews on the basis of race. The Saar referendum earlier in the year has already led to a sharp increase in Germans arriving in France. Now the number of Jewish refugees seeking asylum begins to grow exponentially.

Eva Tichauer is still living away from home when she learns that her younger brother Felix has died of the lung condition that has plagued him since birth. His death leaves her the sole child of her parents, their only hope for the future.

The German Popular Front

Over a hundred people turn up for the meeting of the Lutetia Committee on 2 February 1936 to mark the official creation of the German Popular Front, an illustrious gathering representing every facet of pre-Nazi German political and intellectual life. Hein-rich Mann takes the chair. Fred Stein snaps photographs of the attendees.

The meeting is another remarkable coup for Münzenberg, but his greatest challenge is not to unite dozens of diverse groups and individuals but to navigate the baggage they bring with them from Germany. Prior to 1933 the Social Democrats were the more influential of the two main opposition parties. In France, the balance of power has shifted, with Communists significantly outnumbering Social Democrats. France has a well-organized Communist Party with strong ties to the KPD, while the German Social Democrat leadership in exile in Prague have no shared strategy with the French Socialist Party, and are opposed to the Popular Front policy. Several SPD members living in France disagree with the policies of their leadership and have formed new political groupings without formally leaving the Party.

Making matters more complicated still is the presence of dozens of minor parties, in addition to the three main groups. Add to this the anti-fascist Catholics and a notable number of unaffiliated 'pacifists and democrats' and Münzenberg's achievement in bringing them together appears all the more miraculous. The KPD's Walter Ulbricht and Wilhelm Pieck, by contrast, are bogged down in negotiations in Prague, neither side willing to overcome the political resentments created by the Comintern-directed 'social fascism' doctrine of the 1920s and early 1930s, which encouraged Communists to link social democracy with fascism. The SPD in turn considered Stalinists as fascists – the result being that the two parties were so busy fighting one another they failed to prevent the Nazis from seizing power. Reports of the meeting at the smart Parisian hotel, with its banqueting room filled with Weimar Germany's most prominent anti-fascist notables, cause Ulbricht and Pieck a violent pang of jealousy. Worse, among the crowd is the former German Minister of the Interior, Rudolf Breitscheid – immediately recognisable by his height and his shock of white hair – and former Prussian Interior Minister Albert Grzesinski, both prominent SPD members who are not part of SOPADE. Already rumours are swirling around Prague that Breitscheid and Grzesinski are seeking to exploit the differences between the tactics of Ulbricht and Pieck in Prague and Münzenberg in Paris.

Immediately after the conference a slew of draft manifestos, programmes and constitutions is published calling, in varying terms, for freedom, equality and unity among the German people, but none of them is couched in terms remotely acceptable to the Communist

Party. Walter Ulbricht is not pleased. The Comintern has instructed the KPD to embrace the Popular Front policy, but its first success is not his. Instead, it belongs to his hated rival, Münzenberg.

A Gestapo spy seeking to identify the major players in émigré politics could well have benefited from Gustav Regler's sketch of Walter Ulbricht: 'He had a face stiff with malice that was conscious of its own ugliness and sought to relieve it with a symbolical Lenin-beard round the plump chin, a hairy appendage that did not, however, rid his faun-like mouth of any of its petty-bourgeois arrogance. His eyes, the right sharply observant and the left half-closed, were hidden behind a schoolmaster's glasses. His forehead, furrowed with the wrinkles of unfruitful thought, was rendered higher, but not more intellectual, by the retreating hair. He had the look of a lapsed priest who visits obscure houses.'

Suspicious Minds

Nobody knows how many Gestapo agents there are in Paris. It doesn't really matter, because their shadowy presence is felt everywhere and that is precisely the point. They follow exiled activists to meetings, note their movements, photograph their contacts. Their aim is not just to find out what the exiles are up to: they want to sow discord, to divide the fragile unity of the émigré community. They steal passports or money, plant leaflets attacking the host country to incriminate them. And, of course, they recruit from among the émigrés themselves. Volunteers are not hard to find among the poor and the desperate. In exchange for the promise of a safe return to Germany, or the release of imprisoned relatives, some luckless soul can be persuaded to inveigle themselves into one of the exile groups and then betray it. And so each new arrival is questioned carefully: What political group did you belong to? Whom did you know? How did you escape Germany? At the Lutetia meetings Willi Münzenberg's secretary Hans Schulz keeps a wary eye out for suspicious faces, while Emil sits discreetly nearby, apparently engrossed in a newspaper but with a pistol ready in his pocket, just in case.

Gustav Regler's girlfriend, Marie Louise Vogeler, is an illustrator and goldsmith. She is a gentle soul with no interest in politics, 'fresh as summer rain, orderly as the cornfields, dreaming as the pine-woods'. She left Germany to join Regler in his exile but she is unhappy. One day she tells him simply, 'I must go home.'

Regler is shattered, blaming himself for her unhappiness. 'What right had I to drag her with me into the hazards and uncertainties of this life of exile? Every day she spent in Paris made her more of an émigré, and perhaps before long the way of return would be finally closed.'

The following evening Marie Louise leaves Paris. As a precaution Regler does not accompany her to the station. Since she won't be able to write to him directly, they arrange that she should write to him by way of a friend. They've been together since 1928. This is not their first crisis, but it is the most serious.

Days go by. Regler hears nothing from her, neither does the friend who is to receive the letters on his behalf. During the day, Münzenberg keeps Regler hard at work, but in the evenings he wanders by the Seine, anxious and preoccupied. Have the Gestapo arrested her? Will he receive a message informing him that she will not be released unless he returns to Germany? Marie Louise is neither political nor Jewish: she should be able to cross into Germany and back again without incident. But anxiety gnaws at him. At one point he nearly loses patience and is about to enter the German Embassy to demand news of her but restrains himself just in time: he knows he is on the Gestapo wanted list. To enter Nazi 'territory' would be to expose himself to danger. The following day Regler visits the Louvre, seeking out Marie Louise's favourite paintings and once again torturing himself with questions: why is he risking the love of his life for the sake of fighting 'those gangsters in Berlin'? Standing in front of Raphael's portrait of Giovanna of Aragon, he takes a decision: he will tell Marie Louise that if only she will return to Paris he will put politics aside.

When he returns to work, Münzenberg calls Regler into his office to meet a man who has just escaped from Germany. The man brings news of Carl von Ossietsky, the imprisoned editor of the liberal review *Weltbühne*. The Nazis have tortured him. They made him stand to attention whenever a Nazi guard passed by. They forced him to kneel in the mud, they beat him and trampled on him, calling him 'Polish swine'. The escapee also brings details of the death of the anarchist Erich Mühsam. 'He had been secretly hanged from a latrine door.'

Of course Regler cannot put politics aside. 'These things were larger than ourselves and our private lives. No one had the right to give up.'

He returns to his work. Among the many tasks at hand is a text denouncing the Nazis' attacks on intellectuals in Germany. Typed in minuscule print, the paper is concealed inside a seed packet featuring a brightly coloured illustration of a tomato plant and the words *Tomato – Miracle of the Markets!* The packet will be distributed and sold to horticultural enthusiasts who will open it and find inside not just their seeds and instructions for the care of the plants, but an eloquently written diatribe against the Third Reich calling for different seeds to be sown. Regler and his comrades conceal anti-Nazi pamphlets not just in seed packets but in instruction booklets, scented shampoo samples, innocuous-looking weather balloons. Longer tracts such as the *Communist Manifesto* are rebound into familiar-looking editions of German classics, such as Schiller's *Maid of Orleans*. These are *Tarnschriften*, 'hidden writings', publications produced covertly by a variety of anti-Nazi groups between 1933 and 1945 as a form of political resistance, with the intention of informing and inspiring dissent in Nazi Germany. The Gestapo confiscate any leaflets they find. In German schools teachers warn children to keep an eye on their parents' letters from abroad.

There is still no word from Marie Louise. Regler – once a Catholic – even goes to Notre-Dame to light a candle. And then the miracle occurs: the following day Marie Louise returns, with her passport renewed and bringing tales of how things back home are not nearly as bad as Regler and his comrades think. She has brought some newspapers and reviews, including a passage from a poet, Gottfried Benn, who assures the exiles that if only they had stayed in Germany they would not have been treated badly by the German people.

'I felt chilled and the most hateful suspicions arose in my mind. Her new passport lay on the table, the photograph embossed with a swastika. What if they had let her come back simply as a spy, telling her that her family would be held accountable for her behaviour? Such things were by no means unknown. I looked at her neat, braided hair, her smooth white neck, the blouse of hand-woven material, everything about her that appeared flawless and unsullied, like a room with Easter curtains opening its windows to the spring. Was she capable of betrayal?

'Perhaps tomorrow she would go home again . . . I turned away my head, but the passport was still there, and she seemed to have become a stranger, herself stamped with the swastika.'

Instructions for the Dollina

Across Europe, the Popular Front movement is gaining pace. Success is in the air, if only the Germans would stop squabbling. Heinrich Mann dutifully makes the Paris–Nice journey several times in as many weeks, a voyage of many exhausting hours by train. In Paris he passes from one meeting to the next as he and Münzenberg tirelessly attempt to soothe the fragile egos and self-absorbed resentments of Germany's political opposition. At least at the Lutetia he has a comfortable bed to sleep in.

In the south of France Mann's fellow exiles, those artists who can afford to live at leisure in a pleasant colony by the sea, pass their time reading from their works, taking tea, drinking wine, and bitching about each other.

Instructions for the Dollina is a pamphlet aimed at photography lovers. Concealed within the pages of this instruction booklet for a 35mm folding camera is material produced by – among others – Heinrich Mann, who has written an essay on behalf of the German Popular Front in an attempt to convince the people back home that, in exile, political opponents to Hitler are unified and ready for action.

On 7 March 1936, Hitler's troops occupy the demilitarized Rhineland.

Elections

When Eva Tichauer returns home for the school holidays in 1936 she finds her parents' flat bustling with visitors. The French have just elected a Popular Front government under the leadership of Léon Blum, who – thrillingly for Eva – turns up at their flat in rue Nollet to visit her parents. After so many disappointments, here is something positive not just for the French but for foreigners too, because almost immediately after the election the new government announces a series of measures designed to alleviate the situation of immigrants in France. Most significant among them is a decree applying to all refugees from Germany, whether or not they have been stripped of their German nationality: they are to be issued with an identity certificate that allows the holder to travel through any country that is a signatory of the Geneva Convention. In order to ensure that these certificates are issued only to genuine refugees, the French government invites four prominent Germans and four French citizens to sit on a committee which is to serve as an advisory body to the Minister of the Interior. One of the German émigrés selected to be on the commission is Eva Tichauer's father, Theodor. The role provides a welcome break for Eva's father after three years of failed attempts to be something he is not. Theodor Tichauer is a lawyer and an intellectual. However much he tries, he cannot just reinvent himself as a metal worker or a tie salesman.

At no other moment in their exile do the German political émigrés feel as much at home in Paris as during those first months of the victorious Popular Front government. It is a time of joy and hope: men, women and children march to the place de la Bastille and the place de la Nation. Workers go on strike, occupying their factories. Strangers bring them food and drink. Everyone joins in. In Spain, too, a Republican Popular Front government has been formed. A cascade of concessions follows: a forty-hour working week, paid holidays, collective bargaining. Anna Seghers takes her children to a huge, boisterous demonstration in Vincennes. The event sticks in Pierre's mind for its joyfulness, along with the memory of an exhibition his mother takes him to afterwards, organized by some of the German exiles and showing the first Nazi concentration camps.

Paperwork

Safely tucked under Adrienne Monnier's protective wing, Gisèle Freund's journey from penniless refugee to citizen of France is almost complete when she enters a *mariage blanc* with a friend of Adrienne's named Pierre Blum. A few months later, the temporarily renamed Gisèle Blum obtains French citizenship. Then it is back to the Faculty of Arts at the Sorbonne to undergo the academic ritual of defending her doctoral dissertation before a panel of academics. Walter Benjamin sits in the amphitheatre to support her, and later pens a favourable review of her ground-breaking study on photography in nineteenth-century France. The thesis is formally accepted. Adrienne Monnier proposes translating it into French and publishing it. Gisèle can now truthfully claim that she has the same publisher as the great James Joyce.

With her studies out of the way and no obstacles to her employment, Gisèle is now free to devote herself entirely to photography. She starts taking on freelance assignments for a new American magazine, *Life*, at the same time building up her portfolio of portrait photographs of writers and intellectuals. In Adrienne, Gisèle has the immense good fortune to have found a patron who can offer her an opportunity to observe, on a full stomach, the constant stream of distinguished guests who turn up for dinner at Adrienne's and then, eventually, photograph them.

It is at one of Adrienne's dinners that Gisèle first meets Joyce. She is too in awe of the famous author to say much to him – they mainly talk about food – but over the next few months Gisèle tries to persuade Joyce to allow her to photograph him. Joyce always refuses, claiming that he isn't feeling well, or that his eyesight is bothering him, or that he has too much work to do.

That autumn, Sylvia Beach returns from her trip abroad to the flat she shares with Adrienne to find that Gisèle Freund has taken her place.

The Spanish War

The optimism that accompanies the formation of the Popular Front government in France does not last long. A fresh crisis convulses Europe in July 1936 when a group of renegade army generals, led by Francisco Franco, rise up against the elected Republican government of Spain and civil war breaks out.

No pasaran! The slogan of Republican Spain echoes across the cafés of the Left Bank. Thousands of German exiles – including Gustav Regler and Alfred Kantorowicz – volunteer to go to Spain as fighters in the International Brigades, as journalists or as medics. A German battalion is swiftly formed, named after the imprisoned German KPD leader, Ernst Thälmann. For the German émigrés this war goes beyond mere sympathy: it is personal, a chance finally to fight fascism directly after years of impotence. While the British and French governments refuse to intervene for fear of provoking a wider war, Hitler and Mussolini openly flout the non-intervention agreement to which they are also signatories and send not just arms but troops, planes and pilots to fight in support of Franco. When the Condor Legion trials its deadly bombing methods on Spanish civilians, the German exiles find they are fighting not just fascism but their compatriots.

In Paris, Willi Münzenberg throws himself into the cause, raising money, funnelling volunteers for the International Brigades over the Pyrenees, publishing pamphlets, and organizing rallies and protest meetings. At the Hotel Lutetia, Heinrich Mann, too old to take up arms, is constantly adopting resolutions of solidarity with Spain. On 13 August 1936 a 'European Conference for the Defence of the Spanish Republic' meets at the hotel. The intellectuals busy themselves signing more petitions.

In the face of Western refusal to arm the Republican government, Spain's foreign supporters can only cheer on the Soviet Union for being the sole country, aside from Mexico, willing to supply weapons and tanks to the Republican army and international brigades.

Hotel Moskva

It is at this inconvenient moment – October 1936, to be precise – that Willi Münzenberg is summoned to Moscow. The atmosphere in the Russian capital is tense following the conclusion of the first show trial, the 'Trial of the Sixteen', during which sixteen prominent, long-standing collaborators with Lenin stood accused of being involved in a Trotskyite plot to assassinate Stalin and other Party leaders. Tortured prior to the proceedings, the men confessed, were found guilty, and will soon be shot.

The air is filled with paranoia. Hundreds of foreign Communists, including many Germans who sought asylum in the Soviet Union, have been targeted and liquidated in Stalin's purge. At the Hotel Lux, KPD officials tiptoe around trying to guess which former friends to avoid in case of compromise. Willi and Babette, guests at the newly built Hotel Moskva, receive no visitors. The fatal stench of those who have fallen out of favour keeps old friends away.

Münzenberg is interrogated about the lack of security and general laxness in his Paris enterprises. At first, he doesn't take the questions seriously but, as the hearings continue, he begins to understand the gravity of his position. The men who formerly provided protection for his maverick operations have been edged out, and will soon be under arrest. The criticisms mount. The accusation that Münzenberg associates with 'suspicious' elements in Paris hits home. And everyone knows that he cannot abide Walter Ulbricht.

Münzenberg is lucky to get off with a reprimand, but he is ordered to remain in Moscow to take over the agitprop division of the Comintern. The danger is clear. It takes all his powers of persuasion to convince his superiors to let him complete his work for the Spanish Republican cause in Paris before taking on his new role. Even so, it is only by the skin of his teeth that he receives his passport and an exit permit to return to France.

André Gide returns from a trip to the Soviet Union in the autumn to publish a short work, *Retour de l'U.R.S.S.*, in which he expresses in frank terms his disillusion with the Soviet regime. In no country, he declares, even Hitler's Germany, is 'thought more unfree, more oppressed, more terrorised and more dependent' than in the Soviet Union. It is a courageous act from a man who has until now been a darling of the intellectual left, and he pays dearly for it. *Pravda* accuses Gide of being a defector to the 'Trotskyist-fascist camp'. Many of his former friends – Louis Aragon and Lion Feuchtwanger among them – join in the smear campaign against him, but Heinrich Mann refuses to take part.

Sick Leave

As soon as Willi Münzenberg returns to Paris, the invitation to return to Moscow is immediately and insistently renewed. How long can he stall? Münzenberg has always suffered from ill health, but when he checks himself into a sanatorium in the Parisian suburb of Châtenay-Malabry for a 'serious cardiac condition' even the French police who track his movements believe he is pretending to be unwell.

Münzenberg spends the winter ensconced at the sanatorium working on a treatise about Hitler's propaganda methods. While he writes, one of his oldest and closest friends in the Party, Karl Radek, is sentenced to death in Moscow. Shortly after this, Münzenberg is forced to surrender his propaganda enterprises.

For the first time in almost twenty years Willi Münzenberg finds himself with an empty dance card, forced to take stock of his loyalties and beliefs. Ulbricht and Pieck, meanwhile, busy themselves spreading rumours about his unreliability, suggesting – whisper it – that Willi is no longer flavour of the month at the court of the Comintern. They do not yet dare attack him openly: he may still go to Moscow, after all. But loyal Party members can read the runes: Münzenberg has been cut adrift. The only reason Moscow has not come down harder on him is probably because all those 'fellow travellers' whom he has single-handedly persuaded to support the Communist cause would raise a stink if 'Willi' were to suddenly disappear.

There is one last throw of the dice to come.

The Beginning and the End

Nearly three hundred delegates squeeze into the President Salon to hear Münzenberg's opening speech, followed by Heinrich Mann's address, at the biggest meeting yet of the German Popular Front, held at the Hotel Lutetia over two days on 10–11 April 1937. The theme is one of solidarity, with Spain at the forefront of many of the discussions.

On the surface, the congress looks like a success. In reality, it simultaneously marks the high point of the Lutetia Committee and the end of the German Popular Front in any meaningful sense. While Münzenberg is eloquently trying to persuade his audience of the need to join together to overthrow Hitler before it is too late, members of the Communist delegation and the SAPD almost come to blows about the fate of the anti-Stalinist Marxist POUM[†] in Spain.

† Partido Obrero de Unificacion Marxista – the Workers' Party of Marxist Unification.

Their violent suppression by Moscow-backed Communists under the guise of clearing out 'Trotskyite' factions has caused deep consternation among many Western supporters of Republican Spain. Meanwhile, Ulbricht is intriguing against Münzenberg, pushing for the primacy of the KPD, trying – in effect – to form his own personal Popular Front, entirely under Communist Party control.

Once the congress is over, Ulbricht finally gets his way: Münzenberg is suspended from his post and replaced by Ulbricht himself, who moves to Paris to keep an eye on his hated rival. Without Münzenberg, the Popular Front committees steadily lose both their autonomy and their wider support, and are eventually shunned by all but the most loyal Communist followers. Even Heinrich Mann, who sticks doggedly with it all long after others have given up, can see that Ulbricht is destroying any chance at consensus among the émigré political factions.

'You see,' he says wearily to Alfred Kantorowicz, 'I cannot sit down with a man who suddenly claims that the table we are sitting at is not a table but a duck pond, and who wants to force me to agree with him.'

Drained and dispirited, Heinrich travels with Nelly to their favourite Alpine spot in Briançon for a summer holiday, where they are joined by Willi and Babette. Despite everything, Mann and Münzenberg remain greatly attached to one another, each admiring in the other the qualities that complement his own: without Münzenberg's extraordinary energy and Mann's powerful sense of responsibility to the German people, the whole enterprise would never have got off the ground at all.

The effects of the show trials in Moscow and the purging of the POUM in Spain are widespread: Manès Sperber experiences the moment he quits the Communist Party as a profound loss from which he has to recover as if from a depression; Arthur Koestler enjoys a sense of liberation at no longer being tied to the rigid demands of 'the Party'; Willi Münzenberg simply transfers the energies he once harnessed in the name of Communism to continuing the fight against fascism, and immediately sets about organizing another propaganda network. Ulbricht and Pieck do their best to undermine it by denouncing it, but with little success.

Fluency

Eva Tichauer is nineteen years old now. Her French is fluent, her accent almost gone. She studies hard in preparation for a career in medicine, that portable profession which her parents are so relieved she has chosen. On 17 January 1937 the family are naturalized. The possession of French citizenship makes no difference to her father's prospects: without French qualifications he still cannot find meaningful employment, but he continues to throw himself into his pro bono work in the service of German refugees. Her mother's translation work just about keeps the family afloat. As their only surviving child, Eva feels the pressure of her parents' grieving love: to live where her brother could not, to thrive where her parents cannot. Sometimes she feels that she is the only reason her parents do not give up.

And perhaps she is right. However hard they try, most older German exiles will never fully assimilate in France. There is always that double-layered barrier that holds them back: the lack of French qualifications, and that damned accent which so embarrasses their children.

Walter Benjamin's dear friend, Franz Hessel, has lived in Paris since 1924. His two sons, Stefan and Ulrich, are now young Frenchmen, their German receding rapidly as they adapt to their adopted home. Like Eva Tichauer, and Pierre and Ruth Radványi, their French schooling has gradually rubbed out the traces of their foreignness, leaving behind a private core in which their past, short, German lives continue to exist, fading with time, precious and vital and yet increasingly vague. As Gisela Freund becomes Gisèle, and Peter Radványi becomes Pierre, so Stefan Hessel will one day become Stéphane, a great Frenchman. Meanwhile, he is a brilliant student taking classes at the prestigious Lycée Louis-Le-Grand, which lies at the heart of the 5th *arrondissement*, on rue Saint-Jacques, opposite the literature faculty of the Sorbonne, beside the Bibliothèque Sainte-Geneviève and the Panthéon. It is here, too, that twelve-year-old Alexis Léon, son of James Joyce's long-suffering, Russian-born Jewish secretary (and dearest friend), Paul Léon, is taking his first steps as a *lycéen* under the watchful eye of his proud father.

World Fair

When the 1937 World Fair opens in May, the streets between the Palais de Chaillot and the Eiffel Tower are lined with flags and messages of welcome, and there is an air of festive gaiety as pavilions from each country vie with one another to showcase their nation's technical and artistic achievements. Everyone in Paris goes at least once. But even here the dark shadow that hovers above Europe cannot be fully dissipated. The Soviet pavilion faces off against the German one: massive bronze figures of a young peasant woman and a youthful worker stride forward, hammer and sickle in hand, as if challenging the silver eagle perched atop the gigantic three-pillared tower opposite. No German exile dares cross into that alien realm, where smiling Nazis hand out sweets and brochures stamped with swastikas.

The Fair is especially popular with children, who wander into the pavilions, trying the Swiss chocolate and the Italian sausage, jumping in and out of the brightly coloured carts that carry visitors around the exhibition's various sites. Anna Seghers takes Pierre and Ruth down to the Spanish Republican pavilion, where Picasso's *Guernica* attracts throngs of eager crowds who pause, momentarily, to contemplate photographs of Spain's suffering before moving on to the next attraction. Beyond this, by the river, is a statue of a naked man on horseback: Mussolini as a Roman emperor, clad only in a cloak. Parisians enjoy a joke at the bald dictator's expense.

Summer, autumn, winter, spring. In Spain the war grinds on as the beleaguered Republic steadily loses ground. Austrians wait in a state of tension for what is to come. The politicians talk. At the Hotel Lutetia, Prime Minister Camille Chautemps – back in power again – delivers a speech at a banquet in honour of veterans and the war wounded. Nobody wants to contemplate the possibility of another generation of young Frenchmen's lives being blighted by bombs and guns.

Anschluss

Anna Seghers takes an evening walk along the leafy avenue in Meudon, reflecting on recent conversations in which she has been asked, repeatedly, by friends and acquaintances, where they will take the children if war breaks out. Anna experienced bombing during the 1914–18 war, then again when she visited Spain. 'But here, in this country, my children have known joy and security; should they not, if need be, also understand pain and danger here?' She passes the milkman, with his freshly painted cart and horse. They stop to chat, briefly, exchange a few words of small talk before they move on, each in a different direction, the milkman on his rounds, Anna walking with no other purpose than to enjoy the quiet of the evening. She wonders if the milkman feels the same intense sense of peace in this suburban street as she does. Probably not. People who are rooted in a place do not appreciate it in the way that those who pass through it do. It is those who are forced to keep moving who truly understand what it means to sit together, as a family, for an evening meal.

Pierre attends a children's group in Paris organized by some of the German anti-fascists. At first his mother accompanies him; later he goes alone. At one point the group attends a conference just round the corner from the Lutetia on rue de Rennes. The theme of the conference: the Nazi threat.

On 9 March 1938, Walter Benjamin writes to the Ministry of Justice applying for French citizenship. He has gathered together the requisite paperwork, testimonials from various French writers in which they declare, to whom it may concern, that the afore-mentioned German writer is an intellectual of sufficient value to merit the award of that precious commodity, a French passport. He waits. And while he waits, he works, burying himself in the endeavour which has preoccupied him for so many years: his Arcades Project. Around him, the world is collapsing again.

James Joyce, too, burrows deep into his books, shutting out the awfulness around him in order to finally push out into the world the work that has been his obsession for so many years. *Finnegans Wake* is due to be published simultaneously in the US and England, the date as yet unconfirmed. His close friends and collaborators – Paul Léon, Eugene and Maria Jolas – gather around Joyce in a protective circle, making last-minute changes, correcting proofs, answering queries, unified in their desire to make this happen before it is too late.

Gisèle Freund is still eager to photograph the great man. A friend encourages her to write to Joyce explaining the importance of good photographic publicity for this latest, most demanding work, and setting out her bona fides as a professional and in-demand photographer. Gisèle has recently been experimenting with colour film, an expensive new format that has only recently become available in France, which comes in slide form and has to be projected in order to be viewed. Thanks to Adrienne, Gisèle has been making portraits of the French writers she has met through her mentor: Paul Valéry, André Gide, François Mauriac, André Breton, Georges Duhamel, André Maurois. Joyce replies to her letter, inviting her to organize a slide show at his home on rue Edmond-Valentin. She arrives and nervously sets up the makeshift screen.

Joyce, whose eyesight is severely damaged, sits so close to the screen he can almost touch the faces that pass before him. Throughout the projection he says not a word, only sighing occasionally, a deep, anxious exhalation. But when Gisèle turns the lights on again he immediately declares himself willing to submit to the process, on condition that she does not use colour film.

They agree that Gisèle will spend a few days with Joyce and

produce a series of photographs, a reportage on 'James Joyce in Paris'. Joyce has very definite ideas about what is required: some shots of him working with his close collaborator Eugene Jolas, the trilingual, US-born, Franco-German editor of *Transition* magazine, as they correct proofs of his book; a series of photos in Sylvia Beach's bookshop, Shakespeare & Company, along with Adrienne Monnier. American and British readers will be aware that it was Sylvia who so courageously published *Ulysses* in 1922; French readers will know that Adrienne published the French translation. The story is to be completed with images of Joyce at home, surrounded by his family. And thus 'Three Days with Joyce' is born, later published in full as a photographic work by Freund. Joyce submits patiently to the process, and the result is a unique series of images of the writer in his last years, his thick round glasses obscuring his eyes, his hat perched on the back of his head, an air of perpetual melancholy on his thoughtful face, a rare smile appearing in the pictures of him playing with his grandson Stephen. Unfortunately for Joyce, publication of *Finnegans Wake* is delayed, and he will have to wait another year before it finally comes out.

While Joyce is wholly absorbed with the painful birth pangs of his great and final work, while Walter Benjamin sits in the Bibliothèque nationale reading, researching, writing, writing, Hitler does what everybody has been predicting without quite believing in it as a real, tangible thing: he annexes Austria.

At the Préfecture de Police in Paris, Austrian refugees watch as officials add 'Ex-' onto their documents. From now on this is who they are: ex-Austrians.

In the same month the third and final show trial begins in Moscow, the 'Trial of the Twenty-One'. Among the defendants is Nikolai Bukharin, accused (among other things and along with his co-defendants) of conspiring to assassinate Lenin and Stalin, poisoning Maxim Gorky, and plotting to overthrow the Soviet Union. Bukharin, the star defendant, has been tortured, his wife and young child threatened. He confesses, retracts the confession, confesses again. To no avail: his fate is death. His young wife is separated from her infant son and spends the next twenty years in prison and internal exile.

'The last mass trials were a great success,' declares Ninotchka, played by Greta Garbo in her first comedic role, in Ernst Lubitsch's 1939 film of the same name. 'There are going to be fewer but better Russians.'

The Fifth Floor

In France, following a series of political crises, a new French government under Édouard Daladier is formed, shortly after which a decree is issued tightening the conditions of residence for foreigners in France.

The decree requires all immigrants to be in possession of an identity card. Penalties for foreigners without a card range from fines to imprisonment, followed by expulsion from French territory. Those who have entered France without authorization, or who have evaded an expulsion order, are liable to imprisonment of between six months and three years. German and Austrian immigrants known to be unable to leave French territory may be placed under house arrest. Legally resident foreign nationals are no longer permitted to travel without having their identity card stamped on departure and arrival, even within the same *département*.

The playwright Theo Balk discovers that, lacking the proper paperwork, he is now regarded 'as an individual dangerous to the public security of France', a criminal, in short. He is taken by police to the Palais de Justice, then it's up to the fifth floor of the Préfecture where he joins a mass of unfortunate souls who have been deposited here to await processing. The deadline he is given to leave France is five days.

'I do not have a passport. I do not have a visa for another country. I also do not have money, not enough money to make a major trip. [. . .] For me, the time of postponements begins. The time of waiting. The time of the fifth floor. On the back of my deportation certificate, one stamp follows the other, each postponing the execution of the deportation for three, five, seven or fourteen days . . .'

When Balk returns to the Préfecture de Police a few days later he takes a book, which he doesn't read because it is impossible to concentrate in the crowded waiting room. When the official finally hands him back his papers the vital stamp is absent.

'I know there is nothing more to be done. I take my paper, my fate held together at the edges with glue, dirty and covered with stamps, and I wander, unaware of where I am heading, toward the Luxembourg, passing between people coming out of lecture halls and offices, hurrying to cafés or home or doing the other things that people tend to do at this time of day. Me, a person who doesn't even know where he is going to spend the night.'

Time Running Out

In May 1938 Willi Münzenberg receives another 'invitation' to go to Moscow for a fortnight to 'settle various questions with the NKVD'. He is not stupid. He will not go. One week later he reports to the French police that he has noticed suspicious individuals lurking outside his home and following him when he goes out. For the first time ever, Münzenberg – who has always brushed off such threats with careless confidence – openly confesses himself concerned about the danger from 'certain organisms of repression' in the service of foreign powers.

And still Walter Benjamin writes, head down in a race against disaster as spring turns to summer and summer to autumn and Hitler once again makes a move on the chessboard of Europe. And yet, in spite of his choking fear, it is with a feeling of triumph that Benjamin finally concludes the second part of the three-part essay he has been planning for nearly fifteen years, the section about the *flâneur* titled 'The Paris of the Second Empire in Baudelaire'. He sends it off to Max Horkheimer and Theodor Adorno in New York just as the Munich Agreement decides the fate of the Sudetenland and shakes Benjamin to his core. 'I do not know how long it will still be physically possible to breathe this European air,' he writes.

Again he waits. Who knows which is more pressing for him, to receive a reply to his application for French citizenship, or to hear what Adorno and Horkheimer think of his essay?

The number of refugees flooding across western Europe is growing daily. One by one, previously liberal countries – France, Holland, Switzerland – close their doors to the 'undesirable aliens' streaming across their borders. By the summer the situation has grown so critical that President Roosevelt convenes an international conference in Évian-les-Bains. Here, government representatives stand up, one after the other, to express their goodwill toward these unfortunate human beings. But no one actually wants to host them in their country, least of all the Americans.

The political crisis engulfing France, and the sense of growing menace from their neighbour to the east, push the French – many of them, at any rate – toward indifference. The fate of thousands of foreign refugees has become a wearyingly familiar concern. People are worried about what will happen to *them*, to *their* family. They do not have the energy to care about foreigners. Little by little, public opinion becomes anxious, then hostile. The threat of war makes people suspicious. What language do these so-called refugees speak? German. Where does the threat come from? Germany. Well, we all know how that played out last time. These Germans claim to be against Hitler. How are we to be sure of that? Are they not in some way responsible, simply because they are Germans, for the threat hanging over France and the French? The right-wing press drips this message into willing ears.

And yet. Heinrich Mann and Nelly spend the summer with the Kantorowiczes, now back from Spain and living in the south of

France. They walk, they talk, they eat in inexpensive restaurants along with the Feuchtwangers, the Marcuses, the Schickeles, the Werfels – couples taking the sun, swimming off rocks. Nelly is tall and talkative. Friedel, by contrast, is small and reserved, but the two women become friends. Kantorowicz is fascinated by the relationship between the elderly, distinguished Heinrich Mann and his beautiful but often uncouth mistress, whose origins in a Baltic fishing village go some way to explaining her propensity to get drunk and swear. At the end of July, Heinrich Mann travels to Paris to attend yet another talking shop, the Third International Writers' Congress. While he is there he attends Alfred Döblin's sixtieth birthday at a Paris restaurant, Le Cercle des Nations, where he and Anna Seghers both give a speech. Döblin's son Wolfgang is there too, a brilliant mathematician who has just received his PhD from the Sorbonne and, later that year, will enlist in the French army.

Nineteen thirty-eight is a moment for finishing works, as if the sense of time running out spurs literary men to desperate achievement. Toward the end of August, Heinrich Mann completes the second volume of *Henri IV*. He manages a discreet visit to his brother in Switzerland, where they walk and talk and drink vermouth, reading one another's works as they have always done. Thomas confides in Heinrich that he has taken the decision to leave Europe before it is too late.

In mid-September, Thomas and Katia Mann arrive in Paris on the first leg of their journey away from Europe. They stay at the Hotel Lutetia, along with Heinrich, who has arrived to make one final, valiant attempt to revive the Popular Front. The cause is evidently hopeless. And yet, Heinrich Mann finds a sense of purpose in his commitment. He feels he is playing his part in the struggle against fascism.

The Seven Spires

The night before the final meeting that is to be held in the now-familiar hotel, a handsome twenty-five-year-old SAPD politician, Willy Brandt, living in exile in Oslo, is introduced to Mann. The older writer is interested to meet a youngster from his native Lübeck, someone who knows Berlin and has been to Spain. Tears come to his eyes as he reminisces about the place they once called home: 'The seven spires, we will never see them again,' he laments. Brandt finds the meeting grim: the sparse remnants of the Lutetia Committee, a group of forty or fifty isolated supporters, no longer wish to be known as the 'Popular Front'. In truth, the era of working together is over: the last men standing are directed from Moscow. Brandt has the impression that Mann is being taken advantage of, reading out glib words written for him by apparatchiks whose desire for ideological control has ended all possibility of co-operation. Mann is the figurehead of this failed enterprise, but in truth he is not the only one unable to abandon his faith in the Soviet Union. He may turn his head away from the ugly reality of the Moscow trials, and wilfully ignore the brutal truth about the regime to which they have been so enthusiastically committed, but what is the alternative? If he turns his head the other way he will see only goose-stepping Nazis, the barbarians who have taken from him his language and his home and who are now standing at the gates of western Europe, about to bring war. 'I tried in vain to make political camaraderie work,' declares Mann. 'It was easier to conquer a new audience in far-off countries than to get several dozen Germans to fight for the defence of their own cause.'

Heinrich Mann has sometimes been derided as 'the Hindenburg of exile', depicted as a senile old man who clung to the orthodoxy of Communist ideology long past the moment when he believed in it. And yet during those years in France he never gave up believing in the power of words to effect change. His output was phenomenal: four hundred works in seven years – essays, speeches, appeals and novels. What energy from a man no longer in his youth! All those words. Yet what did they achieve?

On 20 September 1938, the German Popular Front is officially dissolved at the Hotel Lutetia, long after its actual demise. The Lutetia Committee is no more. Across Europe, the dreams of the Popular Front lie in tatters. Meanwhile, meanwhile . . . the appeasers keep giving in to Hitler's insatiable demands.

The German exiles counted on the Western democracies to resist the dictator, and the governments of these democracies have instead rolled over and given Hitler everything he asked for, endorsing and legalizing his crimes, his annexations and his conquests. Willi Münzenberg saddles his horse for one last battle, a knight errant calling into being a slew of new organizations aimed at demonstrating his intent to unite the various factions of the German émigré left. He has a new publishing venture, too, a weekly publication optimistically titled *Die Zukunft – The Future* – its staff consisting of a loyal group of former *Münzenberg-Leute*, disenchanted former Communists all. But the magazine never achieves anything more than a mediocre success. The time for words is past.

Waiting

Nobody wants another war. It is scarcely twenty years since the end of the last one, the one that was supposed to end all wars. Those who were young in the first decades of the twentieth century now have children to fear for. The battlefields of Europe are still raw, the scent of slaughter too fresh. Last time around France lost nearly 1.4 million of its men – significantly more than Britain's losses. For days and nights before the Munich Agreement is signed, the people of Paris live in a state of powerless anxiety. 'What will Hitler do?' they ask. 'What is going to happen?' For a while the street lights are screened and the streets dark, as though a surprise air raid is expected at any moment. Municipal carts deposit piles of sand in front of buildings, annoying the concierges who complain about the mess.

Anna Seghers and her family are taking a short break in Haute-Savoie when the Munich Agreement is signed. Pierre and Ruth must be accustomed, by now, to holidays cut short by political events as the family head back to Paris to be with their friends. Pierre, who is twelve now and beginning to listen with greater awareness to his parents' discussions, feels the fear rising among the émigrés. It is clear to them, if not yet to the French, that war is now inevitable. And yet still his parents believe, or want to believe, that the Germans will revolt against Hitler. Why are they waiting so long before they act? Surely, if there is a time to revolt, that time is now!

This is the moment when some far-sighted individuals begin the lengthy process of acquiring an American visa.

Walter Benjamin has just returned from a visit to Brecht when, on 7 November 1938, a seventeen-year-old Polish Jew, Herschel Grynszpan, shoots a German embassy official in Paris. The response in Nazi Germany is immediate and terrifying. *Kristallnacht*, it is called. A night of shattered glass. Theodor Adorno's father's offices are destroyed; the old man suffers an eye injury during the violence. Adorno later writes to Benjamin with the shocking news that his parents were arrested in Frankfurt during the violent pogroms that followed. Benjamin derives some comfort from the news that his son, Stefan, has made it to England. Stefan's mother, Benjamin's ex-wife Dora, will follow soon after. But he fears for his brother, in prison in Berlin.

Once again Benjamin attempts to contact the Ministry of Justice about his application for French citizenship. Still there is no response. Then more bad news arrives in a lengthy letter from Adorno: Benjamin's essay on Baudelaire has not met with the approval of his editors in New York. Adorno sets out in detail why the essay regrettably falls short of his expectations: excited as he was to read the long-awaited chapter, much as he admires Benjamin for being able to finish the text on time, he regrets to say (on behalf of everyone on the editorial team) that the piece poses more questions than answers – 'many riddles pose themselves anew' – and the chapter 'represents not so much a model for the Arcades as a prelude to that project'. Benjamin's equally lengthy rebuttal cannot alter the fact that, if he wishes it to be published, he has little choice but to accept the 'improvements' and revise his work.

After *Kristallnacht* the number of refugees arriving in France reaches an unprecedented level. By the end of the year there are roughly 60,000 Jewish refugees from east and central Europe, most of whom have entered the country illegally. It leads to a massive crackdown on 'undesirables'.

In early December, the Nazi Foreign Minister Joachim von Ribbentrop pays a visit to Paris, staying in the Hotel George V, just off the Champs-Élysées. With a view to possible negotiations with the Reich, the French government is keen to show that their tolerance of the anti-Hitler refugees is strictly limited, and in anticipation of the visit numerous immigrants are arrested. Some German refugees are even summoned to the Préfecture de Police and taken directly to a provincial town where they are placed under house arrest. On the second day of his visit, von Ribbentrop raises the possibility of a common struggle against Bolshevism and makes a point of mentioning the unwelcome presence of numerous German refugees in Paris.

To be a German in France in 1938 is to be suspect. As Heinrich Mann noted back in 1933, for many foreign observers the National Socialist regime, by virtue of its continued existence, *was* Germany. An exile from Germany is thus not an opponent of the government in power, but an individual who has in some way failed or disgraced himself. Writer Hans Marchwitza, under house arrest in Moulins in December 1938, later recalled a conversation with a nurse who did not understand why he could not return to his country if, as he claimed, he had committed no offence. 'Why didn't you stay?' she asks. And she concludes sententiously: 'If you don't make trouble for others, you don't have to fear persecution.'

*

In Nice, Heinrich Mann's partner, Nelly, is increasingly turning to a combination of alcohol and the drug Veronal to quieten her anxiety. One night she is taken by ambulance to a clinic, possibly as a result of having accidentally combined too much Veronal with alcohol. More likely it is her first attempt at suicide.

Throughout the years of her Paris exile, Willi Münzenberg's partner, Babette Gross, has not seen her son Peter once. Her former husband Fritz's parents have kept him safe, hopeful that he can reach the end of his schooling without having to follow his mother and father into exile. But Peter belongs to a new, official category of human being: he is a *Halb Jude* (Category 1), with two Jewish grandparents – the ones who have dedicated the last thirteen years to caring for him. After the events of Kristallnacht his grandparents conclude that they cannot afford to wait for him to finish his education: Peter must leave Germany now and join his father in exile in England. Since the Gestapo have confiscated his passport, in early January 1939 the fifteen-year-old must undergo an interrogation before the document can be released. At a Gestapo office in Potsdam they question him. They want to know about the letters he receives from abroad, where they come from and who sends them. They show him pictures: *Do you recognize these people?* In the face of the boy's silence they are more precise: *Come on now, we know who your parents are. Do they write to you? Where are they hiding?* Peter pleads ignorance. Indeed, he can state without lying that he has had no word from his mother in seven years.

Luck is on his side: his passport is returned to him. He arrives in England in March 1939 to be reunited with his father.

Joyce in Colour

Winter. Barcelona falls. Thousands of Republican refugees cross the snow-covered Pyrenees and stagger over the border into France, where they are promptly locked up in internment camps.

*

In early March 1939, *Time* Magazine contacts Gisèle Freund asking for a colour portrait of James Joyce to celebrate the publication of *Finnegans Wake*, which is finally about to make its formal appearance on the world stage.

Freund is reluctant to approach Joyce again, especially given the writer's unwillingness to be photographed in colour. But a cover of *Time* would be quite the publicity coup, especially with a book as difficult as this. Sylvia Beach hits upon an unusual solution: she knows that Joyce is deeply superstitious; Freund's *mariage blanc* has resulted in a new surname, Blum, the same as that of the hero of *Ulysses*.

'Write to him,' urges Sylvia, 'sign it in your married name.'

Joyce accepts the proposition straight away.

It is Joyce himself who opens the door to his flat, dressed in a red velvet dinner jacket, his hands adorned with rings. He is nervous, glancing uneasily toward Gisèle's camera apparatus. Soon his nervousness has infected her, too: she starts tripping over cables and dropping things. The atmosphere grows tense. Then – alas! – as Joyce gropes his way to the armchair which Gisèle has asked him to sit in, he knocks his head on one of her lamps. He lets out a high-pitched cry, clutching his forehead with both hands. Blood has been drawn. The great man even swears.

Nora enters to calm him down. Gisèle inspects the cut – just a scratch, she declares, pressing a pair of cold steel scissors against it to prevent swelling. Finally settled, Joyce begins to study a book with a magnifying glass. Freund clicks the shutter and finishes her film as quickly as possible before promising the writer that this time she really will never bother him again.

She exits in haste, jumps into a taxi, and instructs the driver to step on it, which he duly does, missing a corner and crashing into another car. Freund, furious and upset, telephones Joyce and accuses him of putting an Irish curse on her photographs, which are surely ruined. Joyce, filled with remorse, immediately invites her to return the next day.

The second time around everything goes smoothly. The session takes only a few minutes. Even better, when she gets to the laboratory

James Joyce, 1939, by Gisèle Freund

Gisèle discovers that the previous day's film is undamaged, so she has two sets of colour photos to choose from.

When *Time* Magazine appears with Joyce on the cover, Freund recounts his delight at the result.

'I said I would never let myself be photographed in colour,' he tells his friends, enjoying the dramatic story that accompanies the photograph. 'Mrs B. got me not once, but twice. She's stronger than the Irish.'

Darkening

It is early spring when Madrid finally concedes defeat. The agony of the Spanish Republic is finally over. Franco is victorious. Yet more Spanish refugees arrive in southern France.

★

At a Comintern hearing in Moscow, Willi Münzenberg's 'deviations' are traced right back to the early 1930s. He is found guilty of intriguing against the KPD during the years of his exile, conspiring with Trotskyists and other enemies of the proletariat, maligning the KPD leadership, and refusing to submit his propagandistic activities to Party discipline. As the Party press reports his expulsion from the KPD, in Paris Münzenberg attempts to gain the upper hand by publishing an official letter of resignation in which he explains his reasons for quitting the Party. It is the fight against fascism, he argues, that ought to be their most urgent concern.

At the end of May 1939 the German Embassy in Paris receives a letter from their government informing them that Walter Benjamin has been stripped of his German citizenship, apparently as a consequence of an article published in 1936, in which he wrote disparagingly about fascist culture. Benjamin is now not only penniless but stateless. His application for French citizenship has received no response. He casts around desperately for a way out. His beloved Paris is no longer a haven but a curse.

For various reasons the publication of *Finnegans Wake* is delayed yet again, and it is not until 4 May 1939 that the book appears simultaneously in New York and London. Unfortunately for Joyce, eagerly scanning the pages of the literary magazines, by this time few people are paying attention.

The Last Summer

Across Europe, it seems that everyone has collectively decided to pretend that life is going on as normal. In France, people make their way south to sit on crowded beaches, hike up mountains, read books in their country retreats. In Britain the Prime Minister, Neville Chamberlain, goes fishing in Scotland, while King George

VI shoots grouse on his Balmoral estate. In Poland, young couples dance on pleasure boats, swaying to the music of Henryk Gold. Are they deluding themselves? Is it the case that, as Manès Sperber suggests, everyone is certain that wars never break out before the autumn? Or is it because there have been so many false alarms that people have stopped believing in the reality of war? And yet, in the cheap neighbourhood cinemas offering a summer deal of two films for the price of one, cinema-goers seated in the hot darkness, smoking and kissing and roaring with laughter at the antics of Charlie Chaplin and Buster Keaton, fall silent when the newsreel comes on. Once again, they are forced to watch that ridiculous little moustachioed fellow whose raging speeches once seemed so comical. Now they stare at this 'grotesque-looking, glassy-eyed, bellowing man' and feel an undercurrent of dread.

The exiles repeat to themselves, as a mantra, that so long as Britain and France stand firm the Soviets will stand with them and there will be no war. 'You had only to repeat it sufficiently often,' writes Arthur Koestler, 'until you were sick of hearing yourself say it. And all the time we knew that this was our last summer for a long time, and perhaps forever.'

Anna Seghers decides to use some of her last remaining money to send the children for swimming lessons in Paris. One day, she reasons, they might have to sail on a ship. And if they have to escape across the ocean, it is imperative that Pierre and Ruth know how to swim.

Gisèle Freund travels to Britain for an extended visit to see her family, who have managed to escape from Germany. Using the introductions provided by her new friend and mentor, the prominent Argentinian writer and critic Victoria Ocampo, she is soon photographing the leading lights of the British literary scene: Vita Sackville-West, Virginia Woolf, T. S. Eliot, Elizabeth Bowen, George Bernard Shaw.

Walter Benjamin's hopes are briefly buoyed when he receives a proposal to give a talk on his Arcades Project at the Institute for

Social Research at Columbia University in New York. The planned date is late September or early October 1939.

At the end of July, Peter Gross is invited to France for a holiday with his mother. When Babette last saw her son he was eight years old. Now here he is, a young man of fifteen crossing the Channel from his new British home. She takes him to their flat in Issy-les-Moulineux, south-west of Paris, where he is reunited with his beloved Emil, the chauffeur who used to drive him around in Willi's shiny black Lincoln, patiently letting him play with the intercom and roll about on the leather seats. Emil is still recovering from an injury sustained during the Spanish Civil War in which he lost an eye. Peter shares a room with him.

In August, they travel with some close friends to a little spot on the northern coast of France near Étretat, between Dieppe and Le Havre, for a short holiday to celebrate Willi's fiftieth birthday, which falls on 14 August. On the day of his birthday the little group goes down to the beach and while Babette and Peter swim out to the Aiguille de Belval, a stone formation in the shape of a needle, the men sit beneath the tall white cliffs with their trousers rolled up, talking. Not one of them knows how to swim. After lunch they gather around a fire in the garden of their rented house and sing, not Communist camp songs, but sentimental German ballads about the past.

And then.

War

No death is so sad and final as the death of an illusion

Arthur Koestler

Rumours that a pact is about to be signed between Hitler and Stalin are initially treated by the French press as propaganda put out by Goebbels to try to derail an imminently expected agreement between the Soviet Union and Western allies. But then the news is reported direct from Moscow.

For those who have continued supporting Stalin in the face of the show trials, the purges and the persecution of the POUM, the announcement of the Molotov–Ribbentrop Pact on 23 August 1939 is not just devastating but utterly disorienting. In Paris rumours swirl around the cafés, the seedy hotels, the bookshops and bars . . . And as they attempt to make sense of it, the Communists tie themselves in knots. Alfred Kantorowicz torments himself as he tries to understand the reasoning behind Stalin's decision. The leader of the French Communists, Maurice Thorez, concludes that the pact is a stroke of genius on Stalin's part: he is guaranteeing peace by tying Hitler's hands. The following morning *L'Humanité*, the official organ of the French Communist Party, explains to its readers without irony that the new treaty is Stalin's last heroic effort to prevent the threatening imperialist war.

For Willi Münzenberg, Arthur Koestler, Manès Sperber and others who have left the Party, 23 August 1939 marks the point at which they are at last permitted to raise their heads and declare: You see? You *see*? There is no joy in being proved right, of course, because the price to be paid is that of war. Naturally, Münzenberg's first reaction is to publish a passionate '*j'accuse*': the pact, he observes, is a Russian 'stab in the back' against the working class and peace.

When Heinrich Mann hears the news about the pact he locks himself in his study in Nice for forty-eight hours and refuses to speak to anyone. A few days later he finally gets around to marrying Nelly.

The war, when it arrives, does so without fanfare or fuss. It has been announced so many times already, after all. Alfred and Friedel Kantorowicz sit on their terrace in the south of France trying to make out what is being broadcast on the radio in the house next door. Only incoherent fragments reach them through the shutters. Eventually the radio falls silent. The couple sit together for a long time, smoking in silence in the warm darkness of the Provençal night, remembering the civil war in Spain and wondering what is to come now that a new war has been declared.

In Paris, in the south of France, all over Europe, the anti-fascist exiles must finally acknowledge that the battle they have been fighting for the soul of Germany has been lost; was, in reality, lost long ago. Heinrich Mann's appeals to the German people have gone unheeded. The intellectuals, the writers, the artists and the politicians with all their committees, their pamphlets and their urgent calls to action, have failed. The barbarians have won.

Lutetia

It is quiet at night in Paris now. Outside the Hotel Lutetia, passers-by hurry along boulevard Raspail. Inside, guests sit at the bar while the barman keeps an observant eye on who is here, and who is not, as he busies himself polishing glasses, checking on stock. Above the quiet murmur of conversation comes the occasional pop of a cork, a burst of laughter. Many of the regular guests have gone home to the provinces to wait for what is to come. Foreigners are leaving. Young men on the staff have been mobilized and the freshly promoted manager, Marcel Chappaz, must make changes to accommodate their absence. Chappaz carries on doing what hotel managers do, ensuring that the cogs in the machine that is the Hotel Lutetia continue to run as smoothly as they have always done. In reality he, like everyone else in Paris, is waiting.

At night the maids move around silently, pulling the blinds down to comply with the new blackout regulations, enclosing the hotel guests in a warm and candlelit embrace. Outside, on boulevard Raspail, sandbags shore up the building.

Fluctuat nec mergitur – the city's motto inscribed beneath a ship, the symbol of Paris. 'Tossed by the waves but does not sink.'

So they must hope.

In the newspapers, in place of the usual advertisements promoting the comforts and attractive prices to be found at the hotel, is a brief announcement confirming that the Hotel Lutetia remains open and has been officially designated as a civilian shelter: *L'Hôtel Lutetia, Bd Raspail est ouvert. Abri agréé par Déf. passive.*

The autumn banquets have been cancelled: gone are the christenings and the annual jollies; in their place are business meetings, discussions of stocks and shares. By December, the regular advertisements have reappeared: *Hôtel Lutetia, prix modérés. Salons pour repas, noces, banquets.* Moderate prices. Function rooms for dinners, weddings, banquets.

> The more we are together,
> together, together
> The more we are together
> the happier we'll be.

Paris café with German officers, 1940

PART II

During: 1939–1944

All this trouble, all this misfortune that had befallen another people had been caused by my people. For it was obvious that they talked like me and whistled the same tunes.

Anna Seghers – *Transit*

Hiatus

Paris in September 1939 is a strange place: at war but not at war, safe but existing with the constant threat of danger. Statues are swathed in sandbags, paintings packed away for safety. Air-raid alerts put nerves on edge, night-time curfews are imposed. The machinery of government grinds slowly into action to place the country on a war footing. Foreigners lucky enough to be in possession of a passport or a pile of money leave the city and hightail it back home. In a flurry of fear and urgency plans are dropped, weddings postponed, holidays cancelled.

And yet, not yet. While Hitler flattens Poland, in France there is a nine-month hiatus before the 'real' war begins. Nine months, the length of time between the conception and birth of a child.

Pierre Radványi goes out to the kiosk in Meudon to buy the paper and sees *Paris Soir* with its huge headlines declaring general mobilization. Every young man between the ages of twenty and forty-nine is called up to serve. At home his parents stick strips of paper on the windows to stop them shattering, and paint them blue to keep the light from escaping at night. When the air-raid siren blares out its warning, they all troop down to the makeshift bomb shelter in the cellar where they sit patiently with their landlords. Elderly M. Bohl is confident of a swift allied victory. They must trust in the Maginot Line, he declares. If the Germans enter France there will be a new and victorious 'battle of the Marne'. He is sure of that.

The French place their faith in the Maginot Line as in a magic amulet that will preserve the wearer from harm. Created after the devastation of the 1914–18 war to ensure that no future German invasion would ever succeed in penetrating French territory, this defensive fortification runs the length of the Franco-German border. Now 30,000 army conscripts patrol its empty space, their discipline eroding along with their belief in the reality of this not-quite-existent war.

One morning, Pierre is in the bathroom when there is a knock on the apartment door. It is the Meudon police, come to arrest his father. László is given half an hour to prepare himself before he is escorted away to a tennis stadium on the outskirts of the city. Pierre doesn't dare mention this terrifying development at his new school, the Lycée Hoche in Versailles, where he has had to move since his own school – like many others in France – did not reopen for the new term. Anna, as usual, tries to preserve an outward appearance of calm. When the children ask why they have taken László she explains that it is just a precautionary measure and that their father will be back in a few days.

For the exiles the declaration of war opens up a new, bizarre stage in their odyssey. Within days, all 'enemy aliens' are scooped up like so much flotsam and deposited in internment camps, where they live in a state of acute anxiety in conditions varying from poor to appalling as they wait for France's snail-paced bureaucracy to acknowledge the fact that they do not constitute a 'fifth column' and pose no threat to the French Republic.

The 'ordinary' enemy aliens are held in the Stade de Colombes sports stadium on the outskirts of the city. All German, Austrian, Czech and Slovak men aged between seventeen and fifty living in Paris receive an invitation from the French government to present themselves at the stadium with a knife and fork and provisions for two days. The men come willingly, some 20,000 of them. Such is their trust in the French authorities that most of them show up in summer clothes and light shoes, a thin blanket tucked under one arm, carrying – as instructed – provisions for one or two days at most. The

Roland Garros tennis stadium near the Bois de Boulogne has been chosen as the holding place for those individuals of neutral or allied countries (Russians, Poles, Hungarians, Italians) considered to be of special interest to the authorities, along with Germans known or suspected to be involved in political activities. The men held here do not receive a polite order: like László Radványi, they are arrested and brought here by police.

Alongside Radványi are Gustav Regler, Arthur Koestler and dozens of writers, artists, intellectuals and political activists, including most of Willi Münzenberg's collaborators. Münzenberg himself, having just turned fifty, is deemed too old to pose a threat to France's security. For ten days the men lie on the terraces, huddle on benches, stroll along the cinder track, play cards or chess, before they are unceremoniously bundled onto buses and taken under military escort to the Gare d'Austerlitz, thence in sealed carriages to hastily improvised internment camps in the French provinces. The political activists are taken to Le Vernet in south-west France near the Pyrenees. Like other camps in the region, such as Gurs and Saint-Cyprien, Le Vernet was originally set up for refugees from Republican Spain. It is to become notorious as the worst internment camp in France.

'The first (and, as the event was to prove, the only) prisoners of war of the French Republic were now safely behind barbed wire,' writes Regler bitterly. 'They amounted to 560 fugitives from every country in Europe. For years, they had found asylum in Paris; their shelter now was a collection of ramshackle wood huts at the foot of the Pyrenees, without beds, without light and without heating. There were possibly a few dozen profiteers among the prisoners, as well as the full strength of the Central Committee of the German Communist Party; but the great majority was composed of opponents of the Third Reich. Not a single National Socialist had been arrested, or any Italian Fascist. Many carried papers showing that they had reported for service with the French Army. We lay on planks and were forgotten.'

Arthur Koestler and Gustav Regler are lucky: thanks to the

intervention of influential friends they are released after only a relatively short stay. Koestler is the first to go, on 17 January 1940; Regler follows shortly afterwards. It is the efforts of his girlfriend, Marie Louise, and friends from Spain that have brought his file to the top of the pile: Ernest Hemingway, Eleanor Roosevelt and Martha Gellhorn have all written pleas in his favour. Regler packs his suitcase in elation. Back to Paris, then, for where else is there to go?

Vive la France

In a moment of clarity – perhaps clairvoyance – in May 1939 Walter Benjamin suggested that, in the event of war, foreigners in France would end up 'in concentration camps'. In September 1939 he, too, lines up to enter the Stade de Colombes, whence he is taken, some days later, to a small camp named Vernuche in Nevers. Benjamin's health, never good, makes him a poor candidate for what is euphemistically called a 'voluntary workers' camp'. He collapses on the five-mile walk from Nevers and is helped by a young man who carries his bag and places himself at Benjamin's disposal, a disciple ready to serve his Master.

'The camp doctors gave me the following order: "at ease – rest," ' writes Benjamin in a letter to Adrienne Monnier on 21 September 1939, reassuring his friend that there is plenty of food and that he is doing as well as can be expected. He asks Monnier to write to him, and requests that she pass on his new address to Gisèle Freund. As ever, most prominent in Benjamin's mind is his work. When he receives a letter from Sylvia Beach – who has chosen to stay put in Paris – his reply to her is as much concerned with a request for chocolate as with his frustration at not being able to correct the proofs of his forthcoming fragment on Baudelaire. Meanwhile, his meagre funds diminish; he is forced to ask Max Horkheimer to advance him money.

After a few days some kind of order begins to emerge among the 288 internees in Vernuche. Men begin sweeping the rooms, hanging laundry out to dry; they organize lectures on the difference between

Freud and Jung, Lenin and Trotsky. Out of chaos and helplessness, a community emerges. Blankets are procured, eating vessels and drinking cups created from old tins. A man who collects stamps is appointed postmaster, while a painter famous for his cookery is appointed chef. Shortly afterwards, Benjamin begins to hold an advanced philosophical course outdoors, for which he receives a lecture fee of three Gauloises or a trouser button – units of camp currency that also include nails, pencils and other useful items. The rates of exchange are calculated by those in the know according to the principle of supply and demand: five cigarettes for a nail; or two cigarettes, a nail, a pencil, and a button for a small notebook.

Unable to participate in physical work, Walter Benjamin develops a fascination with a pair of inmates who have managed to convince the camp commandant that they are going to make a film entitled *Vive la France*, for which they need to collect material from the local town library. The commandant is delighted by the idea and provides the men with armbands that allow them to leave the camp unhindered. They return in the evenings smelling of wine and whispering stories of the first-class restaurants in which they have dined.

One day Benjamin takes his friend, the poet Hans Sahl, aside.

'It's about the armband,' he whispers. 'No, don't laugh. I have a plan.' He wants to suggest to the commandant that they publish a literary magazine, 'of course at the highest level', a camp newspaper for intellectuals that will show the French just who it is they have imprisoned here as 'enemies of France'.

'Come and see me tomorrow at 4 o'clock. We're going to hold our first editorial meeting.'

Benjamin lives in a hovel at the foot of a flight of stairs that forms a makeshift roof over his straw bed. A curtain fashioned from a piece of old sackcloth by his young disciple hides him from the eyes of others. The newspaper is to be called *Bulletin de Vernuche, Journal des Travailleurs du 54 Régiment*. It will appear weekly or fortnightly, for prisoners and their relatives, in French and German, and will include articles on sociology and philosophy, reviews of the improvised performances held in the camp, as well as a book section.

The newspaper never materializes; nor does the coveted armband, but its preparation gives Benjamin a sense of purpose that distracts him from his misfortune (as does his attempt to give up smoking).

Benjamin's letter to Adrienne Monnier bears fruit. Horrified to hear that the eccentric genius has been interned, Monnier sets to work lobbying the French PEN Club and other influential friends to obtain his release. By November 1939 Walter Benjamin is back in his apartment on rue Dombasle.

What a change a few weeks have made! Paris is unrecognizable: grey, drab, nervous. Windows are blacked out, air-raid sirens wail sporadically, uniforms are everywhere. At night, darkness, the streets empty, cars travelling slowly.

The experience of being interned has profoundly affected Benjamin. The din, the lack of privacy, 'the impossibility of getting away from people, if only for one hour' has left him 'so tired that I must frequently pause halfway down the street because I am unable to go on'. His doctor diagnoses myocarditis (inflammation of the heart muscle), but Benjamin is unable to find a specialist who can order a cardiogram. Twice he meets up with his sister Dora, herself suffering from heart disease, but he does not yield to her entreaties to leave Paris and get himself to safety. Nor does he act on an invitation to travel to Sweden. Instead, he renews his reader's pass at the Bibliothèque nationale, which has reopened after a brief closure, and returns to the matter that concerns him most: his work on Baudelaire. At home he mainly writes in bed because his apartment is so cold. The gas mask hanging on the wall looks to him like 'a disconcerting replica of the skulls with which studious monks decorated their cells'. He has not entirely rejected the idea of leaving France: convinced that emigration to the US is now the only viable option, he starts looking – unsuccessfully and perhaps without much energy – for someone to teach him English.

Gisèle Freund returns to Paris in October from an extended stay in England, where she has spent several months visiting her family and making a tour of prominent British writers whose photographic portraits she has taken. She picks up little bits of work: a report on fashion for *Life* magazine to show the Americans how the Parisian ladies are coping in wartime, some propaganda photos for the French government. Fellow photographer Fred Stein, meanwhile, is interned in the Stade de Colombes before being sent to a camp of *prestataires* – voluntary workers – and given hard manual work to do. His wife, Lilo, is evacuated to Brittany with their baby daughter, Marion, where she feels desperately alone.

Mann

Since his return from Spain Alfred Kantorowicz has been living with his partner, Friedel, at Le Lavandou in the south of France. When war is declared he decides not to return to Paris, thus avoiding the fate of his communist friends, who end up in Le Vernet. Instead, he spends the next ten days in relative luxury in some army barracks near Toulon before being shunted off to the camp of Les Milles, a former brickwork factory near Aix-en-Provence. The camp is to become a collection point for all men of German or Austrian origin living on the French Riviera. Kantorowicz is grateful that his political file remains in Paris: the local French officials assume that he is simply one of those 'relatively well-off refugees' who can afford to spend their exile in the south of France and he is soon freed.

So delighted is Kantorowicz at his release that he applies for a *sauf conduit* – the official permit required for foreigners in wartime – for a trip to Nice to visit Heinrich Mann.

Seated in Mann's study with the windows open, the two men spend a pleasant autumn afternoon discussing the prospects for the war: Mann seems 'clear-sighted, if not very optimistic'. He does not appear to be considering leaving France. As they talk, dozens of little birds fly in and out of the room, twittering, chirping, fetching food from open cages set up by Nelly, who has trained them to enter without fear. Mann seems oblivious to them.

Afterwards, Kantorowicz takes advantage of his permit to pay a visit to other exiled friends in Sanary where he succumbs to what, in retrospect, he recognizes as a form of delusion: 'Without reading my diaries I would never have thought possible the unholy optimism with which I, who was considered a pessimist, wanted to convince my friends in Sanary that victory over Hitler was within reach – I babbled about the prospect of being "back home" the following year.'

'Memory,' he notes, 'has a life of its own.'

Cold Comfort

James Joyce has recently returned from Brittany to the family flat on rue des Vignes in the 16th *arrondissement*. He is as fretful and harried as any man might be at such a time, though the war is merely a distant bass-line to the insistent melody of his concerns, which centre on his family, his health, his work. Poor Joyce, whose eyesight is so damaged, can no longer venture forth for night-time walks in streets made impassable by the wartime blackout. His personal life is fraught: his daughter-in-law, Helen, is in a fragile mental state, her marriage to his son, Giorgio, falling apart; his daughter, Lucia, is in a psychiatric clinic on the Brittany coast, where he has just been visiting her, and what will happen to her in a time of war? All his foreign-born friends are leaving the city. As for the work which has absorbed so many years of Joyce's life and ought to have been his crowning achievement . . . When *Finnegans Wake* was finally published in May 1939 the international crisis ensured that the attention of the world was elsewhere. Worse, those who were paying attention dubbed the book 'crazy', 'impenetrable', 'the work of a madman'.

It is mid-October when the Joyces return to find their apartment building almost empty and the heating turned off. For Nora it is the last straw in a domestic life that is in constant and growing disarray. With Helen close to a mental breakdown, James and Nora have taken it upon themselves to look after their beloved grandson,

Stephen. The family need some modicum of order in their lives, so they decide to move out of their freezing home and into the warm, familiar embrace of the Hotel Lutetia, taking Stephen with them. At the Lutetia, Nora will not have to cook or clean, Joyce can receive his friends in the bar downstairs and play the piano there if the fancy takes him; there will be space, sociability, comfort. Most importantly, there will be warmth.

Like Paris, the Hotel Lutetia is caught in a state of suspended animation. When the kitchen service is over, the head chef sometimes likes to sit down with the *chef caviste* (head of wine), Marcel Weber, in the private dining room next to the basement wine cellar. Here, before the war, the chef hosted food suppliers while Weber entertained merchants eager to add their vintages to the Lutetia's distinguished wine list. Sometimes they are joined by the manager, Monsieur Chappaz. The talk turns to the last war, when two-thirds of the staff were laid off and rooms were requisitioned for senior French officers. The Lutetia remained open to such guests as there were, a pair of banqueting rooms transformed into a Red Cross hospital. There were concerts to entertain the French soldiers, fundraising events organized by well-off, well-meaning ladies. Perhaps this is what they can expect this time around? Nobody knows.

For the moment, guests continue to enter via the revolving door, to be greeted by the concierge before proceeding to reception to register – white forms for the French, green for foreigners – a requirement of the French police. *Monsieur and Madame Joyce, ah yes!* A familiar face, the old Irishman with his bottle-bottom glasses and his cane. *Fill out the form here, if you please.* The old fellow knows the drill. Every morning the forms are taken by a runner to the police station. Occasionally a form is missed, when the staff discreetly 'forget' to register a regular who has arrived with a woman who is not his wife. The long-term guests – the *sédentaires* – stay on, for now.

James Joyce and Samuel Beckett have known each other for over a decade now, having met in 1928 when Beckett was an exchange student at the École Normale Supérieure. They share much in common, in addition to their city of residence: both studied French and Italian, love Dante and loathe religion, and are obsessed with words, puns, rhymes and songs; both are dauntingly brilliant, with a disconcerting tendency to lapse into silence – a habit which the two men enjoy together unselfconsciously, engaging in conversations which consist often of silences directed toward each other, 'both suffused with sadness. Beckett mostly for the world, Joyce for himself.'

Now, as Beckett accompanies Joyce from the Lutetia back to rue des Vignes to fetch some books, he takes the older man's arm carefully as they cross the street, for Joyce does not like being treated as if he were blind. Joyce is jumpy, irascible: the crisis between his son and daughter-in-law has led to a rift with his devoted secretary and friend, Paul Léon, who blames Helen's worsening mental condition on Giorgio's behaviour and objects to the removal of a child from his mother. The stooping, scholarly, Russian-born Léon occupies his position with Joyce entirely voluntarily, never agreeing to accept payment for his devotion. When asked why, he replies, 'This way, the day I do not feel like seeing Joyce I do not have to do so,' adding that it also means that he is free to speak his mind. Which he sometimes does.

An argument usually begins with Paul saying, 'Sir,' – they are always formal with each other – 'I think you are quite wrong . . . I want to scold you . . . I think you are making an error . . .' There is a violent eruption which soon dies down again. Everyone is gloomy for a few days, then the men make it up and everything is back to normal. This rift, though, is a serious one, for it involves Joyce's family and Joyce will brook no criticism of his children. In truth, Joyce is highly reliant on Léon, who has for over a decade been not just his secretary, dealing with publishers, lawyers, contracts, royalties and many other pressing matters, but his closest friend. A standoff ensues between the two stubborn men: Joyce formally requests (via an intermediary) that Léon return his publishing contracts. Léon, disbelieving, calls Joyce to ascertain if this is indeed the author's desire. Joyce frostily responds in the affirmative. Well, then. So be it. If that is what the old man wants. Léon pens an equally formal letter in which he undertakes to return the contracts and requests a signed receipt from Joyce.

There was once a rupture between Joyce and Beckett, too, this one caused by the unrequited passion of Joyce's daughter for her father's young Irish friend – a passion which Beckett eventually, somewhat tardily, rejected.

At rue des Vignes Joyce jumps nervously to the piano and sings at the top of his voice for half an hour.

For two months the Joyces live at the Lutetia, looking after Stephen and entertaining the usual – though diminishing – circle of close friends. With Paul Léon in the doghouse and other friends and collaborators gone from Paris, Joyce spends much of his time with his son, Giorgio, and with Beckett, who comes to the Lutetia to read to him and make notes. In November Joyce decides that they should send Stephen to stay with their close friend Maria Jolas in the country so that the boy can attend school. Maria runs a bilingual school for the children of expatriate Americans, which she must somehow keep going while she still has pupils to look after. As a precautionary measure she has moved the school to a village near Vichy in the south of France, named Saint-Gérand-le-Puy. Her husband, Eugene, is in the United States. As Christmas approaches, Maria suggests to the Joyces that they join her in the country for a few days. She cannot offer to host the family herself but there is a nice little hotel in the village, the optimistically named Hotel de la Paix, and she and her two daughters can temporarily stay in the greenhouse at the property that serves as a school. And so James, Nora and Giorgio Joyce leave the Hotel Lutetia on 23 December 1939, intending to return to Paris in the New Year. Excepting a brief visit in January, this will be the last time Joyce sees the city that has been his home for so long.

On arrival at Saint-Gérand Joyce immediately falls ill, enduring excruciating stomach pains which he explains to his friends as the result of the stresses of recent months. At the Christmas table he sits morosely, almost blind, drinking little, visibly in pain. Eventually he grows merrier, breaking into song as he was always wont to do. At the end of the evening, he jumps up and takes Maria Jolas by the waist to whirl her into an impromptu dance.

'Come on, come on!' he cries. 'You know very well that this is the last Christmas.'

The Collapse

Paris is quiet, the weather warm. An atmosphere of expectation lies heavy over the city. On 10 May 1940 the German army invaded Belgium, Luxembourg, the Netherlands, France. Luxembourg falls almost immediately, swiftly followed by Holland and Belgium. The magic spell of the Maginot Line has been broken: the German army simply went around it and entered France from Belgium.

Quietly, hurriedly, people start to pack up their belongings, strapping them on top of their cars and slipping off, heading south. It is not yet the grand exodus. More like a slow leak from a pipe that is destined, soon, to burst. In late May, refugees start pouring in from the north. In Britain, Prime Minister Winston Churchill finds his finest oratorical hour in the face of the British defeat in France.

After his release from Le Vernet Arthur Koestler has been living a hand-to-mouth existence with his girlfriend in Paris, passing from one police department to another in search of the correct paperwork to legitimize his continued presence in France. Their apartment block is almost empty. Most of the tenants are either interned in camps or have been mobilized. Nobody pays the rent, so the landlord doesn't bother about repairs. Gradually, the building comes to a halt. 'First the central heating in the house broke down, then the hot water, then the lift . . . Next, the telephone was cut off . . . it was like rigor mortis slowly gaining one limb after another.' Koestler manages to acquire some fake papers in the name of Albert Dubert, a Swiss national, and signs up to join the Foreign Legion in the hope of escaping France and somehow making his way to England.

★

The war is close now: air raids become more frequent, bombs land nearby. With László still in Le Vernet, Anna Seghers is alone with Pierre and Ruth in the flat in Meudon. Their landlords have left to stay with their nephew in the Auvergne. While the children try on their new gas masks their mother pays a hasty visit to the post office to send the manuscript of her new novel, *The Seventh Cross*, to her friend F. C. Weiskopf in New York, asking him to find a publisher. As a precaution she sends a second copy to another friend in the US, Wieland Herzfelde, gives a third to Bruno Frei, a fourth to a friend of László's. The last she keeps for herself.

In mid-May, news arrives that the Germans are only days away from Paris. Pierre is fourteen years old and still in short trousers; Ruth is twelve. The seven years of their French exile are almost all they can remember, a peaceful existence in a pleasant Parisian suburb which Anna has carefully built for them on the ruins of their German past. That afternoon the three of them leave on foot, each carrying a bag and a suitcase, along with a gas mask and a blanket. Pierre brings his telescope, because he loves it so much.

They walk for a while, then hitchhike, leaving behind the heavy, useless gas masks. They find a farm where a farmer offers them an omelette and a place to sleep on straw for the night. As they try to reach Orléans to cross the Loire they join crowds of refugees making their way slowly south, an endless human tide on the move. Pierre is in charge of map-reading. It makes him feel grown-up, partly responsible for their little family. The following day they manage to get on a train. Every time German planes appear the train stops and everyone scrambles out, throwing themselves on the ground. People curse the French government for abandoning them. One hysterical woman prays to the Holy Virgin, adding 'God Save the King!' several times.

They take shelter overnight in a house in a village named Pithiviers-le-Vieil where they eat their last tin of sardines. The following morning they wake to see German tanks entering the village square.

On Monday, 3 June 1940, bombs fall on Paris for the first time. Everyone who can, leaves. Cars speed down the streets, furniture and bedding piled high on the roof. The metro and train stations are crowded with families carrying suitcases, baskets, bedding, children, pets. The SNCF have laid on extra trains, but they cannot meet the demand. People are offering crazy prices for a taxi to get out of the city. They fight each other for petrol. Nobody can think straight: everyone is possessed by an urgent desire to run from the storm that is about to be unleashed, no matter to where. Grabbing whatever they can carry, they squeeze themselves into tiny cars, sit on the backs of trucks, ride on bicycles, push carts. An endless, slow-moving river flows from Paris.

Numbers

During the German advance into France between 6 and 10 million people took to the roads in a mass exodus from northern France toward the south.

Over 2 million citizens fled Paris. Many did not return.

More than 90,000 French soldiers died in combat between May and June 1940.

200,000 were wounded.

1,850,000 were taken prisoner.

Meanwhile the German Exiles

During the German offensive, the 'enemy aliens' who were interned at the outbreak of the war are interned a second time. 'It was a dirty trick,' complains Lion Feuchtwanger on hearing the announcement that all German nationals, or stateless persons born in Germany, now resident in France, men and women between the ages of seventeen and fifty-five, are to report on such-and-such a day to such-and-such a place. 'For nine months now I have been stuck in this mousetrap of a France, unable to obtain a permit to go anywhere else. And now

I was going to have to sample a concentration camp for a second time.'

In Paris, the famous indoor cycle track, Le Vélodrome d'Hiver, is crowded with women from every kind of background whose only point in common is their connection to Germany: women who have lived in France for decades; French women married to German men; shop workers; leisured ladies who parade around the camp in full make-up; intellectuals, artists and, of course, political activists. Anna Seghers is fortunate in possessing a Hungarian passport, it allows her to remain free, with her children, but everyone else is here: Babette Gross, Hannah Arendt, a young German anti-fascist named Lisa Fittko who recollects that the last time she was at the Vel d'Hiv was for a rally of the Front Populaire, where her ears rang with cries of *'Des Avions – Des Canons – Pour l'Espagne!'*

After a week or two the women, like the men before them, are taken in buses to the Gare d'Austerlitz. The windows are blacked out. Signs on the buses say: 'Refugees from the Restricted Zone (northeastern France)', presumably to avoid the grim possibility that a French citizen might spot these enemy aliens, these lady-*Boches*, and – what? Attack them? Hurl abuse as they pass by? The women sit pressed close together in the darkness, the air fizzing with fear. It is hot and stuffy inside. From the buses they are loaded onto a train. They travel for hours, right down to the south-west of France where eventually they arrive at the camp of Gurs, first built for Spanish Republicans fleeing Spain. Now, those Spanish men are carted off to Le Vernet to make room for the influx of new arrivals: all women of German origin aged between seventeen and sixty-five are to be interned here.

On the same day, a German pianist named Margot Rauch, formerly of Berlin, recently resident in Italy, is arrested in Limoges along with her nineteen-year-old daughter Ruth, a dancer, and sent on to Gurs. Marta Feuchtwanger and Friedel Kantorowicz are scooped up in the south.

The chaos of the Nazi invasion has spread to every corner of the French administration: neither the sentries nor the officers at Gurs know what to do, not even the special police commissioner who is supposed to be in charge. There are no orders; from their superiors there is only silence. Meanwhile new trucks keep arriving, packed with women, many of them refugees from France's newly conquered neighbouring countries. They call to one another through the barbed wire:

'Where do you come from?'

'We're Belgians.'

'We come from Holland.'

Soon there are over six thousand women in the camp.

This time around they take the older men too: Willi Münzenberg is briefly interned in a camp at Chambaran, south of Lyons. As German troops approach, the camp is evacuated and the prisoners led on a forced march heading south. During the march, discipline disintegrates; soldiers and internees end up going their separate ways. Willi tells a friend that he is heading toward the Pyrenees to try to reach Babette in Gurs. It is the last time anyone sees him alive.

The Mousetrap

The panic induced by the German advance spares no one, especially not a camp filled with anti-fascist German exiles, many of them Jews. A delegation of internees, headed by Lion Feuchtwanger, approaches the commandant of Les Milles camp urging him to act before it is too late: there are thousands of Germans here who are in mortal danger from the Nazis, they explain. If they are captured, they will all be sent to concentration camps. They try to impress upon the commandant the absolute necessity of getting these men as far away from the German army as possible.

Given the general chaos in the French administrative system it is all the more surprising that Feuchtwanger's pleas – backed up by the persuasive powers of several German lawyers also interned in the camp – convince the commandant to act. On a warm day in early June 1940 approximately 2,000 men – among them Lion Feuchtwanger, Alfred Kantorowicz and the artist Max Ernst – are told to board a train organized by the French authorities. The train is to take them on a 500-mile journey from Les Milles in Provence to Bayonne on the Atlantic coast, there to deposit them to make their own arrangements for an onward journey out of France.

The train travels westwards at a snail's pace, in pouring rain, the men crammed into cattle wagons with no toilets and little food. As they finally near their destination the train grinds to a halt. News filters through that *'les Boches'* are advancing toward Bayonne. A slow-motion panic ensues. The train lurches into reverse and proceeds to trundle back in the direction from which it came. At this point many of the passengers lose faith in this French 'rescue' and decide to make their own escape, heading on foot toward Spain or Marseilles. Lion Feuchtwanger stays put. He is by nature a cautious man, at fifty-six no longer young, with settled habits, an internationally successful author whose financial means have so far managed to cushion the pain of exile. The past seven years spent in a spacious villa in the south of France with his wife and the company of friends may not have been ideal, but it has not involved hunger, cold, sickness, want. He cannot make up his mind to flee into the unknown without the all-important transit documents which are currently being held by the train's driver. When, during one of the train's frequent stops, Alfred Kantorowicz clambers up into Feuchtwanger's carriage to inform him that he intends to take the next best opportunity to reach Marseilles, Feuchtwanger scribbles a note to the American Vice-Consul, Hirem 'Harry' Bingham, in the faint hope that something might be done to help him.

Eventually, the remaining internees are deposited at a temporary camp on a hill near Nîmes, where they discover that the *'Boches'* in question are, in fact, themselves: someone had thoughtfully radioed ahead to Bayonne to assure food and supplies for two thousand German internees. In the general panic this message had been garbled into 'the Germans are coming'.

The men scramble up the dusty path in the early summer heat, the older ones stopping every few yards to rest. Some leave their luggage behind, others carry large, unwieldy pieces of cardboard under one arm. These are the painters and graphic artists – Max Ernst among them – who are reluctant to part with the drawings they have made during their sojourn at Les Milles. Kantorowicz seizes his moment to slip away through the bushes to make his way to Arles. 'My luggage was light. I had put on my best and sturdiest suit, but it was too warm for the time of year. I rolled up a few shirts, some underwear and washing things in a coat and hung the bundle over my shoulder on a strong rope.'

At the new camp Feuchtwanger is constantly asked by others, younger and bolder than himself, why he chooses to remain with the incompetently run convoy. Feuchtwanger realizes that, despite all the privations he has endured in recent months, at the back of his mind is the unshakeable conviction that somewhere in the world – in the US, in Britain or in France – a publisher, an agent, a loyal admirer will be agitating on his behalf, arranging to spring the author from the 'mousetrap' country he once loved so much.

Being outdoors in the south of France in June is not all bad. Near the makeshift camp is a pleasant bathing spot and a local restaurant serving decent French food. One day in June, Feuchtwanger and some friends decide to pay a visit to the restaurant, spending the morning bathing before retiring to the shade for an excellent lunch which the landlord has conjured up. It is not a small meal. A plate of mixed *hors d'oeuvres* is followed by a first course of fish, a main dish of guinea fowl, salad and potatoes, then dessert, fruit and cheeses. Each course is accompanied by wine (a light Alsace, a fine Burgundy, a heavy Algerian) and rounded off with coffee and brandy. During lunch the guests discuss politics, literature and French cuisine, the landlord joining in with his own political opinions which are, in Feuchtwanger's view, 'considerably more sensible than those that had been advanced all this time by leading French professional politicians'.

After lunch the guests take a siesta in the nearby meadow. But Feuchtwanger cannot sleep. After months of deprivation and a recent bout of an excruciating stomach bug, this is the first meal in a very long while at which he has been able to sate his appetite and drink his fill of alcohol. The result is indigestion and a headache. Eventually he and a friend decide to walk back to the camp, leaving the rest of their party asleep on the grass.

On their way Feuchtwanger encounters a female acquaintance who has evidently been waiting for him.

'I was told you had gone for a bathe,' she says hurriedly. 'I have news for you from your wife.' The woman hands Feuchtwanger a letter, urging him to read it straight away.

The instructions from his wife are short and to the point: 'Do what you're told,' she writes in French. 'Don't waste time wondering.'

The woman points to a smart car which has drawn up at the roadside. A young man, immaculately dressed in a white suit and string gloves, gets out of the car. Feuchtwanger recognizes him as Miles Standish, US Vice-Consul in charge of visas.

'Please don't ask questions,' says the young man, in English.

Feuchtwanger hesitates, conscious of his shabby short-sleeved shirt, his patched trousers, his rubber-soled sandals.

'Do get in,' urges Standish. 'You'll find a coat in the car.'

Feuchtwanger hesitates again. The friend who has accompanied him from the restaurant steps back, understanding what is about to occur: this is Feuchtwanger's moment to run, not his. They shake hands, bid each other a hasty farewell, and Feuchtwanger climbs into the car.

In the back is a woman's coat with an English brooch on it, a pair of dark glasses and a coloured shawl. Standish instructs Feuchtwanger to put on the clothes, then drives off at speed.

When the car is stopped by police on the way to Marseilles, Standish declares that the elderly English lady seated behind him is his mother-in-law.

Jesus on a Donkey

When she moved south with her school, Maria Jolas told all her friends that if things went pear-shaped they should come to join her in Saint-Gérand-le-Puy. She might well rue the breezy generosity of that invitation, issued in the quiet of the first months of the war. Until now she has been leading a peaceful existence in the little village with her dwindling band of students, her daughters, and the three Joyces for company: James, Nora and little Stephen.

First Giorgio Joyce appears, hoping to pass himself off as an Italian teacher to avoid conscription. Then come the Léons, Lucie and Alexis, followed the next day by Paul, who arrives in a wooden cart drawn by a donkey.

'The Lord Jesus Christ rode into Jerusalem on a donkey!' he cries as his family rush to meet him.

'But he wore a white robe and his path was strewn with flowers,' they remind him.

'It was a white ass, anyway,' adds Lucie, pragmatically, and: 'You'd better have a bath.'

Several other friends from Paris turn up, and friends of friends to whom Maria once blithely offered hospitality, plus there are about fifty refugees who annoy everyone else by buying up all available toothbrushes, shaving equipment and underwear. Maria plays musical chairs as she tries to accommodate the crowd: the Léons move into the Hotel du Commerce, which she has been using for some of her boys, who are now relocated to a nearby farm. The Joyces leave their little flat to join the Léons in the hotel, but then Maria has to vacate the chateau which has acted as the main school building, which means the Léons have to move out of the hotel to make space for her. They, too, find a room in a nearby farm.

It is 17 June 1940. The mood is unexpectedly cheerful, but nobody quite knows what to do. Choices must be made and soon. Whether to stay or go. And if go, then where? If stay, then how?

In the evenings the friends gather in the hotel dining room to listen to the news on an ancient radio.

The General

The stiff-limbed, patrician-looking general who enters the lobby of the Lutetia is greeted as a regular by Monsieur Chappaz, who accompanies the honoured guest to the desk to check in for a stay of – how long? Perhaps a few days, possibly more? It is hard to say under current circumstances. As the manager assures the gentleman that the room is entirely at his disposal for as long as he would like it and directs a porter to take the guest's luggage up to his room, Chappaz might have observed the air of distraction, the hurried gait of the lanky general as he strides toward the lift. He might recall a younger version of the man when he came, in 1921, to spend his wedding night at the Lutetia with his new bride, en route to their honeymoon in Italy. A few minutes later, Chappaz watches as the man hastens back down the stairs, *sans* luggage, passes through the lobby and disappears through the revolving doors.

For the next two weeks this is pretty much all the staff at the Lutetia will see of the freshly promoted Brigadier General Charles de Gaulle as he engages in a frenetic attempt to convince the French government not to conclude an armistice with Hitler.

Everyone in the French government knows that the defeat of France is inevitable, but an armistice is not. Charles de Gaulle, forty-nine years old and newly promoted not only to the rank of Brigadier General but to a junior post in the government too, believes passionately that the struggle against Nazi Germany can be continued from abroad. His conviction is not shared by France's elderly generals, the seventy-two-year-old commander-in-chief of the French forces, General Maxime Weygand, and the eighty-three-year-old war hero Marshal Philippe Pétain. The bloody losses of the Great War weigh heavily on the shoulders of these old men, haunted by the spectre of France's decimated youth. Never again. Better to be conquered than annihilated. No, never again. De Gaulle's argument: the governments of Belgium, the Netherlands and Poland have chosen exile. Let France do the same.

Three times in the space of a week de Gaulle meets the British Prime Minister, Winston Churchill. The night before his first visit he manages to find the time to telephone his eighteen-year-old son Philippe – a student at the nearby Collège Stanislas – inviting him to dine at the Lutetia. Over dinner the father informs his son of the death in battle of his cousin, says little about his own military exploits, and instructs Philippe that he and his sister Elizabeth, also at school in Paris, must immediately travel to join their mother and sister Anne in the Loiret region south of Paris, before moving on to Brittany. To Philippe's objections that, although not yet mobilized, he is undergoing military training and hopes to defend his country, de Gaulle *père* responds sternly that there is nothing to be gained by remaining in the capital. Far better, he insists, to escape now in order to be ready to fight later. 'For the moment, and this is a formal instruction I insist on: under no circumstances allow yourself to be overtaken by the enemy. Otherwise, you'll find yourself behind barbed wire like the young men who hadn't yet been mobilized in the invaded countries of 1914.'

At de Gaulle's first visit to London on 9 June Churchill is impressed by the vigour of the young(ish) general, in stark contrast to the defeatism that holds sway among France's leaders. But the following morning, back in Paris, de Gaulle is woken in his hotel room by the news that the Germans will soon reach the French capital. His argument that the city should be defended falls on deaf ears: the government has fled. That night he, too, leaves Paris in the company of Prime Minister Paul Reynaud, and spends the next few days driving between various government ministers, hastily installed in castles dotted around the Loire region. Communication is difficult, almost impossible; the roads are clogged with refugees. With the government gone, there is nothing to hold back the panic-stricken populace.

At his second meeting with Churchill, this time in France, at the

Château de Muguet near Briare, de Gaulle listens as his country's leaders spell out the dire situation of the French army. Later, at a separate meeting, General Weygand declares that he desires an armistice. That night de Gaulle drafts a resignation letter which he does not yet send.

Open City

By 13 June, Paris is deserted. Shops are shuttered, offices closed. The streets that were clogged with people trying to escape are now silent. Under the threat of imminent conquest, Paris has been declared an open city. According to international convention, this means that it will not be defended.

Early in the morning of 14 June 1940, German infantry enter Paris and head toward the city centre, an immense column of motorized troops: first, motorbikes with sidecars, their drivers clad in leather overcoats; then armoured vehicles and tanks. Behind the closed shutters, those who are awake listen to the deep rumble that heralds the arrival of the conquering enemy. They are mainly women, the elderly, children. The men have gone to fight and who knows if or when they will return? A coffee cup trembles on its saucer; a dog whimpers, sensing the strangeness, the danger, the change. Even birdsong is absent. The bombing of the petrol dumps on the Seine Estuary created a huge, black, oily cloud that has emptied the skies of bird life.

Although France has not yet formally capitulated, General Kurt von Briesen cannot resist: instead of bypassing the capital he leads his men on an impromptu victory parade along the Champs-Élysées, complete with marching band. Von Briesen takes the salute from his horse, nodding and smiling in delight. *Well done, boys, well done.* For the German army this is not just any victory: this is the erasure of a past humiliation, the washing away of the pain of 1918. And to enter this celebrated city not amid gunshot and smoke, but freely, without impediment . . .

And yet, there is something about the nature of their entry into Paris, its almost indecent ease, something akin to a man who has threatened a woman with violence if she does not let him enter her home. Unexpectedly she opens the door and steps aside with a disdainful gesture: enter, take it, you can have it. She yields, but the disdain remains.

On the Left Bank, oblivious to the passage of the invaders through their city, the early-morning staff at the Hotel Lutetia carry on cleaning, polishing, laying out the breakfast plates. The cooks prepare the coffee; the baker pulls a batch of croissants from the oven.

By mid-morning, swastikas are flying from public buildings. At the Hotel Crillon the temporary military governor of Paris, General von Studnitz, receives the chief of the Paris police and the prefect for the Seine region, offering them French champagne which they politely accept. Across the street, the American Embassy preserves an awkward neutrality, while the Soviet Embassy on rue de Grenelle must welcome the Germans as allies.

Into Exile

With his resignation letter still unsent and German troops approaching the Loire, General de Gaulle follows the government as it retreats to Bordeaux. Here he finds Prime Minister Reynaud apparently ready to move the government to North Africa. Seizing on this last hope of avoiding an armistice, de Gaulle offers to make a final dash to London to discuss the transfer of French troops across the Mediterranean. Since there is no plane available, he drives all the way, crossing to Plymouth in the early hours of the morning and arriving in London at dawn on 16 June. He is too late: as he is settling in at the Hyde Park Hotel he discovers that, in the interim, Reynaud has bowed to pressure from Pétain and Weygand and has asked the British government how it would respond if France approached Germany about signing an armistice. De Gaulle returns to France immediately, this time in a British plane. The arguments that follow are bitter but short-lived: Reynaud prefers the option of fighting from abroad, Pétain will not budge from his position that it is better to conclude an armistice and remain in France. Presented with the choice between two unpalatable options, the cabinet choose the latter. Reynaud resigns and the President of the Republic, Albert Lebrun, calls on Marshal Pétain to form a government.

The following morning, de Gaulle packs two suitcases, gathers together a small supply of francs and sets off for London in the same plane in which he arrived the previous day. In his haste he forgets that he has left behind at the Lutetia an army trunk, which the hotel staff duly store in the basement, along with all the other lost property, to be kept until his return. As his plane flies over La Rochelle and Rochefort, de Gaulle sees ships burning from German bombs. Then they pass over Paimpont, where his mother lies ill. It is only once he arrives in London and must find somewhere to live that he begins to feel the magnitude of what he has done: 'I appeared to myself, alone and deprived of everything, like a man on the edge of an ocean that he was hoping to swim across . . .'

Charles de Gaulle has left behind his home, his country and his family to take up the cudgels in a fight that his government has already conceded. Alone in a city he does not know, with few connections and little knowledge of English, unable to call on the support of the French diplomatic service, de Gaulle has set off to lead where, for the moment, few are willing to follow. The tall, standoffish, brilliant general sits in his London hotel room contemplating his self-imposed exile.

Conquerors

Another cast of characters now strides across the stage. They arrive as conquerors to occupy the city, its people, and its hotels. How are we to write about them? They are human beings, after all. But it is because of them, and of what they represent, that all of this is happening. The dramas of 'before' and 'after' are both a consequence of an ideology enacted by the German people who are now present, here in Paris, dressed in field grey and black leather jackboots, pacing the carpeted corridors of the city's hotels with the air of new owners inspecting a recent acquisition.

Within days the face of Paris has been transformed: signposts are erected everywhere to direct military traffic. Clocks are brought forward by one hour to correspond to German time. A curfew is imposed. The machinery of military government, enormous and complex, requires buildings, staff, vehicles, supplies. It needs hospitals, prisons, canteens, barracks, banking and telegraph facilities. Paris is so vital to the Reich that every element of military and civilian government in Berlin is replicated here. And what choices are on offer in this sublime city! So many splendid buildings, such history, such elegance and style! The staff of the quartermaster general vie with one another to follow the example of General von Studnitz and hasten to requisition the city's finest hotels.

The first addresses to be snapped up are those in the swankiest *arrondissements* on the Right Bank: the 1st, the 8th, the 16th: the logistical military command of Greater Paris has already laid claim to the famous Hotel Crillon on the place de la Concorde; the commander of Greater Paris takes over the Meurice nearby; the general staff get the George V, while the military high command in France, led by General Otto von Stülpnagel, take a fancy to the Majestic near the Arc de Triomphe, along with propaganda and censorship services. The German Embassy remains on rue de Lille, where the former art teacher Otto Abetz is soon installed as German Ambassador to Paris, a role that ought to be redundant in an occupied country, but this is von Ribbentrop's domain and he does not want to be left out.

The various branches of the German police present a confusing profusion of initials to the uninitiated French, who are yet to discover the subtle but important distinctions between the SS, the SD (the

Sicherheitsdienst, the intelligence branch of the SS), the Gestapo (secret police) or the *Geheime Feldpolizei* (GFP, secret military police). Their activities are of such a nature that one public building does not suffice: they require private addresses, branch offices, cellars, garages to keep their fleets of black cars. For Parisians the building that will come to symbolize their presence is 11 rue des Saussaies, formerly the headquarters of the Sûreté nationale. And that other infamous address, avenue Foch, where the SD have taken over three buildings at the far end, near Porte Dauphine, numbers 72, 82 and 84. Parisians will refer to all or any of these addresses as 'Gestapo HQ'. Senior staff of these services often prefer the discretion of an apartment or a house left empty by its owners, probably British or Jewish. Neuilly is a favourite spot, although larger apartments in the centre will also do.

And so the grand hotels in Paris are no longer accessible to the French. Instead of a porter, soldiers now guard their entrances. Across France, the scene is being repeated: the entrance of the victors into town and village squares, the requisitioning of buildings, the hoisting of the Nazi flag.

The Lutetia Section

Marcel Weber is on his way up from the wine cellar to visit the manager when he sees them for the first time: men and women in grey uniforms, wandering freely about the hotel. 'We couldn't believe our eyes!' No announcement, no warning, nothing. 'There was no sound of boots, it was more like being in a silent film.' And there is Chappaz himself, standing in the lobby greeting a German officer with the formal politeness with which he greets every guest.

The Hotel Lutetia is a little out of the way from the centre of Nazi power in Paris. How appropriate, then, that it is requisitioned by the Abwehr, the intelligence service of the German military, an organization that itself stands uncomfortably on the fringes of the Nazi regime. At its head, the complex, controversial figure of Admiral Wilhelm Canaris, a fluent French speaker and connoisseur of fine cuisine, a German nationalist who ends up in a concentration camp; a man who will finally send himself into irreversible exile.

Despite rumours that he chose it for its role at the centre of German resistance against Nazism, in reality Canaris's main interest in the Lutetia is its location: the Left Bank of Paris has always been associated with artists and intellectuals, a reliably anti-Nazi group. Planting the Abwehr in their midst makes sense.

There is no immediately discernible difference in the manner with which Monsieur Chappaz greets the new 'guests'. *Un client, c'est un client*, after all. But anyone observing the discussion would immediately understand that it is no longer Chappaz who is the boss of this establishment, but the sturdy middle-aged man with the polished boots who is demonstrating, with an air of pride, his excellent command of French as he issues orders about accommodation, furniture, food. Reality has shifted.

'So, it is true, they were there. One of them immediately asked me what there was to eat.'

Colonel Friedrich Rudolph is one of the Abwehr's most experienced officers. He has been in the service since 1924 and since 1935 has been in charge of Ast (*Abwehrstelle*, or station) Frankfurt, working in military espionage covering southern and eastern France. Receiving the order to travel to Paris to take over command of the new French Abwehr station, Alst (*Abwehrleitstelle*, sub-station) Frankreich, Rudolph quits his job in Cologne and arrives at the Lutetia on 15 June 1940, several days before the official French capitulation.

If Weber and the other Lutetia staff are astonished by the sudden presence of uniformed Germans in their midst, they must have been amazed at the rapid transformation wrought by Colonel Rudolph, who without delay sets about reorganizing the hotel to serve not just as living quarters for Abwehr staff but as their place of work. The first change is to make the building inaccessible to the public: the patisserie and brasserie are closed, the windows at street level covered with tree branches, wire fencing placed over the façade and main entrance. Some of the banqueting rooms are designated as storerooms or meeting rooms, a switchboard is installed, the mail room becomes a dormitory and refectory for the soldiers who guard the hotel. The President Salon – that same banqueting room where another set of Germans held their meetings just a couple of years ago – will serve as an officers' mess.

Staff begin to arrive: secretaries, radio operators, clerks, as well as senior Abwehr officers to take charge of the three departments that will be run from the hotel. The Lutetia Section is to be set up in line with the principles used by the Abwehr in peacetime, consisting of three main sections: Group I, information services, has the task of carrying out military reconnaissance in enemy territory, at the moment mainly in England. At the head of this group is Major Alexander Waag, a nephew of Admiral Canaris. Group II, responsible for psychological warfare, sabotage and subversion in enemy territory, is currently unstaffed. In line with all Abwehr units at home, Group III is the most heavily staffed. In overall command is Frigate Captain Langendorf. The man who has been chosen to run sub-section IIIF, responsible for the crucial task of military counter-espionage, is Colonel Oscar Reile.

The Dreamer

'Reile is an odd character,' remarks a French intelligence officer after interviewing the Abwehr colonel after the war. 'He is both naive and perceptive. He writes poetry, loves nature, is a dreamer, and yet he appears to have run his counter-espionage organization with some success.'

Aged forty-four, Oscar Reile has a long career behind him, first as Chief of Police in Danzig, then as a counter-intelligence officer in Admiral Canaris's newly reformed Abwehr. Following the re-militarization of the Rhineland in 1936, Reile was transferred from his post in Kassel to Trier where, under the guise of a businessman and furnished with fake ID, invisible ink and cameras, he was responsible

Colonel Oscar Reile

for recruiting agents to gather intelligence. Reile's physical appearance suggests his suitability for undercover work, for – as noted in a
1945 British intelligence report – there is nothing that stands out: '5'9",
thin sharp face, piercing eyes, wears glasses, greying hair, blue eyes,
clear complexion, fairly big nose, pointed chin, clean-shaven. Very
upright and stiff. Speaks English and German, bad French.'

On 19 June Reile is in Nancy (now renamed Nanzig) heading an
Abwehr-*kommando,* or unit, when he receives an order to travel to
Paris immediately. He is to report to Colonel Friedrich Rudolph
prior to taking charge of Section IIIF in the newly established
Abwehr post in occupied Paris. The address Reile is given is of a
hotel on boulevard Raspail.

    That night, Reile lies awake worrying about the weighty task ahead
of him. 'Would I be able to fulfil it according to the expectations of

my Berlin superiors? Didn't [they] know that I came from East Germany and had never seen the French metropolis?'

By morning, Reile's doubts have gone: 'After all, I had been conducting counter-espionage against France since 1935, had studied French history in depth and had about thirty agents who spoke French well. By reading French historians and poets, I believed I had also gained a sufficient understanding of the customs and traditions as well as the cultural achievements of the French people.'

With this reassuring vision in mind, Reile takes leave of his men, climbs into his car and sets off for Paris.

The journey from Nancy to Paris crosses most of eastern France. Initially it is Reile's companion, Corporal Hoffman, who does the driving, leaving Reile free to enjoy the scenery and reflect on what lies ahead. As they pass Metz and head west via Verdun and Châlons-sur-Marne, Reile takes the wheel. What a pleasure to drive through France on a glorious early summer's day! It is almost like being on holiday. There is just a sliver of anxious anticipation at the prospect of entering this famous, brilliant city for the first time. Reile does not know it, but he is in august company: two days after his arrival it is the Führer's turn to feel that same frisson as he finally realizes his lifelong dream of visiting the City of Light.

It is afternoon when the silhouette of Paris finally appears on the horizon. As they pass the Bois de Vincennes and enter the historical centre, Reile is struck by the city's emptiness. There are no honking cars, no taxi drivers, no delivery vans. Shops are shuttered, cafés closed. With a map of Paris in hand, Reile and Hoffman navigate their way speedily toward boulevard Raspail. Pulling up outside the elegant façade Reile jumps out of the car, shows his credentials to the guards stationed outside, and enters the Hotel Lutetia.

Colonel Rudolph greets Reile as an old acquaintance, briefing him briskly on the current situation and the tasks of the Paris Defence Force. Reile admires Rudolph, describing him as a 'self-assured gentleman', a former cavalry officer with a wealth of experience,

Colonel Friedrich Rudolph in Paris, 1940 (*left*), and in British custody, 1945 (*right*)

professional and yet approachable: 'In his official behaviour, whether toward superiors or subordinates, he always remained clear and brief. In personal conversations, on the other hand, he appreciated jokes and humour.' These virtues of character are matched by his appearance: 'Colonel Rudolph looked good,' writes Reile admiringly. Aged forty-five, he is 'about 1.80m tall, blond, blue-eyed and of sturdy build.' Looking at a photograph of Rudolph taken just after the war one is led to wonder whether Reile has endowed his former boss with Aryan features that in reality he lacked, for Colonel Rudolph evidently had dark hair. His sturdy build is less courteously depicted in British reports as having a 'tendency to grow stout' or 'podgy'; he is described variously as 'distinguished', having the air of an 'arrogant officer', with a 'very pleasant gentlemanly face' or – less charitably – a '*Gourmandgesicht*' ('foodie face'). The post-war photograph depicts a man no longer stout: a spell in a Nazi prison after the July 1944 attack on Hitler, followed by events at the end of the war, evidently put an end to the sleekness acquired during his comfortable stay in Paris.

Colonel Rudolph interrupts his remarks to call for champagne from one of the French staff hovering discreetly nearby. Before Reile has time to reflect on this unaccustomed luxury Rudolph is raising a glass to drink to his health and to their successful co-operation. He assures his 'dear Reile' that he will be leaving him a free hand in the field of counter-intelligence. 'But first,' he adds, 'a special assignment awaits you.' The German army have seized a large number of secret documents from various French cities and towns. Reile's first task will be to bring these documents together, analyse and evaluate them. At the moment there is only one person to help him, but more units are on their way. 'Make yourself comfortable in the two rooms I have reserved for you,' concludes Rudolph. 'Tonight we'll have dinner together.'

'My driver had already found a place to stay. So I was able to let the French hotel staff show me to my accommodation. The two rooms were on the third floor of the Lutetia Hotel. They offered a magnificent view of half of Paris, especially the Latin Quarter. I gazed at this panorama for a while, mesmerized. When I looked around my rooms, I found that they were furnished with every comfort, even luxurious.' Even more delightful to Reile is the fact that he can take a long, refreshing bath. 'After the eventful weeks of the campaign, during which I had often spent the night in half-destroyed or inhospitable houses, it seemed almost incomprehensible to me that I was now housed in such palatial surroundings. Of course, I had no idea at the time that I would be living in these rooms for four years.'

Down to Work

The following morning, Reile moves into his office in the room adjacent to his bedroom (number 350) and is introduced to Captain Leyerer ('svelte, elegant, lively, full of drive'), a former police officer familiar with intelligence work and an enthusiast for 'thorny' cases. Reile asks Leyerer to make a list of all the buildings in Paris where secret documents have been secured, intending to visit them the next day to obtain a precise picture of the quantities of written material that he is to be responsible for storing and analysing.

Leyerer then introduces Reile to the Abwehr staff who have already started work in Paris: around twenty-five officers, twenty female auxiliaries, twenty or thirty junior officers, as well as radio operators, chauffeurs and other auxiliaries. Eventually there will be over a hundred Abwehr staff quartered at the hotel, taking up almost all of the rooms. Officers and operational staff are given rooms on the lower floors while valets, couriers and chauffeurs live on the seventh floor, at the very top of the hotel. Senior officers like Reile have two rooms, one serving as a bedroom, the other as an office where a secretary sits at a desk with a typewriter dealing with his administrative work. Specialist offices containing safes, type-writers, telephones and radios are located in other parts of the hotel.

So far, so normal, as far as Reile is concerned. When it comes to the living arrangements, however, he is shocked to discover that the measures taken by Colonel Rudolph 'deviated greatly from the usual customs in Germany and seemed questionable to me'. The entire service staff, including cooks, waiters, valets and chambermaids, are French. Colonel Rudolph has allowed seventy-five members of the French staff to keep their jobs, almost a third of the pre-war total. Given that most of the German personnel live in the hotel and eat their meals there, this seems to Reile to be not only unusual but to pose a serious security risk. The manager, too, the unflappable Marcel Chappaz, remains in post, and for the next four years will have the delicate task of acting as intermediary between the occupiers and his staff.

It does not take long for Reile's concerns to fade. By the second day of his stay in Paris, he is enthralled: 'The French waiters served us in the large dining room with the utmost courtesy, as if we were the most pleasant of guests. I had the impression that the manager of the hotel and his staff were keen to demonstrate to us what they understood by good French cuisine and home cooking. The food was skilfully prepared and the wines and champagne, which we were offered at ridiculously low prices, were of excellent quality.'

The ridiculously low prices are, of course, only possible because it is the Germans themselves who have set the rate of exchange.

The invisible staff cook, clean, open doors, sweep floors, prepare food, serve drinks. Breakfast, lunch, dinner. Sometimes senior officers are served in their rooms, drinks brought to the door with a discreet knock. And the reply, amid a burst of laughter – is it *Entrez*, or *Herein?* Rudolph and Reile, proud of their linguistic prowess, undoubtedly address the Lutetia staff in French, but the rest of them? Do they ever pick up the rudiments required to communicate to staff whose skill is such that soon the men and women of the Abwehr forget that they are even there?

Armistice

The following morning Colonel Reile and Captain Leyerer spend hours driving around Paris inspecting the buildings in which the secret written material is stored. The only other people they see are German soldiers wandering around the French metropolis admiring the sights. Reile, busy with his work, regrets not having the time to explore.

They find government offices open, their archives untouched and unguarded, mountains of files left behind in the abandoned buildings of French ministries and the police authorities. Reile loses no time in sending men to collect the documents to secure them somewhere where they can be organized, analysed and – crucially – protected against prying eyes. The Abwehr want to keep their treasure to themselves; they certainly have no wish to share it with the Gestapo or the SD.

On his way back to the Lutetia, Reile learns that German troops have seized a train loaded with archives from the Ministry of War, including most of the records of the French intelligence service, the Deuxième Bureau. As he enters the hotel he is formulating a plan to deal with this cornucopia of information when his thoughts are interrupted by the sight of Abwehr staff rushing excitedly around the lobby.

It is 22 June 1940, and in the forest at Compiègne, in the very same railway carriage where German generals surrendered to Marshal Foch after their defeat in the 1914–18 war, Marshal Philippe Pétain has signed an armistice with Hitler. Pétain declares on the radio: 'A collaboration between our two countries has been envisaged. I have accepted it in principle.' The northern half of the country and the entire western coast is to be occupied by the German army. The rest, the so-called 'free zone', comes under the control of Pétain's collaborationist government, based in the southern city of Vichy. A demarcation line separates the two zones.

The military campaign is officially over. France has been cut in two.

Dizzy with joy, Abwehr staff stop work and gather in the dining room to celebrate with champagne. As the Germans grow merry, engaging in animated discussions about what this extraordinary moment might mean (many of them assume that the armistice will soon be followed by a peace treaty with both France and Britain) the staff of the Lutetia watch in silence.

Service

What does it mean, to serve? *Un client, c'est un client.* Yes. Service is a uniform that you put on and take off again when you go home. Yes. Discretion, tact – those attributes of the staff in good hotels, the ability to make a guest feel that they are uniquely important – yes, all that. But to serve the enemy? There is no book of rules by which staff in requisitioned hotels in an occupied country, the government of which has just signed an armistice, might be guided in their behaviour toward their new 'guests'.

All over Paris thousands of cooks, waiters, chambermaids and shopkeepers are faced with the same dilemma. How are they to behave toward the enemy who is now their ruler? Relief at no longer being at war is tempered by the fear of these unfamiliar figures who have suddenly appeared in every corner of their city. What are Parisians to expect from these tall, well-fed men in field-grey uniforms and polished boots who wander around, cameras and maps in hand, snapping photographs of one another before the Eiffel Tower and the Arc de Triomphe? The Wehrmacht soldiers are just boys, some of them, pink-cheeked, innocent-looking lads from rural villages. The officers are tall and courteous; they hold themselves with dignity (or is it pride?). Some of them smile, try out their heavily accented schoolboy French. Meanwhile, the waiter must serve them dinner, or an aperitif, he must clear the table and polish the glasses just as he has always done, with professional pride. The chambermaid must clean the room, turn the bed, change the towels, plump the pillows just as she has always done. The boot boys must polish the long leather boots that line the hotel corridors, the chefs must provide dinner for hungry guests. And there is pride, too: the pride in a job well done, in showing these *Krauts*, these *Fritzes, Frises, Fridolins* that there is no food finer than French *haute cuisine*, no waiter more efficient than a French *serveur*, no wine more refined than a French Bordeaux or Burgundy. A form of resistance? To say: we will show them who they are dealing with so that they will never be able to say, 'Things are better back home.'

Marcel Weber is used to spending much of his time underground. Under the Lutetia lies a labyrinth in several layers: in the first is the hotel kitchen; beneath this is the vast wine cellar, organized by region, and a dining room where Weber once received his guests. Below this lie two more levels of cellars, enormous spaces mainly used as storage for old furniture and unclaimed items left by guests (including General de Gaulle's forgotten army trunk).

During the invasion Weber thought about his cellar, with its wonderful vintage wines and fine champagnes. He imagined his precious bottles being opened by foreign hands, their contents poured down undiscerning throats. And he decided that, even though his country's leaders had admitted defeat, he would not allow the Lutetia's finest wines to fall to the barbarians. So, with the help of some of the staff, Weber moved all the best wines and champagnes into a corner of the cellar which they then walled up. When Colonel Rudolph requests a map of the basement area he is duly provided with one on which the hidden wines do not feature.

The Germans later dig two tunnels of their own in the lowest cellars in case of attack, one leading to the Banque de France on the opposite side of boulevard Raspail, and a second that emerges at the Sèvres–Babylone crossroads. They never discover the hidden treasures that lie beneath them, and Weber derives enormous pleasure from knowing that the wines about which the Abwehr officers wax so lyrical are not the very best the hotel has to offer. If the Germans cannot tell the difference between a good wine and an excellent one, well, it just shows you what an unsophisticated lot they are.

If Marcel Weber is to be believed, it was not just wine that lay hidden in the cavernous cellars but a group of escaped French POWs. Helped by staff, who brought them food and clothes, they in turn helped out – with what precisely we do not know. It is a pleasing image, symbolic of a kind of passive resistance, or resistance as performance. The Lutetia staff are polite, if reserved; they cater with professional pride to the needs and demands of their unwanted guests. Their rebellion lies not in poisoning the Germans' soup but in keeping something hidden from their masters, right under their noses: the finest wine, and perhaps a few men, too.

And so the delicate dance has begun, as the conquerors seek to convince the conquered that they are really not so bad. The hand of friendship is extended – *Look, we are going to be together like this for quite some time (our Reich is going to last a thousand years, after all) so you might as well get used to us. And we're really most appreciative of everything your beautiful city has to offer.*

Posters go up around the city showing a blond, blue-eyed soldier gazing tenderly at a child in his arms with the slogan: *Populations abandonnées, faites confiance au soldat allemand* ('Abandoned citizens, put your trust in German soldiers').

Article 19

The signing of the armistice marks a pivotal moment in the harried existence of the German exiles. Article 19 of the agreement states that, 'The French Government is obliged to surrender upon demand all Germans named by the German Government in France as well as in French possessions, colonies, protectorate territories, and mandates.'

German and Austrian exiles are now at direct risk of arrest, imprisonment, death, just as they were in 1933. And not just them: any person deemed hostile to Nazi ideology – someone like Arthur Koestler, for example – might find themselves on a Gestapo list. Most urgently in need of help is anyone who happens to be stateless, or Jewish, which often boils down to the same thing.

Once again, the exiles find themselves in a world dominated by the overwhelming need to obtain papers, stamps, visas. The goal now is to head south to Marseilles, the only major port still functioning in the unoccupied zone, there to catch a boat and get away from France and reach the safety of – where? Where next?

It is at this moment that Heinrich Mann finally sees the urgency of leaving France. Once more, it is Nelly who takes on the practical tasks of closing bank accounts, paying bills, finding homes for their pets and their books as they prepare to join Thomas in the United States. Heinrich Mann is fortunate in one respect: as a prominent anti-Nazi who features at the top of the Gestapo's wanted list, he is also top of all the other lists being frantically put together by those who see the urgency of getting certain people out of France. Among these clear-eyed souls is a young American journalist named Varian Fry, who arrives in Marseilles with a small budget and a long list of mainly Jewish artists, writers and other prominent figures under imminent threat. Fry is at the head of the recently formed Emergency Rescue Committee (ERC), a grand name for a small group of dedicated volunteers who, over the next few months, will help over two thousand people escape from France.

Heinrich and Nelly Mann don't have too far to go to get from Nice to Marseilles. On arrival they move into the Hotel Normandie to await their exit visas. Opposite them is the Hotel Splendide, and Varian Fry, who is going to sort everything out for them.

Hitler's Dream

The sculptor Arno Breker is at home in Berlin when the Gestapo arrive at his door and order him to be ready to leave in one hour. As he dresses hurriedly, Breker spots two SS officers waiting outside. To his wife, who is Greek and with whom Breker speaks only in French, he barely has time to whisper a few hasty words before he is escorted to a car and driven at speed to Berlin's military airport, where he is placed on a military transport plane. After a three-hour flight, during which Breker grows increasingly anxious and very hot, the plane lands and Breker is again bundled into a car.

They turn off into a forest at Brûly-de-Pesche, close to the Belgian–French border, and pull up outside a bunker from which a familiar figure emerges. It is the architect Albert Speer, followed by another architect colleague, Hermann Giesler.

'You must have been scared,' remarks Speer maliciously, peering at Breker's sweaty face.

Adolf Hitler is in excellent spirits as he explains to Breker the reason for his presence at the bunker from which the Führer has been directing the French campaign. The following morning the group will travel to Paris, where Breker's task is to act as Hitler's guide to the French capital. The Führer unfortunately has little time to devote to the excursion, so he wants Breker – as a long-time *Parisien* who knows the city well – to come up with a plan for a tour that will take in all the most important architectural and cultural sights in the couple of hours available.

Hitler, the failed artist, has long been fascinated by Paris, but has never visited the city. He tells Breker that this burning desire has always been frustrated by events, until now. 'Now the gates of Paris have opened for me! Since that moment I have had no other thought in my mind but to visit this metropolis of art with my artists.'

My artists.

Hitler has two objectives: he wants to visit the monuments he has always dreamed of seeing, and he wants to study Paris with a view to surpassing it when he realizes his vision of rebuilding Berlin. Hence the presence of his two favourite architects and of Breker, who has the twin benefit of being both a Reich sculptor involved in the urban planning of the future capital, and a connoisseur of Paris. Hitler is optimistic that the war will soon be won. Britain will be defeated, and he will be the ruler of the most powerful country on earth. Buoyed up by recent victories, the Führer can afford to be magnanimous toward the French, choosing neither to destroy Paris nor enter it at the head of a victory parade.

Breker is profoundly unsettled by Hitler's words: to visit Paris, the place he considers his second home, where he spent his formative years, alongside the leader of the winning side in a terrible war, seems to him an almost unbearable moral burden.

The party sets off briskly at 3 a.m. on 23 June. After a short flight they arrive at Le Bourget airport, where a convoy of cars awaits them. Hitler takes his place next to the driver in the first, open-topped vehicle, inviting Speer, Giesler and Breker to sit in the back.

As they enter the city centre, Breker looks around in shock. His last visit to Paris was during the World Fair of 1937. Now, 'Paris seemed dead. Not a soul.' Even Hitler is silent as they speed down the deserted streets. Their tour is to take in the kinds of sites that today might be observed from an open-top bus: the place de la Concorde, the Arc de Triomphe, the Eiffel Tower, Les Invalides, Notre-Dame, the Tuileries, Montmartre. The whistle-stop itinerary is hardly designed to offer an in-depth examination of Paris architecture, but Hitler has done his homework and demonstrates a keen interest in what he sees. First stop is the Führer's favourite: the neo-baroque Opéra, the architectural plans of which he has studied in great detail. Breker is impressed and not a little astonished: Hitler knows the precise dimensions of the building, along with a thousand other details. Approaching the entrance, the first French person they encounter is a terrified janitor who has been sent to let them in. The man does his best to ignore the visitors, his face evincing not the slightest trace of curiosity, and for the first time Breker feels the 'tragic gulf' that separates the French from what he now represents.

Hitler is bowled over by the auditorium: 'The most beautiful theatre in the world!' he exclaims, before asking the janitor to show them the path the French President would take to reach his box. At the end of the visit the janitor remains behind, 'rigid, motionless, petrified, his expression empty'. Breker is impressed by the man's icy yet dignified demeanour. When an adjutant attempts to tip the man, he refuses. Hitler asks Breker to try again, but he is firmly rebuffed.

At Hitler's request, the convoy proceeds slowly along the Champs-Élysées toward the Arc de Triomphe. Hitler is thinking of how his capital, to be renamed 'Germania', will look. His triumphal arch will have to be twice the size of the Arc de Triomphe, the boulevard leading up to it twice as wide. Plans for this project, first conceived by Hitler when he was in hospital recovering from his injuries during the 1914–18 war, are already well advanced. Speer and Breker are both closely involved.

After a brief stop for a photo opportunity in front of the Eiffel Tower it is on to Les Invalides, where Hitler pays his respects at Napoleon's tomb, bowing solemnly to his fellow conqueror, his cap clasped to his chest. The Panthéon does not impress him, but he enjoys being taken through the student district along boulevard Saint-Michel and boulevard de Montparnasse, where Breker once worked. As they head back toward Le Châtelet they pass

Hitler with Albert Speer and Arno Breker at the Eiffel Tower, 23 June 1940

Notre-Dame, the Hôtel de Ville, Les Halles, where for the first time in the deserted city they see some signs of life: a newspaper vendor with the morning edition, and a little group of stout fishwives who, catching sight of the passing convoy, exclaim, 'It's him! It's him!' before scuttling away in fear.

The last stop is Sacré Coeur. Here, with Paris laid out before him, Hitler stands lost in thought for a moment before thanking 'destiny' for allowing him to realize his life's dream. 'This marvel of western culture, spread out before us, absolutely had to be preserved, it had to be kept intact for posterity. We have succeeded.'

The optics of the tour are carefully managed. For the sake of future Franco-German entente, Hitler makes a great show of not wishing to rub French noses in their defeat; nevertheless, the group is accompanied by Hitler's official photographer and the visit is captured on newsreel, enabling Hitler both to project a reassuring image to the rest of the world and to show people back home what victory looks like. As he stops to pose in front of the Eiffel Tower, he makes sure to place 'his artists' next to him, a demonstration both of his vanity and his insecurity. It is notable that they have been asked to wear military uniform for the occasion.

By 8.15 a.m. the visit is over. By 10 they are back in Hitler's bunker at Brûly-de-Pesche. If Hitler's dream was to admire the architecture of Paris he has achieved his aim. But, as in a dream, he has walked out onto the stage alone, a solitary figure standing before an empty auditorium. His journey down the deserted boulevards was accompanied by a ghostly quiet. There were no crowds to welcome him, the cafés and bistros remained empty and shuttered.

As their plane takes off, Hitler asks the pilot to circle over Paris so that he can see it all below him one more time before it disappears beneath the clouds. He will never see the French capital again.

Tourists

'In the summer of 1940, Paris took on a very special look,' writes Oscar Reile. 'German soldiers were everywhere, sometimes accompanied by charming young women. In the evenings, places of entertainment such as the Lido, Folies-Bergères, and Schéhérazade were full. Military tourists invaded all the artistic and historical sites, such as Versailles and Fontainebleau.'

Over the weeks following the armistice the streets of Paris gradually come back to life. People who had fled return, shops reopen. Everyone is desperate to embrace some semblance of normality. The military authorities, too, are keen to demonstrate that nothing much has changed: museums, post offices, banks, the metro are soon back in service. Schools and universities reopen. Newspapers and magazines continue publishing. Bars, restaurants and nightclubs are back in operation. Even the sparrows have returned.

★

The sight of German soldiers seated on café terraces is initially a shock, no doubt about that, but very soon the fact that these men do not behave like philistines, do not get roaring drunk and make a scene, look smart in their grey uniforms, do not harass the women, say *s'il vous plait* and *merci* when they order a *bière*, allows many – if only temporarily – to convince themselves that this is just another kind of tourist come to admire the City of Light.

Signs pop up outside cafés declaring *Hier spricht man Deutsch* instead of *English spoken*. The Deutsche Institut on rue Talleyrand sees Parisians enrolling in their thousands to learn German, fuelling a demand for teachers. Advertisements require these to be 'Aryan, and if possible of German origins'. There are lectures and concerts, readings of German poetry.

Germans in Paris are under strict instructions to be on their best behaviour. Stiff Teutonic manners may not match Gallic charm, but since the French population is predominantly female, and the occupying forces overwhelmingly male, the Germans go out of their way to convey an impression of correctness, discipline and courtesy.

Paris is of such importance to Hitler that he orders that all his men be sent to the city, not just to admire it but to prepare them 'so they will not be surprised once we start building our new Berlin'. German soldiers on leave are sent to Paris under a programme named *Jeder einmal nach Paris* (Everyone to Paris once). They are placed in specially requisitioned hotels or *Soldatenheime*, most of them around boulevard Haussmann, avenue de Wagram, and République. Airmen have lodgings on the Champs-Élysées, while Luftwaffe officers stay on rue du Faubourg Saint-Honoré. They are taken on tours much like the one Hitler himself enjoyed, traipsing around the top tourist spots with their cameras round their necks: up the Eiffel Tower – *snap!* – along the Seine in a *bateau-mouche* – *snap!* – down the Champs-Élysées and up again to Montmartre. The cultural section of the occupying authorities even produces a bi-monthly magazine, *Deutscher Wegleiter für Paris* (German Guide to Paris), which publishes illustrated stories from the city and lists the cultural events

German soldiers buying postcards, Versailles 1940

and tours of the day. Later in the war, when German troops are freezing on the Eastern Front, this magazine proves more popular than stories from back home.

Although all soldiers visiting France are issued with an official copy of Fritz Sablatnig's photo journal of the French capital's architectural highlights, published by the German National Education Office (also available as stereoscopic images), the propaganda department is keen to encourage them to photograph what they see themselves in order to bring home the scale of the German victory and wipe clean forever the humiliation of 1918. Little is left to chance: soldiers are shepherded around with photo opportunities suggested at every stop. The highlight is a trip to Versailles, where a snapshot taken in the Hall of Mirrors, scene of the signing of the hated Versailles Treaty in 1919, sends a powerful signal of national triumph.

Like most tourists, German military personnel on leave rarely stray from the path set out by their superiors and encounter few Parisians beyond those who serve them in cafés and restaurants. There are *Soldatenkinos*, cinemas reserved exclusively for occupation troops and showing only German films or entertainment. There are theatres and nightclubs, too, reserved for Germans only. All over Paris are *Lokale*, army canteens, mostly in former restaurants, from which the French are banned unless they show a permit. There is a German bookshop on the place de la Sorbonne, an Italian one on boulevard Saint-Germain.

Few enlisted men speak French; many come from the countryside or small villages. To them the geography of a capital city, with its complex transport system and unfamiliar habits and routines, is bewildering. How much more reassuring then, after a quick tour of the major sights, to join with a few comrades and indulge in that other favourite tourist pastime – duty-free shopping, using their spending allowance to purchase miniature models of the Eiffel Tower, alcohol, food and – most enticingly – those mysteriously feminine, quintessentially French items such as silk stockings and perfume, all of which can be wrapped up and sent off from the Gare de l'Est to a sweetheart waiting for her beloved back home.

The Victors

Paris is not just the premier tourist destination for German soldiers on leave, it is the most prized posting in occupied western Europe. Anyone who is anyone in the Third Reich feels the need to send a representative to France, creating in Paris a miniature version of Berlin, with all its petty rivalries and intrigues. While Germany's foot soldiers are shuttled around Paris on tourist trips, those at the top of the Nazi administration vie with one another to entertain their guests in the style to which they believe Parisian society is accustomed: dress uniforms, soldier-servants in white gloves, silver cutlery, expensive linen, excellent food and wine, distinguished French guests, especially women to balance the numbers.

Many of the high-ranking German officers stationed in Paris see themselves not as foreigners, but as members of a cultural elite that stands above the divisions that separate conqueror from conquered, German from French. Familiar with French literature and culture, enamoured of French food, wine and women, these are the self-declared standard-bearers of western civilization. It seems rude even to suggest the notion of 'collaboration' to these high-minded, high-ranking individuals. And yet, their posting places them in the ambiguous position of being both superior and desiring to be accepted, wanting to be on equal terms with their distinguished French guests, but always with the niggling suspicion that those who drink and eat with them might secretly despise them.

There are some among the occupiers who experience a profound disquiet at their position. Beautiful as the city is, they know – deep down, like their fellow German exiles before them – that they do not belong here. They can stand with their brother soldiers and drink beer and sing songs, or sit on a café terrace sipping an *apéro* with a charming young Frenchwoman, but at the end of it all each man is here because of his uniform. It is a different kind of exile, to enter another man's home uninvited, to sit at his table and eat his food and drink his wine while he looks on impotently. And sometimes a soldier on leave in Paris begins to question: where do I belong in all this? What is my culture, my history? Where is my home? Berlin may be destined to fulfil the Führer's dreams, but for the moment it represents only a dislocation from the past and an uncertain picture of the future. Lothar-Günther Buchheim, a naval officer and later the author of the best-selling novel *Das Boot*, asks himself: 'Who really is the victor here? The boot-wearing privates in their breeches and their made-to-order military jackets? Or the Parisian people?'

One evening at the Lutetia, the chef serves artichokes at dinner. A member of the Abwehr staff, not knowing the proper way to eat this complicated vegetable, starts to choke. Furious, his comrades call the chef to their table, angrily accusing him of sabotage. One of the more sophisticated officers, familiar with French cuisine, steps in and explains that there was no ill intent. The man has simply eaten the wrong part of the artichoke. The intervention saves the chef from arrest. It does little to assuage the uninitiated officer's sense of wounded pride.

They are, at heart, insecure, these occupiers.

Oh la la!

The Hotel Lutetia has a different rhythm these days. The sound of typewriters emerges from the bedrooms, radio operators make calls from the banqueting rooms, messengers come and go purposefully. So many uniforms! The blue redingote and red collar of the concierge is now set against the field grey and jackboots of the Abwehr officers, the chambermaids' black and white against the *souris grises* ('grey mice', the nickname for female auxiliaries) in their heavy grey skirts and jackets. No wonder the German girls want to buy French stockings and spritz their uniforms with a mist of French perfume! The romance of Paris has dazzled them all. They are feverish with the newly awakened desire to live life as the French do. There is romance in a posting in a beautiful city so far removed from the brutal violence of the war. And with so many young men and women thrown together (though female staff are billeted at a small hotel nearby), it is hardly surprising that the euphoria of victory leads to a certain *frisson* between colleagues.

Oscar Reile, middle-aged and married, observes his younger staff with paternal fondness. 'In this summer, Victory is naturally celebrated and, just as naturally, more tender relations were established between the male and female members of the service.'

The female Abwehr staff serve mainly in administrative roles as typists, secretaries or mail clerks. Reile's secretary, Käthe Winkler (aged twenty-eight, 'brown hair, blue eyes, long nose, clear brow, oval face, slim') has worked for Reile since 1936. Out of eight female staff in the department she runs, three marry during their stay in Paris. Even Colonel Rudolph is not immune: separated from his wife, he employs a twenty-six-year-old secretary named Erika Juhl who becomes his mistress and, later in the war, his second wife. With all the euphoria of their recent victory it is a wonder any of them get any work done at all.

The staff look on with a certain dry amusement at the antics of their unwanted guests. 'At the beginning, everything was very strict and disciplined, military style if you like. But that soon changed. They discovered Paris, they went off shopping and came back with their arms full of packets for their dear wives, saying: *Oh la la, shoes and so many other things, at amazing prices*. Yes, and then they started appreciating French food.'

It is around this time that the head of the Abwehr, Admiral Canaris, pays his first visit to the Lutetia.

La vie est belle!

'As soon as German troops entered Paris, the Abwehr moved into the comfortable premises of the Hotel Lutetia. People lived there "like God in France" (according to the famous saying). The most luxurious requisitioned French cars were parked at the entrance, and the chefs were busy in the kitchens, where the *cordons-bleus* worked ceaselessly to craft delectable, complex dishes. The members of the Abwehr indulge day and night in the pleasures of the table, for there is no shortage of anything and everything is available in abundance, without coupons.

'A *mélange* of the most varied perfumes drifts through the lobby and along corridors of the hotel: the female staff have made a point of reading up on French perfumery. These ladies wear the finest silk stockings, giving their legs a more attractive curve; they sport elegant new outfits, of which there is no shortage in Paris. In the rooms that have been converted into offices, men and women sip champagne and enjoy liqueurs. They make conversation: *la vie est belle!*'

★

The German anti-Nazi journalist Curt Riess honed his energetic writing style as foreign correspondent for *Paris Soir* in the US during the 1930s. After the war he settled in Zurich, where, in 1951, he wrote an article for the Swiss weekly *Die Weltwoche*, titled 'The Secret of Admiral Canaris', the main subject of which was the relative effectiveness of pre-war French and German intelligence services. The opening section of his article describing Admiral Canaris's arrival at the Hotel Lutetia in July 1940 offers a vivid sketch of Abwehr life in occupied Paris, with a nervous Colonel Rudolph making frantic preparations for the arrival of his boss. Given that Riess spent the war in America, the piece is largely a product of his journalistic imagination. It is no less entertaining for that.

'In a blink of an eye the luxurious cars disappear, perhaps replaced by German military vehicles. The lobby and corridors are given a good airing and the female staff are invited to give up – at least temporarily – the perfume they are so fond of and to take their inspiration from the *"Tirpitzufer"* fashion rather than rue de la Paix.[†] To the great disappointment of the Abwehr staff, the French chefs must give way to a Wehrmacht cook. The officers who are already wearing bespoke suits made for them by the finest tailors on the Champs-Élysées must put their uniforms back on again.

'Admiral Canaris emerges from his car, accompanied by his deputy, Colonel Hans Oster, and another officer. Canaris barely glances at the commandant who stands at the door to welcome him. With long strides, he enters the building. He appears to see nothing or to wish to see nothing. He nods a few times in greeting and disappears into the room that has been reserved for him.'

Riess certainly captures the atmosphere of hedonistic pleasure which held sway in those early days of the Occupation. However, the likelihood that Admiral Canaris, a keen gourmand who regularly had delicacies flown into Berlin from all over occupied Europe, would eschew fine food and wine in favour of army stew is slim indeed. Likewise, the image of Canaris striding manfully into the

---

† The headquarters of the Abwehr was at 76–78 Tirpitzufer in Berlin.

hotel lobby conjures up a personality far removed from reality: at 5'3", Canaris was significantly shorter than almost everyone around him, and was far more likely to be followed by his two beloved dachshunds than by his fellow officers.

Canaris

When Admiral Wilhelm Canaris was asked to reorganize the Abwehr in 1935 he made a poor first impression on his staff: he arrived at Abwehr headquarters looking 'colourless and impersonal' in a shabby tunic, on which was pinned the Iron Cross First Class. Short, white-haired, with bushy eyebrows and the ruddy complexion of a sailor, Canaris spoke in a quiet, almost inaudible voice, paid more attention to the two hairy sausage dogs that accompanied him than to his staff, and promptly installed a camp bed in his office.

The Abwehr's taciturn new chief soon revealed himself to be a man of formidable talents with an untiring appetite for work. The camp bed was frequently in use, not just because Canaris was a workaholic but because he disliked going home. His marriage to Erika Waag was unsuccessful; family life with two daughters, one of whom suffered from mental illness, brought him no joy. By contrast, his two beloved wire-haired dachshunds, Sabine and Seppel (later Kasper), accompanied him everywhere. Canaris found in his dogs a sense of safety and companionship which eluded him in human relationships: in Berlin he brought the dogs to work in his black government Mercedes, where they sat in his office, occasionally fouling the carpet. In the rare moments when he stopped working, Canaris would play with his canine friends, or else make notes about their habits and behaviour.

Workaholic, shy, solitary, reserved, unhappy at home . . . Canaris was all these things, as well as a keen amateur cook, and a fan of Spanish culture. He was also a brilliant linguist and a highly effective diplomat, a skill which was to prove essential in navigating the minefield of competing organizations within the Nazi hierarchy.

As a military organization devoted to espionage and counter-espionage the responsibilities of the Abwehr frequently overlapped with those of the Gestapo and the SD, who often tried to muscle in on Abwehr territory in their pursuit of enemies of the Nazi regime. Admiral Canaris's efforts to preserve Abwehr independence in the face of such political pressures inevitably placed him in conflict with SS chief Heinrich Himmler and SD head Reinhard Heydrich, once a friend and protégé of Canaris, now his rival. Himmler hated the Abwehr, considering it a breeding-ground for traitors. His suspicions were not unfounded: most Abwehr officers were not Nazis, and several of its highest-ranking staff were actively involved in the anti-Hitler resistance. Canaris himself, while never participating directly in resistance activities, was sympathetic to their beliefs and frequently turned a blind eye to their plotting.

But these dramas are still to come. For now, Germany is victorious over France and Admiral Canaris has just arrived at the Lutetia to inspect occupied Europe's most important new Abwehr outpost. The porter takes the Admiral's luggage up to the first floor to one of the best rooms in the hotel, number 109, which offers a direct view of the Sèvres–Babylone crossroads, and where Canaris will stay on all his future visits to the French capital.

When travelling on official business Admiral Canaris usually booked a twin room so that his dachshunds could sleep on the bed beside him. If he was obliged to leave them behind, he would telephone daily for news of their bowel movements and emotional state. In the absence of concrete information (his diaries disappeared in 1945), it is impossible to confirm whether Canaris was accompanied by his beloved dogs on his visits to the Lutetia. If they were present, they would surely have enjoyed a thoroughly professional welcome from the staff, a bed of their own, and tasty leftovers from the Admiral's plate. If, on the other hand, Canaris was obliged to travel without them, and if the British happened to be listening in on Abwehr calls (as he suspected they were), they might have made the same mistake as the chief of the Spanish secret police who, when monitoring Canaris's telephone conversations in Spain, was said to have declared himself perplexed at the Admiral's avid interest in the digestive habits of a pair of Abwehr agents called Seppel and Sabine.

Intelligence

While most German soldiers are running around Paris shopping and celebrating their victory, Oscar Reile has been hard at work examining the thousands of French secret files that have fallen into his hands and which he is supposed to analyse. Admiral Canaris has come to see what he has discovered and is expecting a report.

Reile is a diligent man. His main task is to set up a counter-intelligence network in France, but he has devoted so much time to analysing this enormous trove of secret documents that he feels very much behind schedule. Alongside a cache of documents that offers up vital information about individuals spying on Germany before the war are the files of the French Sûreté nationale, discovered – amazingly – to have been left intact. Documents belonging to France's foreign intelligence service, the Deuxième Bureau, captured in a train near Charité-sur-Loire, yield further significant findings, including references to individuals who supplied intelligence to the French, and fresh insights into the espionage activities of France's secret services.

As he sets out his findings, Reile observes his leader without quite knowing what to make of him. 'The admiral was a good listener. He sat quietly in front of me. His clear blue eyes seemed to look right through me. His snow-white hair shone, but his features seemed impassive to me.' The documents offer useful and fascinating information about the past, explains Reile. Many of them will need to be sent to Abwehr headquarters in Berlin, where the information will be used to identify and neutralize French agents who may still be working against the Reich. However, the pressing need, as Reile sees it, is to establish what is going on in France now. Section IIIF of the Abwehr is responsible for gathering intelligence on potential resistance networks in the occupied zone. He needs to find out if the British are active in France, and to recruit a new network of agents.

Canaris seems thoroughly reassured by Reile's diligence: he approves Reile's proposals and leaves him to it. After the conclusion of the inspection Canaris and Rudolph dine together with other senior officers at the Lutetia. As he notes with pleasure the quality of the food and wine, Canaris can congratulate himself on his excellent choice of headquarters. And then it is back to Berlin.

Unlike many of the Abwehr officers in Paris, Colonel Reile is less interested in the perks of his posting than in the professional task that lies before him: as soon as Canaris is gone, he begins his search to put together a network of trusted agents – known as *V-leute* ('trusted people', from *V-mann*, *Vertrauensmann*, trusted man) – to work in Paris and the occupied zone. As a first step he brings in several experienced *V-leute* who had worked as agents before the war, most of them not German nationals, all fluent French speakers, and currently waiting in Belgium and Luxembourg to be deployed again. At a time when thousands of French citizens from Alsace-Lorraine, Belgium and Luxembourg are still on the move looking for new accommodation and employment in France, it seems a propitious moment to integrate these agents under cover names in various French cities as refugees. One of their first tasks will be to seek out new recruits to work with the Abwehr: Reile cannot risk sending established agents into the unoccupied zone where they might be recognized by French counter-intelligence. Fresh faces must be found, and quickly.

Return to Paris

James Joyce and Paul Léon are men of habit.

That summer of 1940, in the little village of Saint-Gérand-le-Puy, the two scholars establish a daily routine. Every morning, at around eleven o'clock, Joyce walks over to fetch Léon from the farm where he is staying. He raps on the fence with his cane.

'*Le voilà!*' cries Paul, hurrying out to meet him.

Sometimes they sit in the garden, watching Lucie hang out the washing, or sit with her while she minds an American child whose parents are packing to go home. More often Joyce and Léon stroll together, arm in arm, down the road to a tree trunk where they sit for hours, sometimes talking, more often in silence. Then they head back and settle down to work on preparations for a new edition of *Finnegans Wake*.

But this pleasant situation cannot last. There must be movement of some sort. Choices have to be made.

The Léons have run out of money. Lucie, the main breadwinner in their household, needs to get back to her work as a fashion correspondent for the *New York Herald Tribune*. The United States is not yet at war, the fashion houses have reopened, American ladies are agog to hear how Parisian ladies are coping with wartime restrictions. For Paul, the pull to return is the desire for the familiar: he wants to sit at his desk surrounded by his books and resume work on the study of Jean-Jacques Rousseau that is preoccupying his thoughts. Most important of all, there is his son Alexis's education to consider: the boy has to get his *baccalauréat*. And besides, they have no warm clothes.

Lucie is the first to leave, setting off for Paris on 16 August. Joyce sees her off at the bus stop in Saint-Gérand. Paul accompanies her as far as the train station in Vichy, begging her to sort out a permit quickly so that he can join her. Two weeks later, Paul Léon is back in Paris, leaving the Joyces alone in the village. Maria Jolas has already left for the States.

'It all seemed reasonable at the time,' wrote Lucie after the war. 'It was only later that we realised what a mistake we had made.'

The Léons are not alone in underestimating the danger they are in. Many foreign-born Jews who had lived in France for decades, as well as French Jews whose families had been in France for generations, could not or would not believe that they could be betrayed by the Republic, where all citizens were equal under the law. When, in October 1940, an official German census required Jews to register their presence, nearly 150,000 Jews in Paris responded. Law-abiding, diligent citizens, they believed that if the state asked them to do something, they must obey.

As naturalized French citizens Eva Tichauer's parents escaped internment. After the armistice, instead of trying to cross into the unoccupied zone or finding another route of escape, they decide that Eva, their sole surviving child, their only hope for the future, must finish her medical studies. Like Anna Seghers, like Paul Léon, the Tichauers value education above everything. If they fear for their own futures, they choose to ignore the risk for the sake of their child's. And besides, they are French citizens. Surely that must count for something. So they return to Paris and Eva takes up where she left off.

Anna Seghers, too, has decided to return to Paris with the children. It is jarring to see the swastikas flying on the buildings, the German uniforms in the streets, the posters of that blond soldier with the child – 'Abandoned citizens, put your trust in German soldiers!' – but she doesn't know what else to do.

Her main preoccupations are their lack of money and the challenge of how to get news of László in his camp in the Pyrenees. She wants at all costs to escape from occupied Paris, but she needs time to work out how to do this. Meanwhile, they have to live somewhere. They cannot go back to their flat: the Gestapo will know the address. She finds a small room on rue Saint-Sulpice where they can stay for a few weeks, and sells the last piece of jewellery that her father had given her. It is enough for them to live off, just. At least the children are never truly hungry.

Even now, Anna never wavers from her conviction that wherever they are, whatever their circumstances, the children must continue learning. When she discovers that some schools are running summer courses, she immediately registers Pierre at the Lycée Louis-Le-Grand near the Sorbonne, where Paul Léon's son Alexis is a pupil. For Ruth she finds a primary school in the 6th *arrondissement*.

As German convoys drive up and down rue Saint-Jacques, Pierre's geography teacher cheers his students up by showing them maps of the world: 'The British have Aden, the Cape and Singapore. All is not yet lost!'

That summer in Paris seems to Pierre at first like a big adventure worthy of his beloved Alexandre Dumas: his mother sends him on secret errands to contact friends and to visit their apartment to find out, discreetly, if it is possible to retrieve some of their things. In Meudon with their friend Else, a neighbour tells Pierre that the Gestapo came looking for Anna and László in July but have not been back since. The house itself is empty. The owners are still away. Pierre and Else slip in through the back door and creep up to the first floor, where they quickly gather up a few belongings. Discovering the manuscript of *The Seventh Cross* hidden in a drawer, Else decides to burn it 'so that it doesn't fall into the hands of the Nazis'. When Pierre later recounts this to his mother, for the first time in his life he sees her cry. Of the five precious copies Anna had made of her novel, this was the only one she had kept for herself.

Their neighbour's account confirms that Anna is on a Nazi wanted list. They must keep moving. For a short while they find lodgings with an elderly couple, then move on again. Anna sends Pierre out, this time to visit her friend Lore Wolf. When he arrives at Lore's flat the concierge pulls him aside and tells him that the Gestapo came that morning and took Lore away. Pierre is dumbfounded. *But what about her son?* The boy is due back from school at any moment. *Don't worry*, says the concierge. She will take care of the boy. For the first time the reality of their situation dawns on Pierre. Terrified, he leaves the building, checking to see if anyone is following him. He gallops down the metro steps four at a time, takes the first train that comes along and changes line several times before eventually running back to tell his mother what has happened.

For a while the family live in hiding, each in a separate place. But they cannot continue like this. They have to try to cross into the unoccupied zone and find László. Anna has no contacts in the south, but they must get out of Paris before it is too late.

In July 1940 the Vichy government sets up a commission to study the cases of 'aliens' naturalized after 1927, many of whom then have their French citizenship revoked, thus depriving thousands of foreign-born citizens – mainly Jews – of the protection of the French state. With the loss of their precious French nationality the Tichauers become, once again, stateless Jews. When new restrictions are brought in excluding Jews from university, Eva has to renounce her medical studies. Her father Theodor's position as a prominent social democrat places him high on a list of those wanted by the Nazis. All the signs are there, telling them that they should flee, and quickly. They should go to Marseilles, where everyone else is heading.

And yet, like the Léons, they choose to stay on in Paris, even as new restrictions limit their freedoms.

Marseilles

I should understand, he said, that French cities aren't there for me to live in, but for me to leave from.

Anna Seghers – *Transit*

Marseilles in the summer of 1940 is a scene from a medieval vision of hell, the streets and cafés packed with thousands of desperate refugees – Germans, Czechs, Poles, Yugoslavs, Belgians, Dutch, Spaniards – all looking for the same prize: a visa, it doesn't matter too much for where, so long as it will get them out of France. Every morning they line up outside the consulates of the countries to which they hope to flee, or through which they need to pass. But the visa, once obtained, is only the first step in a process so byzantine it has the quality of a particularly troubling dream: a visa allows a refugee to apply to the French authorities to stay in Marseilles for a limited period to prepare for their departure. They then must find a ship that will get them to their final destination, or to a staging post along the way. In every case a French exit permit is required, which for those on the Nazis' extradition list is impossible because Vichy France will not grant them one. All visas and permits are only temporary, so the effort to co-ordinate the necessary entry, transit and exit visas requires a balancing act of rare delicacy. In the meantime, the refugees must survive with the help of aid committees, which provide them with food, meal tickets, handouts, cash.

They meet one another in the cafés on the old harbour or on La Canebière, where they show each other 'their valid or invalid papers, passports, makeshift passports, identity cards, makeshift identity cards, chase after rumours about incoming and outgoing ships – always with the risk of being picked up in one of the raids and taken to prison or deported to an internment camp'. But the risk has to be taken. Those who stand on the sidelines are lost. The Vichy government enthusiastically enforces the armistice agreement, handing over fugitives to the Gestapo.

Arthur Koestler's brief stint in the Foreign Legion has – if nothing else – exempted him from a second internment. Determined to get to England, he has been slowly making his way toward Marseilles. As he exits the train station the very first person he sees – immediately recognizable in the crowd by his height and shock of white hair – is Dr Rudolf Breitscheid, the former German Minister of the Interior, leading member of the SPD, erstwhile participant in the Lutetia Committee, and one of the Nazis' most wanted political fugitives.

'What is this fancy dress?' asks Breitscheid, staring at Koestler's uniform.

The pair retire to the third floor of the Hotel Normandie, where Breitscheid's wife makes coffee on a spirit stove while Breitscheid knocks on the wall of the next room. Seconds later, the former Minister of Finance, Dr Rudolf Hilferding, appears in his dressing-gown. Hilferding, another leading Social Democrat, is also high on the Nazis' wanted list.

The little group sit on the bed drinking coffee and eating grapes, exchanging news about friends and colleagues. Both politicians have visas for the US but – the usual story – no French exit visas. When Koestler asks them why they don't try some unofficial route, the men reply in outraged tones that they refuse to contemplate such a course, confident that the Vichy authorities will grant them what they need. Koestler listens in disbelief as Breitscheid declares that Article 19 is a 'mere formality, to humiliate the French'. It will never be executed.

Six months later, Breitscheid and Hilferding are still in Marseilles. On 11 February 1941 they are handed over by the French authorities to the Germans.

If Breitscheid and Hilferding remain trapped by their dogged faith in the forces of 'legality and righteousness', the majority of those who feature on the Nazi wanted lists know precisely what to expect if they don't leave France. Varian Fry and his volunteers also understand what is at stake. Given the continuing uncertainty surrounding the possibility of leaving Marseilles by boat, Fry decides to risk another route, leading his charges across the Pyrenees and over the Spanish border, through neutral Spain to Portugal, where they can await a ship to take them on their onward journey.

One of the first to risk this dangerous mountain crossing is also one of the oldest.

Crossing the Pyrenees

When Alfred Kantorowicz arrives in Marseilles on a two-week permit with his wife, Friedel, to arrange the final pieces in the jigsaw of their departure to Mexico, he finds the city 'stuffed full of Nobel Prize winners, poets, professors, senate presidents, clergymen, princes, ministers, excellencies, all grateful if they can pass as Müller or Meier, Dupont or Durant'. When he learns that Heinrich Mann is among the throng, Kantorowicz telephones his friend and mentor to suggest a meeting. Mann explains that it is too risky to meet at his hotel. The city centre must be avoided, too. He suggests a spot on the outskirts of the city at twelve noon, an hour when even the gendarmes take a break for lunch.

Picture Heinrich Mann waiting beneath a palm tree, dressed formally as always, baggy linen trousers and a summer jacket, a hat to shade him from the sun and prying eyes, his hang-dog face still recognizable to those who know him well: the thin moustache, behind his glinting glasses those familiar, pale-blue eyes. Kantorowicz, always lean, is thinner now than ever, eyes shining in delight as he strides forward to greet Mann hastily, not wanting to draw attention to themselves. Mann tells Kantorowicz that he knows a good restaurant which they can reach via side streets. The two wanted men set off in silence in pursuit of lunch.

From the outside, the restaurant looks like nothing much. Inside, it reveals a cornucopia of traditional French cuisine laid out in a menu of astonishing length. Mann reaches for the wine list, examines it carefully and suggests they start with a rosé.

'We ate and drank in silence. After we had emptied the bottle of rosé, he ordered a 1912 Burgundy. [. . .] After we had finished this bottle too, he leaned back in the old-fashioned plush seat, looked around as if lost and said to himself in his North German dialect: "*Tjä*, I'm supposed to go to America . . . There'll probably only be fast food restaurants there . . ."'

As they part, again in silence, Kantorowicz wonders what it means for this writer, whose life and work are so intimately connected with France, who speaks the language fluently, who writes about its kings, to have to flee his second home, just as he fled his country of birth seven years earlier.

Heinrich, Nelly and Heinrich's nephew Golo Mann leave Marseilles by train at dawn on 12 September 1940. With them are Franz Werfel and Alma Mahler-Werfel, widow of the composer Gustav Mahler. The group is led by Varian Fry. Alma arrives accompanied by a dozen suitcases containing Mahler's scores as well as her extensive wardrobe. Since she will not countenance the idea of leaving any of it behind, Fry has to take the luggage himself, travelling separately. He ushers the little party into their first-class carriage and reminds them that they are supposed to be tourists on a day out. It is a twelve-hour journey to reach Spain, a long time to keep up such a pretence.

Everything goes smoothly until they reach Cerbère on the French border, where they are met by one of Fry's volunteers, sent to tell them that the train journey to the first Spanish town, Portbou, is no longer safe. They will have to cross the mountains on foot, continuing the pretence that they are holidaymakers taking a leisurely hike.

The route over the Pyrenees is well marked, but even so, they nearly lose their way. Franz Werfel is overweight and has heart problems. Heinrich Mann is almost seventy and has to be supported, almost carried at times, by Nelly or Golo. But when, eventually, they arrive at the Spanish border the guards let them by without a glance. At Portbou station they are reunited with their luggage and with Varian Fry, who has bribed the Spanish guards to turn a blind eye to the peculiar group of perspiring foreigners about to board the Barcelona train. Their onward journey will take them to Barcelona, Madrid, then Lisbon.

In October 1940, Heinrich Mann and his family leave Lisbon for New York on a Greek passenger liner. On board are Leopold Schwarzchild, the Werfels, Alfred Döblin and his family, and many others. These are the luckiest ones, those who have got out quickly. In New York, Heinrich is met by his brother Thomas, who takes him to the Hotel Bedford, where they drink vermouth, eat a good lunch, and travel on to Princeton, where Thomas Mann is living. Thus begins his second exile.

The Gestapo agents who have been pursuing Heinrich Mann arrive in Cerbère the day after his departure from France.

Der alte Benjamin

Lisa Fittko is asleep in a little garret room in the coastal village of Port-Vendres when she is woken by someone knocking at the door.

It is early in the morning of 23 September 1940, just a couple of weeks after Heinrich Mann left Marseilles.

'It had to be the little girl from downstairs; I got out of bed and opened the door. But it wasn't the child. I rubbed my half-closed eyes. It was one of our friends, Walter Benjamin . . . *Der alte Benjamin*, Old Benjamin, I called him – I really don't know why; he was only forty-eight or so.

'"*Gnädige Frau*," he said. "Please forgive the intrusion – I hope this is not an inopportune time."

'The world is falling to pieces, I thought, but Benjamin's courtesy is unshakeable.

'"*Ihr Herr Gemahl*," he continued, "explained to me how I could find you. He said, 'She will take you over the border to Spain.'"

'What had he said, my honoured spouse? That was just like him, always taking it for granted that I'd manage. [. . .]

'"But are you sure you understand that I'm not an experienced guide in this area? I don't even actually know the way, I myself have never been up there yet. All I have is a piece of paper with a sketch of the route, one the mayor drew from memory. [. . .] Do you want to take the risk?"

'"Certainly," he said without hesitation. "Not to go, that would be the real risk."'

Lisa Fittko escaped from Gurs in the chaos of the German advance, made her way to Marseilles on false papers and was eventually reunited with her husband, Hans, a journalist who was interned with Walter Benjamin at Vernuche at the beginning of the war. Like everyone else, Hans and Lisa have been trying to work out how to get out of France and have concluded that the idea of waiting for a ship is close to lunacy. They are young, they are organized, they are determined: they will try the route across the Pyrenees. Lisa bases herself in Port-Vendres, a harbour town in the foothills of the eastern Pyrenees, to try to gain more information. The easiest route, the one taken by Heinrich Mann, is no longer safe. Lisa makes contact with a sympathetic Socialist mayor in Banyuls who tells her about a path named 'the Lister Route' after the Republican General Lister who used it during the Spanish Civil War. The mayor describes the route in great detail, and even draws Lisa a map, but he cannot risk acting as a guide, so it is up to her to try it for herself.

Walter Benjamin, meanwhile, has travelled from Paris to Lourdes and from Lourdes to Marseilles, where he has now been waiting weeks for a French exit visa that is evidently never going to materialize. Thanks to the efforts of Max Horkheimer, Benjamin is finally in possession of an emergency visa to the United States. He has the requisite transit visas for Spain and Portugal. The only thing missing is this damned exit visa from France. Perhaps encouraged by the success of Heinrich Mann, Benjamin decides to try his luck over the Pyrenees. If old Mann can do it, why shouldn't he? He is twenty years younger, after all.

The Lister route passes high over the mountains, avoiding the German patrols stationed on the more direct route below. It is a rough path and Lisa is concerned about Benjamin's heart condition, but he is determined to make the trip. On the first day the group – consisting of Benjamin, Lisa and two fellow Germans, Henny Gurland and her teenage son Joseph – make a recce of the first section of the route with the aim of returning to the village for the night and setting out again the following morning, but Benjamin is so exhausted by the climb he insists on spending the night outside. His goal is to cross the border, he explains. He has attained one-third of this goal. If he returns to the village now only to have to repeat the whole ascent the next day, his heart will probably give out. It follows, he reasons, that he will remain where he is. Reluctantly they leave him seated under a tree, clutching a black leather briefcase which he says contains a manuscript of vital importance to him.

When they return in the morning, Lisa is relieved to find Benjamin unharmed if a little chilly, still clutching his briefcase. They set off, but Benjamin is so short of breath he has to stop every ten minutes to rest. Lisa and Joseph take it in turns to carry the case.

At one point they even have to carry Benjamin himself. Once they reach a high point in the mountains they sit down for a picnic lunch.

'By your leave, *gnädige Frau,*' says Benjamin as Lisa passes him the tomatoes, 'may I serve myself?'

They begin their descent, walking on until, finally, they reach the Spanish frontier at Portbou. Lisa hands over their transit visas, suppressing her excitement at being so near their final goal. But the Guardia Civil shake their heads. *You cannot pass*, they say. *Your transit visas for Spain are no longer valid.* Lisa is shocked. *Since when? Since yesterday.* They changed the rules.

The group are taken, under guard, to a hotel in Portbou, to be escorted back to the French border by train in the morning.

Walter Benjamin's death is registered at 10 p.m. on 26 September 1940, confirmed by a judge who was called to attend the 'foreign traveller' and found Benjamin dead on his bed, fully clothed. The cause of death on record is given as 'cerebral haemorrhage', a conclusion offered either because the doctor misunderstood or deliberately avoided a suicide verdict out of compassion, since suicide was a penal offence in Spain and would have had to be referred to the police.

On the previous evening of 25 September Walter Benjamin sent a postcard to Geneva to the Institute of Social Research and made four telephone calls from the hotel, it is not known to whom. That night a Spanish doctor attended Benjamin. It is not clear who called him or precisely why. Walter Benjamin's last words were written on a postcard addressed to Henny Gurland, which she destroyed during her flight and later reconstructed from memory:

'Finding myself with no way out, I have no choice but to end it all. It is in a small village in the Pyrenees, where nobody knows me, that my life will come to an end. Please pass on my thoughts to my friend Adorno and explain to him the situation I find myself in. I do not have enough time left to write all the letters I would have liked to write.'

The following day the border is reopened. Had Benjamin travelled either a day earlier or a day later he would probably have survived. That was his particular tragedy. He lost hope, as so many other exiles had in the preceding years, and gave up at this final, seemingly insurmountable, hurdle.

The last time Arthur Koestler saw Walter Benjamin was in Marseilles a few weeks before his departure. Benjamin asked him, 'If anything goes wrong, have you got anything to take?' It was a common-enough question in those days: everyone carried something, 'just in case'. Koestler had nothing, so Benjamin offered to share what he had with his friend, 'Sixty-two tablets of a sedative, procured in Berlin during the week which followed the burning of the Reichstag. He did it reluctantly, for he did not know whether the thirty-one remaining tablets left him would be enough.'

For seven years Benjamin had been carrying the tablets around, 'just in case' the worst should happen. Now it seems it had, and thirty-one tablets were more than enough.

The 'manuscript' which Benjamin was carrying, to which he was so much attached, was never found. The possessions handed over to the court in Figueras on 5 October 1940 were described as follows: 'a leather briefcase like businessmen use, a man's watch, a pipe, six photographs, an x-ray picture, glasses, various letters, magazines and a few other papers whose content is unknown, and also some money.'

Arthur Koestler made it to London via North Africa in the company of a group of escaped British POWs and only heard the news many weeks later: 'Walter Benjamin, author and critic, my neighbour in 10 rue Dombasle in Paris, fourth at our Saturday poker parties, and one of the most bizarre and witty persons I have known.'

It is as good an epitaph as any.

The End of Willi Münzenberg

Not long after Benjamin's death, in October 1940 a brief notice in a French newspaper announces the discovery of the body of the well-known left-wing propagandist Willi Münzenberg in a forest near Grenoble. All that remains of the squat frame and powerful shoulders is a decomposing corpse, found by hunters with a rope around his neck, the other piece still hanging from the branch of a nearby tree. When police examined the contents of the dead man's pockets they found a pair of glasses, a medical certificate declaring that the bearer suffers from a stomach ulcer, an identity card for a foreigner with no right to work, a membership card of PEN, a statement of the loss of German nationality, and a postcard, dated 18 June 1940, from a Mme B. Gross, Barrack S in the camp of Gurs in the Pyrenees.

The official verdict of suicide is believed by no one who is paying attention at the time, although the world is busy with the war and Münzenberg's death little reported in the international press. When death came for Willi in that forest near Grenoble there are only two guises it could have taken: as an agent of the Gestapo or of the NKVD.

Babette and Willi's friends are in no doubt: Willi Münzenberg was a well-known former Communist who had openly broken with the Comintern and rejected Stalin. Stalin never forgot a grudge; the reach of the NKVD was long. Only a few weeks previously, news of Trotsky's violent death in Mexico had hit the headlines.

In the absence of facts, there remain only theories: Willi Münzenberg was last seen on 21 June 1940 when he left his companions to search for a car to take him to Gurs to find Babette. Somebody mentioned a 'third man' who is said to have appeared mysteriously at the Chambaran camp and encouraged Willi's plans to escape before disappearing again. Aside from that, nobody knows.

Plenty

Colonel Rudolph has already established a routine. In the evenings he comes downstairs, greets the waiter in his accented French – *Bonsssoir!* – makes his way to his favourite table and settles back to ask, with gusto, what is on the menu tonight. The waiter recites the day's specials, consisting of the kind of fare that Parisians once took for granted and now can only dream of. Meat, game, poultry, fish, cream, Chantelle mushrooms, asparagus in season, artichokes, ripe tomatoes ... And then it is Weber's turn, Weber, with his German-sounding name. *What do you recommend to go with tonight's dish, Weber? We have guests from Berlin, so something special, eh?*

Colonel Rudolph has no operational duties himself. He is responsible for overseeing the running of the Lutetia Section and for entertaining visiting high-ranking Abwehr officers. When he dines alone his upright posture is immediately recognizable from behind – straight shoulders, fork poised between plate and mouth, head bowed in pursuit of the interesting business of eating. Often he is joined by his secretary, Fräulein Juhl, and they are soon deep in discussion of some matter of great interest to them both. Everyone knows, of course, that they are lovers. As soon as his divorce comes through, they will tie the knot. Meanwhile, Juhl runs Rudolph's office; rules it, some say, makes the decisions, wears the trousers. Perhaps. Juhl leaves little trace in the official records, not even a first name, so it is hard to say for sure.

Do she and Rudolph wander together through the empty streets of Paris at night? Do they stand hand in hand on the Pont Saint-Michel and gaze down at the inky river Seine, the dark silhouette of Notre-Dame rising before them, and talk of what they will do when the war is over?

While the Germans are filling their bellies, the inhabitants of Paris have two things on their mind: food and fuel. From September 1940 rationing is imposed on the French, who now need coupons to obtain basics like bread, eggs and meat. As supplies run short, Parisians must replace their morning coffee with chicory and find inventive ways to render the infamous *rutabaga* (swede) edible. It is a vegetable normally fed to cattle, now a common item on the menu.

★

One day staff at the Hotel Lutetia see a large quantity of cases, boxes and bottles being packaged up. Who is it for? Nobody has ordered anything.

'Yes, yes, it's for Admiral Canaris. He's in Berlin. A mistake, surely? Well, now, it was not a mistake. A plane had come specially from Berlin to Paris to take it all away: foie gras, good wine, and the rest. In the middle of a war!'

Admiral Canaris's expensive tastes set the tone for the rest of the Abwehr. It is not just Paris that provides him with delicacies: he imports his favourite foods from whichever country happens to produce them, with a particular penchant for strawberries from Spain. He is also known to be lavish in his gifts, offering one of his favourites a diamond-encrusted tobacco jar said to belong to Napoleon, presumably filched from France. With decent salaries, generous expense allowances and little scrutiny from Berlin, few Abwehr staff in the various *Abwehrstellen* dotted all over Europe can resist the lure of high living, and the Lutetia Section is no exception. The general attitude of take-what-you-can derives not just from Canaris, but from the very nature of the German occupation.

On a small scale, German soldiers can go shopping to their hearts' content and ship luxury goods back to their families, thanks to a highly favourable exchange rate that is set by the occupiers. On a large scale, everything is geared to sate the hunger of the German war effort: the Vichy government is forced to pay for the German occupation to the tune of millions of Reichsmarks a day, while the bulk of France's agricultural and industrial production is to be sent to Germany. If it means that the French have to live off *rutabaga* and chicory, so be it.

Bureau Otto

One of the most egregious mechanisms by which the German administration systematically despoils its conquered territory is a system of official purchase offices, known as *bureaux d'achats*. Every department has one: the Luftwaffe, the Kriegsmarine, the Gestapo, the SD – everyone has their fingers in the collective pie. The *bureaux d'achats* connected to the Abwehr serve a dual purpose, providing a front for the activities of Abwehr agents while also subsidizing them in a manner that is almost entirely free from scrutiny. The man chosen to run the office in Paris is to become so notorious it is named after him.

Hermann Brandl, known as Otto, is a suave Bavarian business-man in his mid-forties who was initially recruited to the Abwehr by Colonel Rudolph in the 1930s, providing small snippets of infor-mation of no great note and recruiting a handful of agents in Brussels. After the armistice, Brandl turned up at the Lutetia and reported to Colonel Rudolph, ready to serve the Abwehr again.

When Rudolph was interrogated by the British in 1946, he claimed that Brandl was employed by the Assistant Quartermaster of the Paris Abwehr section, Captain Wilhelm Radecke, as a kind of general factotum, initially dealing with problems relating to accommodation before being asked in September 1940 to run a new organization that had been set up to make large-scale purchases of goods in short supply in Germany. In this version of events, Brandl simply receives orders from the German military, purchases the goods specified, and Captain Radecke organizes their transport to Germany. In this task they are assisted by a couple of members of administrative staff, including a secretary, Mary Waldtraut-Jacobson, a South African with German nationality who keeps the accounts, runs the personnel department, and happens to be Brandl's mistress.

The reality is somewhat less anodyne.

Bureau Otto is run out of the Hotel Lutetia with the official aim of financing the operations of the Abwehr. With almost complete freedom to act as he sees fit, supervised with the lightest of touch by Colonel Rudolph, Brandl cultivates relationships with anyone and everyone who can be of use to his business affairs, building up a network of paid informers who seek out goods for purchase as well as providing a rich source of intelligence to be passed on to Oscar Reile's counter-espionage department. Simultaneously,

Brandl cultivates contacts with the Gestapo and the SS. Whatever they want, Otto can obtain it: champagne, vintage wines, jewellery, rubber boots, sheepskins, textiles. The organization grows so large it occupies vast warehouses along the quayside at Saint-Ouen, which are stuffed to the gills with silk fabric, crates of vintage champagne, ladies' perfume, medicines, gentlemen's hats, furniture, paintings, carpets, car tyres, cars, coal, leather, wool, steel. Brandl himself lives in a private hotel on the Square du Bois de Boulogne not far from avenue Foch. Business expands to such an extent that several buildings on the same street are requisitioned for his use, before the bureau has to move to larger premises in the 16th *arrondissement*.

Brandl is a busy man, wining and dining the great and the good of French society, using his extensive connections to seek supplies, favours, contacts, leads. Then off he goes to the Gestapo or the SS with a little gift for someone, a tip for someone else, a service rendered, a service returned . . . Amid all this, he is purchasing not just goods but information, tip-offs, intelligence, securing the services of agents with loyalty-inducing gifts. He is also enriching himself, earning a 1 per cent commission on every transaction made and acquiring a vast fortune in the process. His girlfriend, Mary Waldtraut-Jacobson, runs the personnel department. With over four hundred employees, it is no small feat.

Brandl is not fussy about how he acquires the goods he wants. Among his employees is a petty criminal named Henri Lafont (real name Henri Chamberlain), who heads a vicious gang known as the Carlingue or Bonny–Lafont gang, alongside his second-in-command, Pierre Bonny, a disgraced police officer who was involved in the Stavisky affair. Lafont was doing time at the Cherche-Midi prison across the road from the Lutetia when the German invasion offered him the opportunity to escape. When Captain Radecke acquired Lafont's services he obligingly ordered the release of twenty-eight men from Fresnes prison on Lafont's behalf, to serve as members of his 'staff'. Later in the war, Bonny and Lafont quit the Abwehr in favour of the Gestapo, who offer even more opportunities for enrichment, providing them with official police identity cards, arms, guns, petrol. Now known as the rue Lauriston gang, after the address where they are based, the pair develop a busy sideline hunting down Jews and breaking up Resistance cells. Another of Brandl's former employees, Frédéric Martin, alias Rudy de Mérode, becomes head of the French Gestapo in Neuilly.

How they must have swaggered when they entered the Lutetia for the first time and sat down with the German officers, ordering champagne from the snooty French waiters. How hard it must have been to preserve a veneer of professional neutrality before these criminals!

The portrait shifts. Colonel Rudolph, that 'self-assured gentleman' and former cavalry officer whom rosy-eyed Oscar Reile admires so much, is said by other Abwehr staff to employ Hermann Brandl as his 'henchman', allowing Brandl and Radecke privileged access to his office while regular Abwehr officers are forced to wait. The image of a busy environment of military professionals simply doing their job cedes to something far seedier: greed has entered by the revolving door of the Lutetia, alongside its companion, corruption.

Cold Comfort

As autumn becomes winter and the temperature drops, the veneer of normality that rendered Paris so strange over the summer peels off, revealing fear beneath, and resentment as Parisians freeze in their apartments and go hungry while the occupiers are living it up in Maxim's or Fouquet's.

The winter of 1940–41 is exceptionally cold. Parisians gather wherever they can to keep warm. Cinemas are popular. Library membership doubles. Some people simply stay at home, writing diaries in bed, working on long-delayed scholarly works, burying their minds in study, trying to forget the ever-present desire to *eat*. In their freezing studio apartment on rue des Favourites, Samuel Beckett constructs a canvas tent in which he and his girlfriend, Suzanne Déchevaux-Dumesnil, huddle together to read or write, swathed in layers of clothes.

Acts of direct resistance are scarce in the early part of the war: the situation remains fluid and unformed. General de Gaulle is a little-known figure broadcasting into the empty ether, and only a few people are ready to hear what he has to say. Those who long to *do* something feel isolated, stranded amid what appears to be a population all too willing to accommodate the new reality.

But change is afoot. The belief that the British will soon be defeated by Nazi Germany fades in the face of the Battle of Britain. A slim current of hope begins to course through the French populace. A few bold souls begin to organize themselves into informal groups: colleagues at work, friends who trust one another. The respected anthropologist Germaine Tillion and her colleagues form a network called the Musée de l'Homme, named after their place of employment. Samuel Beckett's good friend, the poetry-loving intellectual Alfred Péron, returns to Paris after demobilization to resume his job as an English teacher at the Lycée Buffon, where he finds in his colleague Suzanne Roussel a like mind and a determination to act.

Resistance networks begin to sprout like mushrooms in the dark, helped by the British, who provide them with money, guidance, direction. For Oscar Reile, this is the moment to make his opening moves in the counter-espionage game that he enjoys so much.

Calamity

For three months James Joyce battled tirelessly with Swiss bureaucracy, while friends did their best to convince uninterested officials in Zurich and Lausanne how vitally important it was to enable one of the world's greatest writers to escape France. In December 1940 he and his family finally arrived in Zurich. Just a few weeks later the ulcer that had tormented him for so long burst. Joyce died of peritonitis on 13 January 1941.

That evening, in Paris, Paul Léon goes out as usual to buy two packs of cigarettes at the bistro on the corner of rue de Bourgogne, where he and Joyce met every day for years. Seeing him, the manager bursts into tears.

'What a calamity, Monsieur – all because of this terrible war!'

At first Léon has no idea what the man is talking about. Then the manager explains: Joyce's death was announced earlier that day on Radio Lausanne.

For days Paul cannot bring himself to speak of his friend. Twelve years of shared endeavour, of scholarship, of ridiculously complicated financial deals, labyrinthine publishing contracts, arguments about matters trivial and grave, meals shared, disappointments endured. Laughter, conversation, silence – shared.

On 2 February 1941, the date of Joyce's birthday, the Léons invite Samuel Beckett, the poet Léon-Paul Fargue and the painter Madame Chériane to dinner at their flat. Somehow, despite rationing, they manage to scrape together a feast: Paul has found smoked eels at the Russian fishmongers; Lucie brings scallops; a local shopkeeper sells them some small pheasants. It is an emotional evening, far from the war. They reminisce about Joyce, listening to recordings of *Anna Livia Plurabelle* just for the pleasure of hearing his voice again.

Hotel Drouot

Not long afterwards, Paul Léon discovers that Joyce's landlord is planning to hold an illegal auction to sell off Joyce's property from the flat on rue des Vignes. The man wants his overdue rent, which obviously cannot be paid. When Léon attempts to persuade the landlord to wait until the end of the war, the landlord threatens to seize everything in the apartment. A public announcement follows:

an auction of Joyce's belongings is to be held on 7 March 1941 at the Hotel Drouot.

Desperate to safeguard Joyce's most valuable documents, Paul Léon defies the night-time curfew to go to rue des Vignes not just once but several times, bluffing his way past the concierge with a bribe and a story about fetching his own things. He rescues as many of Joyce's papers and books as he can carry, hoping desperately that he will not meet a German patrol as he walks the dark streets with a pushcart, accompanied by a handyman.

Léon places the most important documents in nineteen brown manila envelopes and takes them to the Irish Embassy with instructions that they are to be turned over to the National Library of Ireland, there to be kept sealed for fifty years. It is his final act of devotion toward his dear, departed friend.

At the Hotel Drouot the auction lots are arranged haphazardly in baskets around the room. Most of the people who have turned up seem more interested in the furniture and other household items than the first editions lying scattered among the clocks, the linen and the crockery. Paul knows precisely which books are worth bidding on. Lucie's brother, Alec, in hiding in the unoccupied zone, has sent them money, enabling Paul to buy back almost all the books of any value. Overcome by a painful sense of nostalgia, Lucie purchases a few household items which she thinks Nora might like: some linen, Joyce's leather writing pad, his paper knife.

Coeurs Vaillants

It is cold in Le Vernet; it gets colder every time they visit. It is hard for Pierre and Ruth to see their father imprisoned behind barbed wire but the internees are kind to the children, making hot soup from their rations to keep them warm. As winter sets in there is an evil wind, *le vent d'autan*, which blows from the Pyrenees, where the peaks are soon covered with snow.

Anna and the children are staying in Pamiers, a small town just a few kilometres from Le Vernet camp. Anna has rented rooms in the house of a clairvoyant, Mme Jeanne, who, despite her air of mystery and her tarot cards, turns out to be kindly and discreet. Ignoring their lack of paperwork and Anna's foreign accent, she suggests simply that the family enter the property by the side door. Every day, toward dusk, Anna watches as shy young girls slip into the house to consult their local oracle. One evening Mme Jeanne reads the palm of Anna's friend, Kurt Stern, declaring solemnly, 'I think, sir, that you will soon be making a long journey.'

The children are at school again: Ruth is in the fourth class at the École supérieure des jeunes filles, Pierre in the second at the Collège des garçons. Even though the pupils have to sing *Maréchal, nous voilà!*', Pierre finds it comforting to be in class with the others. In between visits to László in Le Vernet Anna writes letters, spends entire days in the local library rereading the works of Balzac; sometimes she travels to Foix, Marseilles, Toulouse, intent on finding a way out of France. She is fortunate in having friends abroad, in New York and Mexico, who have not forgotten her. The Mexican Consul General in Marseilles has lists of well-known figures who are under threat. When Anna learns that she and her family have been granted a Mexican visa her delight soon turns to dismay when she discovers that the papers have been made out in her pen name, not her legal name of Netty Radványi. More time is lost as she works to rectify the mistake. Meanwhile, humiliating interviews: appearing before an aid committee for intellectuals, a German writer asks her: 'And can you at least show us one or two of your works, Miss Seghers, so that our American colleagues see that they are dealing with a real writer?'

The children's great comfort at this time is to read the adventures of Tintin in the French comic-book series *Coeurs Vaillants*. When they are feeling down Anna cheers them up with the refrain: 'Who is frightened of nothing, and I mean nothing? Tintin! And who follows him everywhere, and I mean everywhere? Snowy!'

During these dark, cold days it is her children who save Anna from despair. It is the absolute necessity of Pierre's and Ruth's survival that gives her energy as she traipses from one consulate to another in her quest to put together the lucky combination of documents that will finally provide the key to their escape.

In mid-December Anna receives the corrected visa and, in early January 1941, an exit visa allowing the family to reach the United States and Mexico via Marseilles. László is transferred to Les Milles, now serving as a transit camp.

The family can finally be together, staying in a shabby little hotel in Marseilles where Anna writes on a suitcase between the bed and the gas cooker. At Pierre's new school one of his classmates gives him a pamphlet which, at first glance, looks like a poem glorifying Hitler but, once folded, becomes an anti-Nazi tract. Pierre is thrilled. He wants to stay in France to fight. He wants to be a Musketeer, Tintin, Edmond Dantès . . . But he also knows what will happen to his parents if they don't leave. The cafés are full of rumours. Food is scarce. On a day off from school, Anna gives the children some money to take the boat out to the Château d'If to follow the trail of the Count of Monte Cristo.

It is not until March 1941 that the family finally collect their very last stamp, *Vu, bon à embarquer* ('Seen, permission to embark') and board a cargo ship, the *Capitaine Paul-Lemerle*, to sail for Martinique, thence to Mexico.

The boat is twenty years old, with the forward hold reserved for cargo and two aft holds for two to three hundred refugees, one for women, the other for men. There are rows of hastily constructed bunk beds, no portholes, only a ladder to the rear bridge. The majority of the passengers are Spanish republicans, some of whom once held important office. Among the political refugees is the Russian revolutionary Victor Serge, with his twenty-year-old son. Alfred and Friedel Kantorowicz are here too; they only just made it after Kantorowicz was nearly arrested just hours before the boat's departure. On the top deck, some privileged French passengers, including André Breton and Claude Levi-Strauss. Sometimes the children catch sight of Breton on the bridge, looking out to sea, a huge scarf wrapped around his neck. He doesn't mix with the crowd on the rear deck.

As they hug the coast of Spain, with Barcelona clearly visible in the distance, the Spaniards weep for their lost republic. Then, the Atlantic, a crossing of around twelve days. All this time, Anna is making notes for the book that will become her most famous work, *Transit*. She asks Pierre: should the hero leave France or stay, in the end? Pierre emphatically replies that he should stay.

The Lucky Few

Those among the exiles who managed to leave France were, by and large, those with money and connections: authors, journalists, scholars, artists, men and women considered to be 'outstanding intellectuals' worthy of rescue. Even for this small number it took weeks and months of waiting, corresponding, queueing up and answering humiliating questions until the magic stamp was placed on their passports and they could leave. Gustav Regler and Babette Gross reached Mexico, Arthur Koestler made it to England, Manès Sperber got to Switzerland, Lion and Marta Feuchtwanger joined Heinrich and Nelly Mann in the United States. Thanks to Varian Fry, Fred and Lilo Stein departed for New York in May 1941, carrying with them their Leica camera, some negatives, and their baby daughter. Gisèle Freund received an invitation to stay in Argentina from another of her influential friends, Victoria Ocampo, who – like Adrienne Monnier – acted as a mentor, offering Freund the opportunity to meet and photograph writers and artists such as Jorge Luis Borges and Pablo Neruda. Lisa and Hans Fittko were about to leave France when Varian Fry begged them to continue acting as guides. For the next few months, working in co-ordination with the Emergency Rescue Committee, the Fittkos guided dozens of refugees over the Pyrenees, bringing people across several times a week. Eventually they, too, managed to escape, to Cuba.

These lucky ones faced an uncertain future in their second exile: they had escaped persecution, but survival was no easier than it had been in France, and who knew how long their stay would be this time around? In 1941 there was no sign of an end to the conflict, no hope that they could one day safely return to Europe. Though physically distant, the war continued to absorb their attention as they agonized about those they had left behind.

The fate of the majority of Germans and Austrians in France was mixed: some remained in camps like Gurs or Le Vernet, eventually to be given up to the Gestapo. Of those who joined the French Army or were called up for auxiliary service as *prestataires*, some managed to escape to England or to unoccupied territory, but many were captured by the French and imprisoned.

After the flurry of departures that followed the armistice, the camp of Gurs went from being a mass prison to a place of refuge for those with nowhere else to go. Here in the remote Pyrenees, forgotten by the outside world, life began to settle into a routine and a cultural life took hold among this isolated community. In the autumn of 1940, the camp grew crowded once more when over 6,500 German Jews were expelled from the southwestern states of Baden, the Palatinate and Saarland. Among the new arrivals were many artists, musicians and intellectuals. More, still, arrived in a transfer from the camp of Saint-Cyprien.

Little by little, the talents present in the camp begin to emerge. The camp authorities don't interfere. The internees build a stage; a grand piano is miraculously obtained. Berlin cabaret artist Alfred Nathan arranges soirées at which Ruth Rauch dances while her mother, Margot, plays piano in the orchestra. Sometimes Margot plays duets with the distinguished pianist Hans Ebbecke, at others it is composer Hans Meyerowitz performing Beethoven and Bach. Fritz Brunner, first violin in the Vienna Philharmonic, organizes a choir and a small orchestra. Soon they are playing Scarlatti, Handel, Palestrina, Corelli, Mozart, their beautiful music echoing around the silent, indifferent mountains.

*

As time goes on the German military presence in Marseilles grows, the work of the Emergency Rescue Committee is gradually curtailed, and Varian Fry is forced to leave France. At the start of the Occupation, the efforts of the German army to create a sense of calm were successful. People would say, 'They're well behaved and polite, after all.' It helped them reconcile themselves to the reality of living under enemy occupation. But this cannot last.

On 22 June 1941 a profound change in the direction of the war occurs when Germany invades the Soviet Union.

Bachot

It is a warm summer's day when Samuel Beckett spots a familiar stooping figure walking along the street. With astonishment and alarm, he recognizes Paul Léon. What on earth is he still doing in Paris? Over the past months Beckett has witnessed the rapid disintegration of the situation for Jews in France. He has seen Jewish friends insulted, beaten in the street, thrown out of their jobs. And things are growing steadily worse. Beckett urges Léon to leave the city at once, as other Jewish families have done.

'I have to wait until tomorrow when my son takes his *bachot*,' replies the devoted father (the *'bachot'* being the *baccalauréat*, which Alexis Léon is sitting, aged sixteen, at the Lycée Louis-Le-Grand).

The following day, 21 August 1941, Paul Léon is arrested in a raid by the Paris police and interned at Drancy camp near the city. Ten days later, Samuel Beckett joins the Resistance. The date is significant not just for the connection it offers between Beckett's decision and the arrest of his friend, but because it reflects a wider trend in France: resistance, at first sporadic, is beginning to grow. Soon, resistance will become the Resistance, albeit still in tiny cells scattered across the country.

The momentous news of the German invasion of the Soviet Union has two direct and interlinked effects: first, thousands of German troops are shifted east, leaving parts of France almost unguarded; a man might hide for weeks or months in the unoccupied zone and not be found. The second effect is to release French Communists from the contorted position into which they have forced themselves since the announcement of the Molotov–Ribbentrop Pact. At last, this is no longer an imperialist war being waged against the proletariat; the barbarians are at the gate and must be stopped. What the Communists bring to the table are established networks, a habit of working underground, and experience of collective action.

Acts of sabotage, once rare, become more frequent, disturbing the fragile status quo that has existed between occupier and occupied since June 1940. When German personnel are attacked, brutal reprisals against the civilian population follow; hundreds of hostages are executed. This leads to more resistance, which in turn leads to a rise in German counter-intelligence efforts to capture Resistance members and saboteurs, which means a greater number of trials by overburdened military courts.

At the same time, repressive policies against Jews grow in severity. The first mass arrest in Paris was in May 1941, when just under four thousand (mainly Polish) Jews were rounded up by the French police. After June 1941, the situation gets steadily worse: over just two days in August 1941 more than four thousand Jewish males aged between eighteen and fifty – among them Paul Léon – are arrested and taken to Drancy. It is a tragic irony that the list of names used by the police was compiled from the index to which so many Jews had diligently contributed in October 1940.

Spy Games

'In Paris, life went on. Every day, at midday, when the guards' company marched up the Champs-Élysées accompanied by a band, hundreds, sometimes thousands of people gathered to watch the parade. One rarely observed an expression of anger or hatred on their faces. Because of their great military tradition the French had a particular taste for manifestations of force and discipline. In the evenings, on the boulevards, in front of the cafés, did one not see German soldiers and civilians in friendly conversation?'

Things are going well for Colonel Reile. He has gathered together a group of highly effective agents who, in 1941, notch up a run of stunning victories over the nascent French Resistance. His happy vision of an acquiescent French populace, admiring and fraternizing with their conquerors, suggests his confidence, in these early days, that those who choose to act against the occupiers are a small minority whose efforts will be easily quashed. His first big coup is Operation 'Porto', run by Andreas Folmer, a cultured Luxembourgeois of German origins whom Reile recruited before the war and who, in Paris, becomes his closest friend. The men spend much of their leisure time together, eschewing the louche pleasures of the city to spend their leave shooting in the French countryside. 'Porto', named by Reile 'after the excellent Portuguese wine', begins in June 1941 with Folmer posing as an intermediary sent by London to run resistance cells in Paris, transmitting instructions to them supposedly from the British but, in reality, from the Lutetia. The operation comes to a head in September when the cell defies Folmer's orders to attack two German officers. Suspecting that his agent's cover is blown, Reile orders mass arrests. Over the course of several days 962 people are put behind bars. All are sent for court martial, many condemned to death.

After 'Porto' comes 'Paul', or 'Interallié'. This complex operation is run by another of Reile's star recruits, Hugo Bleicher, a German from Hamburg who proves himself to be an agent of exceptional talent. Bleicher is astute, capable, educated, a highly competent interrogator, adept at obtaining information without resorting to violence. Like Reile, Bleicher dislikes and mistrusts the Gestapo, hates Nazi methods, and is determined to work in his own way. The 'Interallié' network is directed from London and run in Paris by a volatile and charismatic Pole, Roman Czerniawski, together with his girlfriend, Mathilde Carré. In November 1941 Bleicher hits the jackpot when he discovers the main address used by the network at Villa Léandre in Montmartre. A raid leads not only to the arrest of Carré and Czerniawski but to a massive haul of documents. When Bleicher succeeds in turning Mathilde Carré to become a double agent he confirms his status as Reile's star recruit.

As one of the Abwehr's most successful operatives, Bleicher is perhaps entitled to a sense of resentment at not being granted officer rank: he is a mere *Feldwebel*, or sergeant, which places him on unequal terms with the Abwehr officers who hang around the office of Reile's deputy, Major Schäfer, at the Lutetia. This rankles, because in his view the Abwehr officers in France – with the exception of Reile – are pretty useless at counter-intelligence, their only discernible talent being 'to supply head office in Berlin with black-market goods unobtainable in Germany' and thus feather the collective German nest. Bleicher doesn't do so badly out of his alliance with the Abwehr: he and his lover, Suzanne Laurent, live in considerable comfort in a variety of hotels and apartments, eventually securing a fine new flat at 76 rue Pergolese in the 16th *arrondissement*, near avenue Foch. But the lack of recognition grates.

Reile's initial success in breaking up Resistance networks makes little impact on the overall picture in France. Irritated by the backed-up military courts, frustrated by the apparent inability of his occupying forces to stamp out resistance, in December 1941 Hitler issues a directive, code-named *Nacht und Nebel* ('Night and Fog'), which permits the German authorities to arrest individuals deemed to be endangering German security without following any of the usual legal procedures. There are to be no more trials. Families of resisters will receive no information. The prisoners will have no right of correspondence; they can receive no parcels. They are taken at night and vanish without a trace.

As the noose tightens, so resentment against the Germans grows. And when the US enters the war in December 1941 a Nazi victory no longer seems inevitable, encouraging more French citizens to act.

The Priest

One cannot simply walk into the Hotel Lutetia these days, especially not when one has espionage in mind. So when a potential
new recruit makes contact with Oscar Reile – and he comes highly
recommended – the Colonel arranges to meet him in a villa near
the Bois de Boulogne, a location so well placed that any observers
will be quickly noticed. Nevertheless, as a precaution, the two men
enter the house in darkness.

The candidate is short, dark-haired, with a high forehead and eyes
like small, hard buttons. He speaks perfect German. His French,
also perfect, is accented but can easily be explained by claiming, for
example, that he comes from the Saar. In reality, he was born in
Luxembourg, studied theology in Freiburg, and was ordained in
Switzerland. The thirty-four-year-old, who has dressed in civvies
for his visit to Reile, has the perfect cover for a would-be spy: since
1935 he has been priest in the parish of La Varenne Saint-Hilaire on
the outskirts of Paris, where he regularly preaches fiery anti-Nazi
sermons. He has a reputation as a fervent patriot and is a member
of a resistance cell offering humanitarian assistance to escapees and
allied airmen attempting to cross into the unoccupied zone. And, of
course, there is the black soutane, a costume which automatically
engenders trust.

The man's name is Robert Alesch. He is to be responsible for the
betrayal of dozens of members of the French Resistance. The effects
of his actions are so devastating that in 1949 he will find himself, after
a lengthy trial, at the receiving end of a French firing squad.

Reile is delighted to accept the services offered: Alesch presents
himself as a keen proponent of Franco-German rapprochement
and later proves (in Reile's rose-tinted view) to be 'a lively, highly
intelligent, cheerful young man who appreciated good wines and
made no secret of the fact that he did not disdain sensual pleasures'.

In reality, Alesch is ambitious and self-obsessed, consumed by a burning desire to be nominated curate of Chapelle Saint-Joseph on rue La Fayette in Paris, a church belonging to the Luxembourg Catholic Mission that occupies a far more prestigious position than Saint-Hilaire. In order to realize this goal, Alesch has first befriended the head of the Luxembourg Nazi Party, then taken German citizenship in order to join the Nazi-affiliated Luxembourg German Popular Party in France.

Alesch's talent for dissimulation soon marks him out as a highly effective agent. Before long he is living a double life, one so utterly divided as to suggest that he is not one person but two, as if he has been riven in some drastic, painful way. He is a priest, steeped in Christian theology, and he is a spy – Agent Axel – who betrays the people who trust him with their lives.

The obvious explanation for Alesch's actions is greed, for he makes a small fortune out of his relationship with the occupiers. The Abwehr pay him a monthly stipend, along with a generous bonus for every member of the Resistance he betrays. He is soon earning enough to lead a life of notable debauchery, spending his evenings drinking with the Abwehr officers at the Lutetia and his nights with his two mistresses at a posh flat on rue Spontini, before returning to his parish in the morning to don his soutane and preach patriotism to his flock.

But human nature is complex and it is not just the promise of money that attracts Alesch to this work: 'The Germans flattered me with compliments that were not undeserved. They admired my knowledge of languages, my psychological finesse, and even my innate sense of adventure. As to myself, I felt that this new occupation took advantage of a weak spot in my soul of which I had previously been unaware, and that it ended up pleasing me.'

Alesch had discovered within himself an appetite which, once awakened, would never be satisfied: it wanted more money, more sex, more power. His first betrayal was perhaps the most egregious, for he betrayed the trust of the young people in his parish who confided in him their resistance activities. He went on to decimate network after network – and for what? Gold coins, sex and a smart flat? Or a sense of importance?

Alesch's actions were not unique, of course. Between them, Andreas Folmer and Hugo Bleicher did more damage to the Resistance than Alesch. But Folmer and Bleicher, like Oscar Reile, engaged in the 'game' of counter-espionage with a certain professional pride. The roles they played on behalf of the Abwehr were fictional, their cover was part of the job, and their enemy played the exact same game in reverse. Alesch's betrayals, by contrast, are bound up with his status as a priest. In betraying others, he was betraying something deep within himself.

There is another reason to speak of him, a connection that binds him to our story.

Gloria

A 1944 British Special Operations Executive (SOE) report describes Samuel Beckett thus: 'Age 38. 6ft. Well built, but stoops. Dark hair. Fresh complexion. Very silent. Paris agent. Acted as secretary and got reports photographed. An Irishman known to GLORIA before the war.'

The Irishman, observes the intelligence officer with unintentional humour, is not just silent, but 'very silent'.

When Samuel Beckett decides to join the Resistance after Paul Léon's arrest it is the urbane, witty, sensitive English teacher Alfred Péron (code names 'Buffon', 'Dickie', 'Moby') who recruits him. Péron is one of Samuel Beckett's closest friends: the pair first met as students at Trinity College, Dublin, in 1926, where Péron spent a year as the French *lecteur*. When he returned to Paris he did so sporting a pair of plus fours, all the rage in Dublin but objects of ridicule in France. When Beckett in turn arrived in Paris as an English *lecteur* the pair resumed their friendship. Over the years they have lunched and played tennis together countless times;

Péron translated Beckett's early work into French, and they collaborated on a translation of a fragment of Joyce's *Anna Livia Plurabelle*.

The network to which Alfred and his Russian-born wife, Maya (known as Mania), belong is known as Gloria SMH (an inversion of HMS – His Majesty's Service). It was co-founded in May 1941 by another mutual friend, Jeannine Picabia, the diminutive twenty-seven-year-old daughter of the surrealist painter Francis Picabia. Jeannine works with several groups under different aliases and runs Gloria SMH with a chemical engineer named Jacques Legrand. Alfred Péron soon becomes an important member of the network, along with his fellow English teacher Suzanne Roussel (code name 'Hélène'). Both she and Alfred play an active role in recruiting additional agents.

Gloria SMH is run from London, its primary purpose the gathering and transmission of information about Nazi operations and movements. Jacques Legrand also works closely with Germaine Tillion, whose network, the Musée de l'Homme, was one of the first to be betrayed. After its collapse Tillion began to co-operate with Gloria SMH.

The leaders of Gloria SMH recruit agents first and foremost among friends whom they feel they can trust. It is an amateurish affair, and a recipe for leaks.

Beckett's job involves typing and translating information reports from French to English. He is good at the work, possessing astonishing powers of concentration and meticulous attention to detail. 'They would bring this information to me on various bits, scraps of paper . . . It was a huge group. It was the boy-scouts! They brought it all in to me. I would type it all out clean.'

Once he has done his bit Beckett takes the typescripts to a man known as 'Jimmy the Greek', who photographs it onto microfilm. This is placed inside a matchbox or printed onto a cigarette paper which is rolled around a needle and inserted into a cigarette. The messages are then transported into the unoccupied zone, most often carried by Jeannine's mother, the tiny, sixty-year-old, innocent-looking Gabrielle Buffet-Picabia. It is Alfred Péron who brings Beckett the material. They have a perfect cover story, which in any case is true: they are working together on a French translation of Beckett's novel, *Murphy*.

Germaine Tillion and her mother, Emilie, have both been active resisters since the early days of the war, sheltering escapees in their house in Saint-Maur des Fossés, which happens to be the neighbouring parish to that of Father Robert Alesch. One day, the nice-looking young priest knocks at Tillion's door and introduces himself, telling her that he has been sent by one of her Resistance colleagues, Maurice Dessinges, and wishes to work with her group. Tillion is diligent: she makes enquiries about the volunteer and receives reassuringly positive responses. So she takes Alesch at face value, as an ardently pro-Gaullist priest, and welcomes him into her cell.

Drancy

Situated on the northeastern edge of Paris, the 'Cité de la Muette' at Drancy was originally designed to provide social housing for people on moderate incomes. The project was a failure, poorly constructed and in the wrong location. Nobody wanted to live there. At the outbreak of the war the housing complex was commandeered by the French government as a prison for Communists. After the armistice the Wehrmacht used it as a temporary detention centre for French and British POWs, and from 1941 Drancy became an internment camp. Situated near the Bourget-Drancy and Bobigny railway stations, the camp was to become the main holding centre for Jews arrested in France who were destined to be transported to concentration camps. Notorious for its poor living conditions and lack of hygiene, at one point the camp held up to seven thousand people. Paul Léon finds himself in a supposedly 'privileged' club at Drancy, known as the 'Lawyers' Group', who are kept in marginally better conditions than the other internees, despite the fact that he had never formally practised law.

Paul Léon's immediate response to the noisy, overcrowded, filthy environment into which he has been thrown is to request paper and pencil, and to embark on a series of letters to his wife, Lucie, which begin on the day after his arrival, 22 August 1941, and end the day before his departure east. Over a total of forty-nine letters, some written in French, others in Russian, Léon reveals a mind tormented by three preoccupations: the fate of his wife and son; his son's education; and his work.

'How is Alexis? I advise you to adopt an attitude of great prudence and patience. Full responsibility for the family rests on your shoulders now. You must manage your nerves and keep a grip on yourself. I will only love you all the more for this, if that were possible.'

Asthmatic, possibly diabetic, terribly unfit, Paul Léon's health goes rapidly downhill as he is tortured first by hunger, then by dysentery, then oedema, which causes his legs to swell up painfully. They feel like jam, he writes. He is barely able to walk.

'I feel tired out and my nerves are frayed. The noise in the room is horrific.'

Ever practical, Lucie immediately tries to find a way to alleviate her husband's suffering. She joins the Red Cross, arranges a reception area for families of internees where they can bring food to be packaged and taken to the camp; she visits Drancy several times and even manages to meet Paul secretly there. When he writes to her begging her to send him his copy of the Bible, which he left on his bedside table, she somehow manages to find a way of getting one into the camp by persuading a Russian Orthodox priest to take it to this eccentric Jewish internee of profound Christian conviction. Léon derives great solace in reading from it to the other men.

Appalled by Léon's plight, Samuel Beckett offers his rations to Lucie so that she can take them to her husband. 'I will never forget this great kindness on his part,' writes Lucie later. 'At that time he was probably in almost as much trouble as we were, and he certainly needed those rations himself.'

As the weeks pass and the prospect of release recedes, Paul Léon's letters grow increasingly desperate:

30 September 1941
I'm worried about Alexis, about his work, and about his future.

6 November
I send you hugs,
I love you.
I'm hungry
I have yet to receive a single food parcel.

8 November
I have no more yellow shoelaces, no laces at all in fact. Could you send me a pair, please. And sugar lumps, cheese, butter, bacon . . .

12 November
My madness is producing dreams of culinary expeditions with you.
'My beard is growing snow white'

Grave as they are, the physical privations endured by Léon are secondary to the mental anguish experienced by this generous and impractical intellectual, this scholar of Constant and Rousseau, this loving father and husband whose warm familiar world of books and conversation has been replaced by incomprehensible brutality.

29 November 1941
How much I long to be close to you and to be doing some real work. [. . .] Here our intelligence weakens and crumbles and numbness takes over. In the morning we awaken still capable of thinking but two hours later everything has vanished, we have lost all our ability to reflect. It's hard, my love, it's hard. [. . .] It's painful, my love, and above all, it's sad. I must stress that Alexis

needs to go at least once a week to a lesson with Bosqui. As it is, last year he lost a whole trimester of instruction and this must not happen again. I beg of you, do whatever it takes, because his whole future is at stake.

On 12 December 1941 Eva Tichauer's father, Theodor, is arrested in Paris, in a further round-up of Jewish men, and taken to Compiègne internment camp in northern France. Rather than flee, Eva's mother is convinced that she and Eva should stay in their apartment, in order to be there to receive news of him.

'Did my mother really think she had any chance of seeing my father again?'

On the same day as Theodor's arrest, many internees in Drancy belonging to the 'Lawyers Group', including Paul Léon, are moved to Compiègne. This transfer coincides with further mass arrests of 743 French Jews in Paris, known as '*la rafle des notables*' (the round-up of prominent citizens): they are all taken to Drancy.

Paul Léon remains in Compiègne until March 1942, in conditions that are even worse than Drancy. Then, the men are divided into two groups. The first are returned to Drancy on 19 March 1942 and later deported east. The second group are sent directly to Auschwitz from Compiègne. On Thursday, 26 March 1942, Léon writes a final letter to his wife:

> Darling – we've been counted and tomorrow we leave – I don't know where we are going or how. [. . .] I pray to God every evening for you and for Alexis, as well as for all our friends. I hope I will see you again but I don't have much hope. But the most important thing for me is to tell you that I love you as much as I did 20 years ago and that – if I don't get to see you again – it is you that I shall love forever.

On 27 March 1942, the first transport of 1,112 Jewish men leaves France for Auschwitz. On it are Paul Léon and Theodor Tichauer. Eva Tichauer's mother, Erna, travels alone to watch the transport leave. She does not want Eva to witness her father's departure.

Lucie and Alexis Léon are there to say goodbye to Paul, who is now so ill he has to be supported by two men. Lucie, undaunted, breaks through the military police cordon and hands Paul some food, but she is pushed back. She and Alexis move to the other side of the station and wave at Paul through an opening in the fence before he is obscured from view. The men leave, singing the 'Marseillaise'.

Lucie returns to Paris. A week later she uses her contacts in the Resistance to get Alexis out of the occupied zone. The day after he leaves, the Gestapo arrive at 6 a.m. They have come for her boy and his bicycle. Lucie herself later escapes to the Free Zone.

Eva Tichauer and her mother return to their flat on rue Nollet. Eva sleeps in her father's bed because her mother does not want to sleep alone.

Yellow Star

In May 1942, Reinhard Heydrich arrives in Paris to personally introduce Himmler's new appointment, Carl Oberg, *Höherer SS- und Polizeiführer Frankreich* (Higher SS and Police Leader, France), to selected officers of the occupying forces. Oberg, a fanatical Nazi who will come to be known by the French as 'The Butcher of Paris', has been sent to France to crack down on the growing Resistance movement. A further meeting between Heydrich and the Secretary General of the French police, René Bousquet, lays out the terms of closer police co-operation not just in respect of suppressing the Resistance, but in the implementation of the decisions taken at the Wannsee Conference in January concerning the 'Final Solution to the Jewish Question'. Bousquet is all too ready to oblige.

The arrival of Carl Oberg not only opens a new and particularly brutal phase of the Nazi occupation, it also fundamentally alters the task of the Abwehr in France, by essentially handing control of all actions concerning the Resistance to Himmler via the Gestapo and the SS. From this point on, the Abwehr is no longer able to decide

independently how or when to take action against spies and saboteurs. Oscar Reile is no longer free to act as he sees fit.

The death of Reinhard Heydrich at the hands of the Czech Resistance just days after his Paris visit does not impede the rollout of the
new and terrifying Nazi policy regarding Jews. The first transport
which took Paul Léon and Theodor Tichauer to Auschwitz on 27
March turns out to be just a foretaste of what is to come.

In June 1942, the head of the Jewish Office in France, SS officer
Theodor Dannecker, issues a decree ordering that all Jews over the
age of six living in the occupied zone must wear a yellow star. Jews
are to report to their local town hall or police station, where they
must either pay for the star or give clothing rations in exchange.
The decree takes effect on 7 June 1942.

This is followed, from 16 to 18 July 1942 and again on 10 August, by
mass arrests of Jews, carried out by the French police.

Vel d'hiv

'We were warned about the *grande rafle*, someone told us not to
answer the door. On 16 July the knock came. My mother opened up.
We had prepared our luggage. At the door were two French policemen, one in uniform, one in plain clothes. They asked us to get
ready. We were to get dressed. My mother asked them if I could go
downstairs to fetch some family photos and papers she'd left with
the concierge. They said yes. I never knew if my mother wanted me
to escape, but I couldn't have abandoned her. I came back upstairs,
and we accompanied these two policemen to the *mairie* of the 17th
where there were lots of Jews waiting.'

The most notorious round-up in Paris takes place at the same indoor
cycle track, the Vélodrome d'Hiver, where the German female
'enemy aliens' were interned in May 1940. On 16 and 17 July 1942
a vast operation by the Paris police targets foreign Jews and their

children, many of whom were born in France and thus have French nationality. In less than two days a total of 12,884 people are arrested and crammed into the baking-hot stadium in the 15th *arrondissement* before being sent off to Drancy camp, thence to Auschwitz. It is the largest round-up in western Europe during the Second World War. To carry it out, the Nazis need the collaboration of the Vichy regime and the French police. In a vain attempt to spare France's indigenous Jewish population, the Vichy government prioritizes the deportation of foreign or stateless Jews.

For several days Eva Tichauer and her mother wait in the burning summer heat at the Vélodrome, crammed in with thousands of others, with little food and almost no water. Once transferred to Drancy, Eva's medical training – so important to her parents that they returned to Paris when it was no longer safe to do so – allows her to volunteer in the camp medical facility, where children are arriving alone and in a terrible state, sick with scarlet fever, measles, covered with rashes and lice. When the medical volunteers realize that the children are being transferred immediately onto transports headed east they begin to manufacture illnesses for them, making false diagnoses, changing mild illnesses to serious ones, inventing infectious fevers so that the children will be evacuated either to the Rothschild Hospital or to the Claude Bernard Hospital for Infectious Diseases. They do this not because they know precisely what is going to happen to the children, but because they instinctively feel that Paris has to be a better bet than a transport to Poland.

Around France, the same scene is being repeated.

Issy l'Évêque

On a beautifully sunny Monday morning on 13 July 1942 a car draws up outside a house in Issy l'Évêque, a village in southern France that lies right on the border between the occupied and the unoccupied zone. Footsteps approach; there is a knock at the door. Two gendarmes stand in the doorway, bearing a summons for the well-known Russian-born writer Irène Némirovsky, who left Paris for Issy in 1940 with her husband, Michel Epstein, and their two daughters, Denise, aged ten, and Elisabeth (Babet), aged five. Like Paul Léon, Irène Némirovsky did not take the chance to flee abroad when she could. She has lived in France since 1920 after her family fled Russia, converted to Catholicism, and established herself as a successful author. Since the outbreak of war she has made no attempt to leave the country, either through a sense of misplaced hope or one of resignation, perhaps a combination of both.

In silence Irène packs a bag. In her haste she forgets to take her pen, her reading glasses, her book. She explains to Denise and Elisabeth that she is setting off on a journey and instructs them to be good. A kiss for her distraught husband. No tears. The car door slams and she is gone.

Just two days previously Némirovsky was walking in the nearby woods on a peaceful, sunny morning doing what she always did: writing, making notes.

'I am sitting on my blue cardigan in the middle of an ocean of leaves, wet and rotting from last night's storm, as if on a raft, my legs tucked under me. In my bag I have Volume II of *Anna Karenina*, K. M.'s Journal and an orange. My friends the bumblebees, delightful insects, seem pleased with themselves and their buzzing is deep and solemn.'

After her arrest Némirovsky writes two letters: the first, on 13 July 1942, in pencil.

My dearest love, for the moment I am at the police station where I ate some blackcurrants and redcurrants while waiting for them to come and get me. It is most important to stay calm, I believe it won't be for very long. [. . .]

I shower my darling daughters with kisses, tell Denise to be good and sensible . . . You are in my heart, as well as Babet, may the good Lord protect you. As for me, I feel calm and strong.

On 16 July, the same day as the Vel d'Hiv round-up in Paris, Némirovsky scribbles a letter in pencil to her family from Pithiviers camp, where she has been taken following her arrest:

My dearest love, my cherished children, I think we are leaving today. Courage and hope. You are in my heart, my loved ones. May God help us all.

Over the summer Irène's husband Michel grows steadily more frantic as he tries every means at his disposal to secure his wife's release. He cannot sleep, can hardly eat, drinks too much wine, falls into rages as he contemplates the inevitable moment when he, too, will be taken and his girls will be left without parents. In his attempts to secure his wife's release he defies a recently introduced edict forbidding Jews from using the telephone: he contacts influential friends, writes endless petitions begging for help. At one point he even offers to take his wife's place. His letter to the German Ambassador to France, Otto Abetz, is so utterly, embarrassingly desperate it was probably never sent on by the intermediary whom Michel begged to help: 'I know, Ambassador, that you are one of the most eminent men in your country's government. I am convinced you are also a just man. And it seems to me both unjust and illogical that the Germans should imprison a woman who, despite being of Jewish descent, has no sympathy whatsoever – all her books prove this – either for Judaism or the Bolshevik regime.'

To no avail. It mattered not that Irène was a novelist, nor that she was Russian, Catholic, anti-Bolshevik or ardently pro-French. She was a foreign-born Jew. And so was Michel.

Betrayal

In August 1942, Robert Alesch asks permission from his Abwehr handler, Major Schäfer, to visit his brother in the Basses Alpes. Schäfer agrees and furnishes the priest with the appropriate paperwork.

When Alesch mentions the trip to his Resistance friends, they ask him if he would be prepared to carry out a mission for them at the same time.

Jacques Legrand asks Alesch to contact their cell in Lyons on his behalf, entrusting him with an important cache of microfilms showing the coastal defence plans at Dieppe, along with further military information and a request for money for the Gloria SMH network (recently renamed WOL – War Office London). He can no longer go himself, explains Legrand; the Gestapo are on his trail. Legrand trusts Alesch implicitly: he prepares him carefully, teaching him all the necessary code names and passwords. The person Alesch will be going to meet is one of SOE's top agents, Virginia Hall, code-named 'Marie Monin'. For the last few months Hall has taken over the transmission of WOL's messages and reports following the arrest of their previous contact, Pierre de Vomécourt.

When a young priest presents himself at the surgery of a Dr Rousset in Lyons, addressing the doctor by his code name, 'Pépin', and introducing himself as the new courier for WOL, with documents to be handed over to Marie Monin, Dr Rousset (a Catholic) is not disposed to mistrust the man in the soutane. When Alesch requests the 200,000 francs owed to cover the network's expenses, as set out in the letter, Dr Rousset explains that, since Marie was not expecting him, the money is not ready. They arrange that Alesch will return the following week to collect the cash.

In Paris, Alesch informs Major Schäfer that another meeting has been set up between him and Germaine Tillion at which he will be handed further microfilmed documents for 'Marie' in Lyons. Schäfer consults Colonel Reile, who in turn must now consult the security police. Reile would almost certainly have wanted to continue the 'game' with WOL but it is no longer up to him: the information the network has been passing to London is considered to be so strategically important, the SD decide it is time to cut them off once and for all.

On 13 August 1942, Germaine Tillion and Jacques Legrand's deputy, Gilbert, arrive for the meeting with Alesch and hand him a matchbox containing the microfilm, along with a letter from

Legrand to Virginia Hall. They enter the Gare de Lyon; Tillion tells Gilbert to leave while she accompanies Alesch to the gate where the tickets are checked. She and Alesch walk together, pushing their bicycles. She watches the priest punch his ticket and head off toward the train. At this moment, someone taps her on the shoulder:

'German police, follow us . . .'

As she is thrust into the back of a black Citroën, and Gilbert too is hauled away, Tillion has time to wonder why the Gestapo have not arrested Alesch. She saw him, from the corner of her eye, walking away quickly toward the train.

The following day, Alfred Péron is picked up in Anjou. Jacques Legrand and several others are next. Between August and September 1942 more than fifty members of the network are arrested and taken to Fresnes or Romainville prisons, then later deported to concentration camps under the Night and Fog decree.

Alfred Péron's wife, Mania, manages to warn Samuel Beckett and Suzanne. '*Alfred arrêté par Gestapo,*' reads her telegram. '*Prière faire nécessaire pour corriger l'erreur.*' (Alfred arrested by the Gestapo. Please do whatever necessary to rectify the mistake.) This cryptic but unmistakable message saves their lives. The couple quickly pack a few belongings and flee their apartment. Shortly afterwards, the Gestapo arrive. Finding the apartment empty, they leave a guard on the door in case they return, later sealing it with lead.

Beckett and Suzanne have no money and no idea where to go. At first they hide with friends in Paris, then move around between small hotels, giving false names and adopting a variety of unconvincing disguises. In October, using false papers provided by friends, they escape into the unoccupied zone, where they eventually find refuge in a small village named Roussillon in the Vaucluse. The little group of strangers who have taken up residence in the village are there either because they are Jewish or because they are in the Resistance. Exiled from their homes, forced into hiding, unable to act, they must sit here and wait. The villagers call them all, collectively, '*les Juifs*'.

★

On the transport to Ravensbrück in October 1943, Germaine Tillion finds herself in a group of five, all of them connected to Jacques Legrand. All were betrayed by Alesch.

But the priest is not done yet. Three weeks later he reappears in Lyons, with no microfilm but asking for the money owed to WOL and insisting on seeing 'Marie' in person. Like everyone else, Virginia Hall allows herself to be convinced of Alesch's bona fides, noting that the priest comes recommended by Jacques Legrand and accepting his explanation for the lack of documents and his non-appearance at their earlier rendezvous (ironically, he cites the arrest of one of his comrades as the reason for his caution). She duly hands him the cash, most of which Alesch pockets for himself.

On instructions from London, and against her better judgement (for there is undoubtedly something about Alesch that is off), for the next couple of months Hall continues interacting with the priest, whom the British have code-named 'Bishop'.

Oscar Reile is delighted that his agent has penetrated such an important network: thanks to Alesch the Abwehr have been able to intercept and break many of Virginia Hall's coded messages. Unfortunately, the Abwehr's successes are no longer their own.

Waning Power

Robert Alesch's success in betraying Gloria SMH turns out to represent a high point in German military counter-intelligence activity in France. The brutal methods employed by Carl Oberg to suppress resistance leads to a drastic reduction in the Abwehr's ability to penetrate Resistance cells because they are always on full alert, while many young Frenchmen opt to join the Resistance rather than submit to being used as forced labour on behalf of the Reich. Worse, a series of intricate counter-espionage games set in play against the British by Hugo Bleicher and Oscar Reile after their early triumphs turn out to yield disappointingly small returns. Hugo Bleicher's success in turning Mathilde Carré fades when she meets SOE agent Pierre de Vomécourt and confesses to the dashing Frenchman that she is working as a double agent. De Vomécourt proposes an extravagant plan, designed to tempt Bleicher and fool the Abwehr, which results in de Vomécourt returning to London unscathed, accompanied by Mathilde Carré. De Vomécourt later returns to France without Abwehr knowledge, while Carré remains in London hoping to be accepted as a triple agent. The British mistrust Carré, judging her to be not just unreliable but extravagant and indiscreet. Rather than run the risk of leaving her at liberty in London, they decide to intern her in a women's prison until the end of the war. De Vomécourt is eventually captured in France, put on trial, sent to Fresnes prison and then to Colditz.

Oscar Reile tries a double-cross strategy of his own with Roman Czerniawski, who since his 'Interallié' network was broken up in 1941 has been sitting in Fresnes prison. Reile's bold idea is to persuade the Pole to work for the Abwehr and then send him to England on a secret mission.

Reile is not in favour of executing prisoners, or torturing them like the Gestapo do. Knocking someone's teeth out might be satisfying to a certain type of brute but it generally does not produce any useful information. He prefers persuasion: get someone to talk and then talk them round, recruit them as an agent, give them some money and let them get on with it. Reile's strategy is to play on Czerniawski's patriotism by convincing him that a victory for the Allies will mean the Soviet Union controlling Poland (an accurate prediction, as it transpires). Spying for Germany, he argues, is therefore the least worst option. To clinch the deal, Reile offers Czerniawski a sweetener, offering to save seventy members of Interallié from court martial if he agrees to work for the Abwehr. The contract is signed in May 1942; Czerniawski is trained in the use of a radio and supplied with some wireless crystals hidden in the heel of his shoe. His 'escape' is arranged for 14 July, Bastille Day, when the streets of Paris are sure to be crowded.

Reile is careful to make the escape look convincing: Czerniawski is transferred from Fresnes in an open truck. As the truck makes its way through the busy city streets of the capital, the prisoner unexpectedly leaps out into the crowd, right in front of the Hotel Lutetia. His guards give convincing pursuit.

The result of Reile's bold ambitions simply proves the point that someone who has shown themselves willing to change sides once is likely to do the same again: as soon as he arrives in London Czerniawski promptly informs the British that he is playing a double game, producing Reile's wireless crystals and offering to act as a triple agent. After lengthy questioning, the British give Czerniawski a new code name, 'Brutus', and he is set to work to play the Germans at their own *Funkspiel* – 'radio game' – using the very same wireless crystals provided by the Abwehr. 'Brutus' feeds the Germans a steady supply of misinformation, most notably in the service of 'Operation Fortitude South', which successfully misdirects Hitler's attention to the Pas de Calais region instead of Normandy as the chosen site for the D-Day Landings of July 1944.

All that is left to Reile in his diminished domain is the battle for radio supremacy. Radios are the only means by which the Allies can rapidly obtain the information they need from occupied countries. As a consequence, the ether is awash with messages, all in constantly evolving codes, broadcast at regularly changing times on different wavelengths by operators using different handles to identify themselves. When an Abwehr tracking unit is put in place in the unoccupied zone, its unexpected success – within a few weeks they have caught eight radio operators and broken up several Resistance groups – is mitigated by the fact that it is the Gestapo who take charge of the arrested agents, while the Abwehr can only look on impotently.

It is a strange kind of exile, this prolonged posting in a smart hotel far from the front line. It has been two years now. The novelty of luxury has worn off, to be replaced by tedium, and fear about the future, and a longing for home. The Abwehr officers will never be

Parisians; their hotel room will never be their home, and, after all, they are still at war. Many of them seek distraction in the pursuit of money, pleasure, material goods, but no amount of champagne or fine cognac can disguise their growing unease. They ask themselves: where is this war taking us? To what end are we here, in this city, stuffing our faces with foie gras while our families are living off rations and our comrades are dying on the Eastern Front?

Diligent Reile, seated in his bedroom office on the third floor of the Lutetia, head bowed as he concentrates on his latest report, carries on working, but he can no longer convince himself that all is well.

Gurs

In the camp of Gurs, in southwest France, the actors, musicians and dancers continue to entertain their fellow internees with concerts and performances to distract them from the ever-growing fear of lists. The rumours can no longer be ignored: the Germans are deporting Jews to Poland, and they are making lists of names. The first transport departs the camp in early August 1942. Almost everyone on it is an artist of some sort. Among them is the twenty-year-old dancer Ruth Rauch.

They are taken first to Drancy, thence directly to Auschwitz on 10 August 1942. Ruth's mother, Margot, is not there to see her daughter leave: in January she was transferred to the camp of Récébédou, one of two so-called 'hospital camps' set up by the Vichy government in response to a public outcry at conditions in internment camps. (The other is Noé, to which Margot is transferred in October 1942.) The inmates there are generally older or infirm Jews. Conditions are slightly better, although the food is worse. Did Margot know? Did communication between mother and daughter simply cease?

Handbags

Eva Tichauer's work at the medical facility at Drancy enables her and her mother to remain in the camp for two months, an unusually long stay. But the day comes when their names are called and they are taken by green Parisian bus to the railway station at Bobigny where, on 23 September 1942, they are crammed on to a train, fifty people in each compartment. Two days later they arrive at Auschwitz at dusk. When the wagon doors are opened Eva can see little in the fading light: just a few shadowy figures in striped uniforms. The SS officers shout *Raus! Raus!* Get out, and leave your luggage.

The women are divided into two groups. One is told they will walk to the camp, the other will be taken by truck. Eva and her mother are separated.

'My mother was exactly fifty years old at the time. Since German was our native language she spoke to the officer separating people and said:

' "I'm a good walker, let me stay with my daughter."

'The man answered in a polite, persuasive manner: "Madame, the trucks are there to save you from walking, get in and you will see your daughter at the camp."

'I watched my mother disappear without even saying goodbye. I didn't see her get into the truck. I never saw her again.

'For my mother, who had always been a very intuitive person, the fact that they told us to leave our luggage . . . even more significant was the order to leave our handbags behind . . . It gave her an understanding of what was in store. All our documents were in our handbags.

'She clung to me, she sensed that the truck full of old people and the sick led to death, and she wanted to choose the walk to the camp, and life. She sensed what was awaiting her. I felt her despair.'

Forty-eight Hours

Three hundred miles away, in Autun on 9 October 1942, Michel Epstein and his daughters are taken to the same police station where Irène Némirovsky was interviewed just a few months previously. A German officer takes pity on the young girls. Removing from his wallet a photograph of his daughter, blonde like Denise, he says, 'I give you forty-eight hours to get away.' Michel's parting injunction to his eldest daughter is never to let go of the suitcase he hands her, since it contains her mother's manuscript. It will be many years before Denise can bring herself to open it and read what is contained within its covers.

Despite the fact that both the girls were born in France, Denise and Elisabeth Epstein's names appear on a list of Jews living in the region and French police have instructions to find them. Their first port of call is the village school where Denise is a pupil, but her teacher has the presence of mind to hide the girl behind her elderly mother's bed. That evening their guardian, Julie Dumot, tears the yellow stars from their clothes, throws some photographs and jewellery into a suitcase and flees the village with the little girls.

Numbers

Between June 1942 and July 1944 approximately 75,000 Jews were deported to concentration camps from France.

Over 60 per cent were foreign Jews, including 6,258 German and 1,746 Austrian Jews.

The vast majority – 67,000, including 6,000 children – were transported from Drancy camp.

Sheep

By now the war is no longer a shocking novelty, but a habit. In November 1942, shortly after the Allied advances in North Africa, a significant territorial change takes place in France when the southern zone is brought under German control. All of France is now occupied. The transports continue, taking Jews and members of the Resistance east. France, meanwhile, is being bled slowly dry of manpower and materials: thousands of young men are sent to Germany to labour for the Reich, or made to work in French mines and other industries deemed essential to the German war effort.

For the Abwehr, the German occupation of the whole of France offers an opportunity to act directly against the growing number of Resistance groups, but it raises other obstacles: as Abwehr posts are installed in Lyons, Marseilles, Toulouse and Limoges, resources are stretched ever thinner. With troops needed on the Eastern and African fronts there are fewer and fewer Germans in France. At the beginning of the Occupation there were around 40,000 German military personnel in Paris. By 1943 this has been reduced to 15,000.

The Abwehr's loss is the Resistance's gain: the French no longer have confidence in the Vichy government and resistance movements continue to multiply. Until now these have been small groups acting independently. Following instructions from London, they start to work together. Support from the British increases; propaganda against Germany is intensified.

In early December 1942 Admiral Canaris pays one of his sporadic visits to the Lutetia on his way back from Spain, accompanied by the head of Section I of the Abwehr, Colonel Piekenbrock.

That evening, a small group of six or seven officers who have been in post longest meet together in room 109 for dinner. While they are waiting for the Admiral to join them, Colonel Piekenbrock recounts an anecdote:

'Canaris and I were driving through Spain, in glorious weather, in an open-top car. We came across a herd of sheep. Canaris stood up and gave them a military salute.

' "Why did you do that, sir?" I asked.

' "Because one never knows if one of our superior officers might be among them," he replied.'

Despite the general good humour, during dinner Canaris remains largely silent. Then, suddenly, he begins to talk, a rapid flow of words expressing his violent revulsion at 'the gangster methods used by Hitler and his creatures'. It is not enough to have committed so many crimes in the East, he declares, the same practices are going to spread to France. The war will be lost, and the German people will be shamed throughout the world. No foreigner will ever be able to trust a German again. Canaris usually enjoys staying up late with friends, but tonight he quits the party shortly after the meal, leaving his subordinates to digest in silence the significance of their boss's outburst.

The Admiral now spends much of his leisure time in Spain, taking refuge from the war in frequent visits to Algeciras, where – on the pretext of visiting the local Abwehr station – he likes to cook and listen to the murmur of voices from the nearby Hotel Reina Cristina, when he is not deep in meditation in a Spanish church. On a visit to Sofia in Bulgaria he speaks with a friend about what they will do after the war. 'We ought to open a little coffee shop in Piraeus harbour,' he says. 'I'll make the coffee and you can wait table. Wouldn't it be great to lead a simple life like that?'

Sometime in 1943, Colonel Rudolph obtains a divorce from his first wife, enabling him to marry his long-term mistress and secretary, the fair-haired, bulbous-eyed Fräulein Juhl who has ruled his office and his heart for so long. They celebrate – where else? – with a champagne dinner at the Lutetia. Official rules mean that after their marriage the new Frau Rudolph is no longer permitted to remain in post alongside her husband. She is transferred to Spain, where Rudolph visits her every fortnight.

★

Life in the Lutetia goes on as comfortably as ever. Perhaps too comfortably for Oscar Reile:

'The streets were busy, shops were open. The menus of good restaurants were still offering excellent dishes. The supplies of wine and champagne appeared endless. One could still obtain almost anything: clothes, furs, jewellery, toiletries. Our secretaries tried to match the elegance of Parisian women in order not to be recognisable in town.'

One high-ranking Berlin visitor, passing through the Lutetia, takes offence at the over-dressed female staff and suggests to Colonel Reile that he intervene. Reile gamely gathers the Abwehr secretaries together and offers them a lecture about uniforms and suitable forms of dress. Afterwards one of the women, Isolde, comes to find Reile in his office:

'If you don't like my make-up,' she says, 'then transfer me to Marseilles. I know someone who works in our department who likes me just the way I am!'

Isolde is duly transferred to be appreciated elsewhere.

That summer, the Abwehr's vast black-market enterprise, Bureau Otto, permanently ceases operation.

By the end of 1943 it is clear to Reile – as it is to many Germans who are not fanatical Nazis – that Germany cannot achieve a decisive victory. The summer landing of the Allies in Sicily has led to the collapse of Italy. Allied bombers now regularly pass over Paris on their way to bomb German cities. On the freezing Eastern Front, German troops are being steadily pushed back by Soviet forces. After their early triumphs, the heavy-handed methods of the Gestapo means the counter-intelligence operations of the Abwehr are also failing to yield results. Major Schäfer has grown tired of Robert Alesch and his insatiable greed. His cover now blown with the British, Alesch is handed over to Hugo Bleicher, who does not have much for the eager priest to do.

Lions

There is always a change in atmosphere among the Abwehr staff when Admiral Canaris pays a visit, a sprucing up, an air of standing-to-attention. But it has been over three years now since the Germans first took possession of the hotel and Marcel Chappaz must surely have noticed the change in the Admiral's demeanour: Canaris seems to be getting smaller, his face has grown sunken, his eyes bloodshot and tired.

When Admiral Canaris visits the Hotel Lutetia again at the end of 1943, he is accompanied by Vice-Admiral Leopold Bürkner, Chief of the Foreign Affairs Section of the Abwehr. After Canaris has done the usual rounds of visits he arrives in Reile's office, where the colonel offers him an unvarnished report on the situation as he sees it. The admiral listens in silence, then asks Reile how much longer he thinks the war will last. Without reflecting, Reile replies that, without a political solution to end it, the war could drag on for another two years. This prospect evidently provokes Canaris to such frustration that he ends the meeting abruptly and walks out.

Yes, he has changed, Canaris: he is nervy, his hands shake, he looks pale and drawn.

That evening, as usual, a small dinner is held in room 109. Since there are two admirals present the conversation opens with a discussion about the war at sea. There is no good news: U-Boat losses are severe, there are too few battleships, and naval officers are having to be used in multiple positions. There is a joke going around that there are more admirals than ships. At the same time Germany is experiencing severe food shortages. A popular joke in Berlin quickly spreads: two hungry lions escape from the zoo and separate to search for food. Two weeks later they bump into one other again. One is skinny; the other fat and content. The skinny one asks the fat one how he has managed to gain weight. The fat one replies: 'I caught a couple of admirals down at the *Tirpitzufer.*'

At dinner, when Canaris mentions that a friend in Berlin has finally been made a rear admiral, a young officer can't resist: he relates the funny story. The anecdote is greeted with frosty silence. Canaris remains tight-lipped. Vice-Admiral Bürkner orders a double Cognac.

Late at night, when dinner is over and the conversation done, Canaris retires to his bedroom. He sleeps little these days, his mind preoccupied not just with the disastrous conduct of the war but with his own increasingly precarious position. The Admiral is more profoundly isolated than he has ever been. Sidelined in office, despairing at the conduct of the war, yet he is somehow unable or unwilling to betray his military oath and join those of his fellow officers who would strike against their leader.

The previous summer, Canaris covered up the efforts of Hans Oster and Hans von Dohnanyi, senior Abwehr officers, close colleagues and (as it happens) leading figures in the anti-Hitler resistance within the Wehrmacht, to enable a group of Berlin Jews threatened with deportation to escape to Switzerland. The Gestapo were told that the Jews were secret agents to be deployed in South America. When, months later, they discovered the truth Dohnanyi was arrested, and Oster placed under house arrest. Inevitably, Gestapo suspicion has turned next to the boss of this nest of spies. It is not the first time Canaris has offered a helping hand to his rebellious friends.

At night the hotel is quiet. Two soldiers remain on guard outside, but boulevard Raspail is silent. Any late-night revellers – officers returning from a nightclub or an assignation – slip quietly into the lobby, walk upstairs to their rooms, collars finally loosened, caps under their arms. *Goodnight, goodnight. Gute Nacht.* Off with the leather boots – leave them outside the door if you want the boot boy to polish them – the jacket placed over the back of a chair, cufflinks on the table, the slow creaking of the mattress springs as the officer finally settles down to sleep off the champagne before another day dawns over the City of Light.

In their meeting the following morning Canaris restricts his discussions with Reile to professional matters: there is no mention this time of Hitler or the Nazi regime. In reality, the Abwehr itself is beginning to unravel: bitter disputes with the SS, the SD and the RSHA (the Reich Security Main Office) have led to a collapse in morale. As Reile bids Canaris goodbye in the hotel lobby he forms the impression that the Admiral has given up any hope of change within Germany and is preparing himself for trouble ahead. It is the last time the men will meet.

A few months later, in February 1944, Hitler finally succumbs to Himmler's energetic persuasion and decides to merge the Abwehr and the SS, allowing Himmler to achieve his aim of taking full control of military defence. Canaris, now almost unrecognizable from the strain, his face 'tired and sunken', is forcibly retired from his position and ordered to proceed to Burg Lauenstein in the Franconian Forest, to await instructions concerning his future employment. The Admiral is accompanied into exile by his chauffeur and his two dachshunds. His family are not present: his wife has been evacuated to escape the bombing, one daughter is at boarding school, the other lives in an institution.

Canaris remains in the remote castle, effectively under house arrest, until he is given a new post as the head of the 'Special Staff for Mercantile Warfare and Economic Combat Measures', an office job of no strategic significance. He makes the journey home to Berlin, where he lives alone save for his dogs, his Arab mare, his Algerian manservant and his Polish cook.

For Reile, the subordination of the Abwehr to the RHSA is a disaster: the Gestapo and the SD are entirely ignorant of the methods or objectives of military espionage. Their men are dispatched to England insufficiently prepared and poorly equipped, ignorant of what they are supposed to be looking for and consequently wasting their efforts on goals of secondary importance. Powerless and frustrated, Reile goes about his daily tasks, analysing intelligence, writing reports. In the morning he rises, bathes, dresses, goes downstairs to take his breakfast and his coffee, before returning to close the door on his private office and begin the day's work. In reality, he is waiting for the war to end.

Izieu

On 6 April 1944, a group of forty-four Jewish children and seven of their adult carers are taken by police from the 'Colonie des enfants réfugiés de l'Hérault' – better known as the 'Maison d'Izieu' after the village where it is situated – and transported to the Montluc prison in nearby Lyons, at that time under the control of the notorious Gestapo chief Klaus Barbie. The Maison d'Izieu is a children's home and school run by the Jewish welfare organization OSE (Œuvre de Secours aux Enfants – Children's Aid Society) for Jewish boys and girls aged between four and seventeen whose parents have been deported, or interned, or are in hiding. In charge of the house is a Polish nurse and social worker, Sabine Zlatin, who works alongside her husband, Miron, a Russian-born agronomist, and several other volunteers.

On the day of the round-up Sabine is away in Montpellier look-ing for alternative accommodation for the children when she learns what has happened thanks to a warning contained in a telegram from a friend: *'Famille malade, maladie contagieuse'* (Family sick – sickness contagious). The details will come later: from Lyons the children and their carers are sent to Drancy, arriving on 8 April 1944. From Drancy they are transported to Auschwitz.

As soon as she hears the news Sabine travels to Vichy, then Paris, where she contacts the Red Cross in a desperate attempt to save the children from deportation. In vain. A few weeks later, she returns to Izieu and discovers that the house has been ransacked by the police. She goes around gathering up what is left: the children's letters and drawings, photographs and other documents. Alone, with no news of Miron or any of the children, she returns to Paris and joins the Resistance.

In the same month the pianist Margot Rauch, who entertained her fellow internees in Gurs with beautiful duets played on the grand piano with Hans Ebbecke, is transferred to Le Vernet camp, then

Drancy. A few days later she is taken from Paris-Bobigny station on transport number 75, arriving in Auschwitz on 30 May 1944.

Waiting

At the Lutetia, Oscar Reile is preoccupied by the imminent Allied landing. All senior Abwehr officers know it is coming. They also know that it will take place on the northern coast of France, perhaps Belgium. Agents in England have signalled the arrival of large contingents of Americans in England's southern ports. All other work has been suspended. The Abwehr staff sit by the radio listening to the BBC, waiting to hear the key words that will signal the landing. The tension is almost unbearable.

Finally, toward 6 p.m. on 1 June 1944, the radio operators at the Lutetia inform Reile that the BBC have just spoken twenty-six phrases that will put Resistance groups on alert. Reile telephones the Commander-in-Chief of the West, the military governor in France and the heads of the Abwehr in Berlin with the news, which he confirms in writing the following morning.

The next few days seem interminable. Reile sits by the radio with his colleagues, listening out for the phrases that will indicate the beginning of the landings. It is almost with relief that on 5 June they hear the BBC announce the phrases signalling that the operation has begun. Reile again informs his superiors by telephone, followed by a written note. Around 10 p.m. that night German army units stationed by the Channel are placed on full alert. The first Allied parachutists jump in the early hours of 6 June in the region of Caen–Cherbourg. The long-anticipated landing has begun.

The Plot

In Berlin, Admiral Canaris has retreated to the life of a pen-pushing public servant. He goes to work and comes home, spends his free time reading, gossiping with neighbours over the garden fence, and cooking an occasional meal. His animals bring him the solace which humans cannot: he plays endlessly with his beloved dachshunds, Sabine and Kasper, and allows his Arab mare to wander through the French windows into the house for a sugar lump.

Canaris has always kept a watchful distance from the group of conspirators whose activities centre around the charismatic figure of Count Claus von Stauffenberg, so he doesn't hear the news of the attempt on Hitler's life until late in the afternoon on 20 July. Hoping that the subsequent clampdown will pass him by, Canaris swiftly pledges his allegiance to Hitler. In vain. In the interrogations that follow the attack his name comes up again and again. He may not have been directly involved, but he is widely seen as a central figure, an enabler, somehow the 'spiritual instigator' of the movement that ultimately led to the plot. An order goes out for his arrest. Walter Schellenberg of the SD is given the task of bringing him in.

The repression carried out by the Nazi regime after this event touches several high-ranking members of the Abwehr, including Colonel Rudolph, who is known to be close to Admiral Canaris. On 26 July 1944 Rudolph is arrested and taken to an SS prison in Berlin for questioning about his possible involvement in the plot. Although he is released in September due to lack of proof, his career in Paris is over. After repeated arrests, trials and interrogations at the hands of the SS, when he is finally captured by the Allies in May 1945 he appears – perhaps conveniently – to have been so affected by these experiences, and by concern about his wife whom he has not been able to contact for months, that his memory has suffered and he is barely able to concentrate. Colonel Rudolph certainly is no longer the plump, pleasure-loving man with the 'Gourmandgesicht' who spent the previous four years living so comfortably at the Lutetia. He is broken, his memory shot, his eyes haunted.

Something in the character of Admiral Canaris prevented him from truly joining those who decided to fight Hitler from within. Instead, he acted passively, tacitly supporting their actions from the early stages of the war, turning a blind eye to their plotting, and helping on many occasions to facilitate the escape of refugees threatened by the Nazi regime. Whatever the reasons for his reluctance to act it makes no difference to the outcome: Admiral Canaris is arrested and taken to a Gestapo prison, thence to Flossenbürg concentration camp where, along with other leading members of the conspiracy, he is hanged on 9 April 1945, right at the very end of the war.

The Abwehr has lost all sense of unity. Most officers are convinced that, short of a miracle, the war is lost, but they only dare speak of it in small groups, terrified of being shot for defeatism.

The last mass transport from Drancy, number 77, leaves Paris-Bobigny station for Auschwitz on 31 July 1944. There are over 1,300 names on the deportation list, including 300 children.

Retreat

As the bombing comes ever closer to the city centre, the spectacle becomes a real, visceral experience. In the evening, there are sorties overhead, shrapnel rains down upon the city. A huge bomber crashes near the Gare de l'Est. By the end of July, Paris is seized by the same panic that took hold in the spring of 1940, only this time it is the Germans who are running, hurriedly emptying their hotels of bedding, mattresses, furniture, loading them onto waiting trucks.

The end, when it comes, is quick: on 17 August 1944, Prime Minister Pierre Laval and others are forcibly removed by the German army, first to Belfort, where they are joined a few days later by Marshal Pétain, then to Sigmaringen in southwest Germany.

On the same day, the German army begins placing explosives around the French capital following orders from Hitler that they defend Paris to the last and, if necessary, leave the city in ruins. His vengeful fury has evidently led him to forget his earlier conviction that Paris must be preserved at all costs. As the bombs close in on the centre of Paris, the president of the Paris Municipal Council, champagne magnate Pierre Taittinger, travels to the Hotel Meurice to request an audience with General von Choltitz, at which he begs him not to follow Hitler's orders. Whether it is thanks to Taittinger's pleas or not, Choltitz disobeys the Führer and the city remains intact.

One final convoy of fifty-one prisoners, mainly members of the Resistance, leaves Drancy that day, destined for Buchenwald. Accompanying them is SS Captain Alois Brunner, the brutal commander of Drancy camp, who is using the train to return to Germany. Twenty-one of the deportees manage to escape before they reach the border. The following day the remaining 1,400 inmates of Drancy are handed over to representatives of the Resistance and the Red Cross. Four days later, the camp is empty.

On 18 August 1944, just over four years since he first arrived, Oscar Reile takes advantage of the quiet that has descended on Paris to empty the Hotel Lutetia of personnel. His colleagues from Section I have already left. It takes all day to prepare for their departure, and it isn't until midnight that they are ready to set off. The hotel and the city beyond lie in deep silence. Of the hotel staff, only one waiter can be reached. Reile has the impression that he is waiting for the last Germans to leave the hotel. '[He] behaved in a rather unfriendly manner when I wanted to enjoy a last bottle of champagne with Major Schäfer and Andreas Folmer,' he complains. 'The hotel's wine cellar was still well stocked. But we contented ourselves with a single bottle of champagne, drank it down peacefully and left around 1 o'clock. Nobody disturbed our departure.'

Marcel Weber, who hid the Lutetia's best wines from these unwanted guests at the beginning of the war, watches their departure at its end. 'Of course, we tried to stop ourselves laughing. You don't provoke a tiger at bay, it's dangerous. And then, suddenly, there was no one left.'

★

On 25 August 1944 the French 2nd Armoured Division and the US 4th Infantry Division liberate Paris. General von Choltitz is arrested; he signs the formal surrender of the German forces to General de Gaulle's provisional government. The following day, General de Gaulle leads a liberation march down the Champs-Élysées.

Now they have gone. The Hotel Lutetia is empty of guests. The German chapter in Paris is over.

Deportees welcomed with cherries as they arrive
by bus at the Hotel Lutetia, May 1945

PART III

After: 1945

The Return

A crowd waits outside the hotel. Their backs are turned. No faces, only a sea of shoulders, shirt sleeves, threadbare jackets, hats, curly hair. Necks twist forward, roaming up and down. What are they looking for? They jostle one another, pushing patiently. There is no aggression, no sense that this is a competition which one of them must win. They are largely silent, the atmosphere tense. Their anxiety is palpable. The heads glide forward, searching, scrutinizing, scanning. A shoal of fish carried by an unseen current. What is it? What is it they are looking for?

Two young girls wearing summer dresses, loose on narrow shoulders, wait anxiously, balancing on tiptoe behind the obstacle of the adults. Their hair is the same colour; it has the same curl. They carry cardboard placards on which are written their names: Denise and Elisabeth Epstein. Denise is thirteen, Elisabeth (Babet) is eight. The last time they saw their parents they were ten and five.

The crowd shifts, and in the space between their heads we catch a brief glimpse of what it is that so engages their attention: a line of long wooden frames, municipal noticeboards of the kind on which local elections are advertised. Pinned on to these boards are hundreds of photographs of the missing, placed there by anxious families. Men, women, children. Wedding pictures, passport photos, family holiday snaps. Cheerful, happy faces posing in front of mountains, with a bicycle or a tennis racket, by the sea. Images that belong to a world that no longer exists.

The sound of an engine causes the shoal to shift, a current of anxious excitement passing through it. As the waiting crowd turns they reveal their faces: anxious, eager, fearful, desperate, the pent-up hope of years. *Let it be her! Please, let it be him!*

Their eyes are fixed on the bus's windows, where rows of passengers are just visible behind the dirty panes. From the hotel entrance a group of young volunteers emerge, clad in scout uniforms. Inside, the passengers do not stir. They seem to be far away, staring blankly across the heads of the people outside. Suddenly a woman in the crowd pushes forward. She holds up a photograph of a smiling young man, pressing it urgently against each window in turn. Another joins her, this time with a photograph of a child dressed in a white summer frock. Then another and another, banging on the windows. *Please!*

The passengers shrink. A shake of the head. A hand raised. *Please, no. Don't ask me.* The young volunteers are stationed like a guard of honour, two on either side of the bus door. The driver presses a switch and the doors fold back with a hiss of compressed air. There is a moment or two of stillness.

The driver turns to the passengers and gestures toward the door.
Nobody moves.

A young boy scout climbs up the steps to guide the first passengers down.

Through here. That door there, see it? I'll help you, shall I?

As they make their way through the crowd the passengers take in with a bewildered gaze the agitated faces, the photographs thrust toward them as those waiting surge forward eagerly.

'We entered the lobby. All those wooden panels covered with photographs.

'*Have you seen so-and-so? He was in this camp, that camp . . .*

'But we were looking for someone from our family.

'These people coming up to us with photographs of a good-looking young man or a young woman with her hair done nicely . . .

'*Did you know so and so?*

'Of course, we only knew the names of a small group around us . . .

'*But she would have been deported to this camp or that camp. You must have known her. She was a brunette . . . blonde . . . she was eighteen . . . thirty . . .*

'How were we to know how to answer them? We were still in shock. People were grabbing us, literally pulling at our clothes. That was the hardest part, passing those mothers crying, pulling at our clothes.'

The passengers shuffle past, unable to meet these eyes which are imploring them for information – no, for hope. Some panic, pushing away the hands that pluck at their striped sleeves. One man accepts the photograph thrust at him by a desperate woman.

'You knew him?' she clutches at his sleeve. The man does not respond. She tries again. 'Is he alive?'

He drops his gaze, pushing the photograph back toward her.

'Is he alive?' she cries again.

The passengers move on, the woman is left alone, the photograph clutched in her hand. She knows what the man did not tell her, and yet she cannot accept it. Not without proof. So she returns to the noticeboards and keeps on scanning.

At the back of the crowd, the two sisters wait in vain. For two months in the spring of 1945 they return to the Hotel Lutetia every day in the hope of finding their parents. Their father, the banker Michel Epstein; their mother, the writer Irène Némirovsky. They will never see either again.

Hiatus (again)

In October 1944 a seventeen-year-old boy named Jacques Desjeunes returns to his home in the Marais after spending three years at a hotel school outside the city. He is hoping to find work as a chef in a restaurant but most of them are closed. The city is still half-dead.

The gap between the liberation of Paris and the end of the war in Europe forms a hiatus almost identical in length to the one that marked the time between the declaration of war and the beginning of the

Occupation: nine months, from August 1944 to May 1945. Once again, Paris is a city that is at war but not at war. The Germans have gone but the world is still busy fighting, and although the restaurants and cafés are free to serve whomsoever they like, rationing, blackouts and shortages persist. There is a provisional feel to life: everyone is waiting for this damned war to finally end. Even General de Gaulle's new government is provisional until elections can be held.

Jacques manages to find a few short-term jobs, but he is a young man looking for a start in life: he needs a stable position. His father suggests they try the Hotel Lutetia. After all, he knows Monsieur Chappaz well. The Lutetia is part of Jacques's family history: his parents married there in 1924, Jacques was christened there in 1928; every year before the war there would have been two or three occasions when the family held a party in one of its banqueting rooms. His father offers to have a word.

Thus it is that Jacques Desjeunes finds himself approaching the familiar curved façade of the Lutetia, only today he is to enter not via the revolving doors on boulevard Raspail but round the back, via the staff entrance. Here, Chappaz will accompany him down to the basement, leading him into the enormous kitchen where he will introduce the boy to the head chef and the team of twenty or so kitchen staff with whom he is to work. He is starting at the bottom, as a *commis de cuisine*, or kitchen help. Jacques knows the deal; his father has drummed it into his head a thousand times: knuckle down, work hard, don't be cheeky, and maybe if you're lucky you won't get fired before the week is out.

Jacques is a hard worker, and for the next four or five months his life follows a steady rhythm as each morning he gets up early to make the short journey on foot across the Seine before descending into the gigantic basement where, bit by bit, he is proving his worth. The hotels of Paris no longer play host to the various departments of the Nazi military administration. Instead, it is the Allied forces who have installed themselves at the city's best addresses. Billeted in the Lutetia are officers attached to the Chief of Staff of the

French army, General Noiret. The chefs serve up food for the officers. It is not onerous work. The hotel is not full. Then, suddenly, in the spring of 1945, kitchen staff are told to expect a large number of people. Nobody specifies who or precisely when. Vast quantities of food begin to arrive, delivered in military trucks: meat, vegetables, butter, milk, food that Jacques has not seen since 1939, when he was thirteen years old. The French officers abruptly disappear. In their place are new faces, young men and women in uniform and civilian clothing bearing clipboards, making lists, holding earnest discussions, pointing here and there, making notes. Partitions are brought in and set up on the ground floor near the lobby, desks arranged in neat rows, there are X-ray machines and medical staff in white uniforms. When Jacques asks his colleagues what this all means they shrug and say they have no idea. He knows better than to bother the head chef with his questions. He longs to ask Monsieur Chappaz, but a seventeen-year-old kitchen help cannot just wander up to the hotel manager and ask him: what on earth is going on?

Les absents

During the short-lived military campaign of May 1940 the German army captured vast numbers of French prisoners of war, and they have been held in a network of POW camps stretching across Europe ever since. During the Occupation, hundreds of thousands of French citizens were conscripted for forced labour and taken to Germany or Poland to work for the Reich. In addition, thousands of deportees were transported from France to concentration camps and prisons, either for political reasons, as members of the Resistance, or on racial grounds, as Jews. Collectively these people are known as '*les absents*' ('the missing').

The provisional government of Free France run by General de Gaulle from North Africa, known as the French Committee of National Liberation, was already thinking about *les absents* in November 1943 when de Gaulle approached Henri Frenay to join his government as head of a newly created Ministry of Prisoners, Deportees and Refugees.

Frenay belonged to that select group known as *résistants de la première heure*, those who had fought the Nazi Occupation right from the outset. Captured and imprisoned by the Nazis in 1940, within three days Frenay had escaped and made his way back to France, where he immediately started producing clandestine literature and founded what would later become one of the three main resistance movements, Combat (the other two being Libération and Franc-Tireur). Frenay accepted de Gaulle's offer with some reluctance. It meant that he would have to forgo the sense of comradeship and active purpose which came with the life of a *résistant*. More importantly, nobody could tell him what his new job would entail. The only figure the government could put forward was so enormous as to deter the bravest individual from the task to come: they estimated that in total there were over 2 million *absents* who would need to return to France once the war was over.

Frenay arrives in Paris at the end of August 1944, choosing the symbolic address of 83 avenue Foch (former 'Gestapo HQ') as the base for his Ministry. The task facing him is complex in the extreme: whereas the number of POWs has been comprehensively documented, and there are fairly accurate numbers for those taken for forced labour, where deportees are concerned information is almost non-existent. The Nazi archives are gone, Vichy records have been dispersed. As to the camps, it is chaos: aside from places such as Buchenwald and Dachau, established before the war, nobody knows where the concentration camps are or even how many exist. The Night and Fog decree of 1941 means that there is little trace of those deported for political reasons, and for those deported for racial reasons there are no records at all. Sometimes there are names in registers at prisons such as the Romainville fort, or in the files of the Compiègne and Drancy transit camps, but nobody has any accurate idea of the numbers involved, where these people are, their state of health or their needs. It is almost impossible to prepare effectively for their return. The process of repatriation is further complicated by the way in which the war in Europe is ending, with two zones of control divided between the Americans and British in the west, and the Soviets in the east.

Frenay gathers around him a team of young men and women most of whom, like him, have a background in the Resistance. They are prominent members of Combat, MLN (*Mouvement de la Liberation nationale* – the National Liberation Movement) and the social services organization COSOR (*Comité des œuvres sociales des organisations de la Résistance* – Committee of Social Work of Organisations of the Resistance). Few have any direct experience of administration. There are no established systems in place. Everything has to be improvised. Resourcefulness is one of the primary qualities of a successful *résistant*. It is a quality that will be thoroughly tested over the coming months.

Olga Jungelson is a history teacher and former resistance member who is awaiting the start of the school year to resume her teaching career when she is approached by a friend who suggests she join the Ministry of Prisoners, Deportees and Refugees to begin the process of locating French deportees. She starts work on 12 September 1944, keeping a detailed diary of the 'nine deadly months' between the liberation of Paris and the end of the war as she tries to document the number and whereabouts of French citizens deported by the Nazis. The task turns out to be both fascinating and profoundly painful.

Jungelson begins in France, travelling around the country during the freezing winter of 1944 trying to glean what information she can in the prisons where deportees were held: she speaks to former prisoners, visits prisons to find names scratched on walls, window frames, stools. 'Shot, deported, interned, tortured, taken hostage – these words begin to dominate my vocabulary.' She goes further afield, travelling to Geneva to see what she can find at the International Committee of the Red Cross. And then comes the dramatic moment when Allied armies open the gates of Buchenwald, Dachau and Belsen – a moment of unspeakable horror that is broadcast around the world.

The opening of the concentration camps at least allows the process of compiling lists to begin. Another member of Frenay's team, Marie-Hélène Lefaucheux from the OCM (*Organisation Civile et Militaire* – the Civil and Military Organisation, another social service branch of the Resistance) travels to Belsen and starts putting together lists of survivors. In April she sends back the first names of French citizens to be liberated from the camp. It is a meagre haul: just 1,200 names out of the many thousands they are looking for. But it is a start.

Numbers

Known in 1945:
1 million prisoners of war
650,000 forced labour conscripts

Not known in 1945:
165,000 people deported to Nazi concentration camps and prisons from France
Of these –
90,000 political deportees and resistance members
75,000 Jews, including 11,400 children

La vraie France

Paris martyrisé! Mais Paris libéré! Libéré par lui-même, libéré par son peuple avec le concours des armées de la France, avec l'appui et le concours de la France tout entière, de la France qui se bat, de la seule France, de la vraie France, de la France éternelle.

Paris has suffered! But Paris has been liberated! Liberated by herself, liberated by her people with the help of French armies, with the support and agreement of the whole of France, of fighting France, of the only France, the true France, eternal France!

When General Charles de Gaulle enters newly liberated Paris on 25 August 1944, he does so with the profound conviction that in order to move forward the country must be united. Four years of occupation have left France deeply divided in every respect. Beneath the simple joy that accompanies the first moments of liberation lie complex, difficult feelings: shame, resentment, anger, the desire for revenge against those who wielded power on behalf of the Nazis. Returning to his home country after his years of exile, de Gaulle puts forward a triumphant narrative that is aimed at bringing the country together: the only *true* France is the France that resisted Nazi rule.

It is spring when the first deportees arrive in Paris, repatriated by air from Buchenwald and arriving at Le Bourget airport on 18 April 1945 to be greeted by officials, journalists, photographers and a band playing the 'Marseillaise'. They are a carefully chosen group of prominent political deportees and members of the Resistance whose return underscores de Gaulle's depiction of a France united in celebration of its courageous heroes. Among them are two major generals, several senior military commanders, members of parliament, professors of law, medicine, literature, science, the head of the Bibliothèque nationale, journalists and doctors. Buchenwald held the greatest number of French prisoners. The camp even had its own Resistance organization, known as the Committee of French Interests. Two of its leaders are among the returnees: trade union activist and Communist Marcel Paul, and Colonel Frédéric-Henri Manhès.

These men (and they are all men, the women will arrive later) belong to the first of two distinct categories of deportee: *deportés politiques* – political deportees, as opposed to *deportés raciaux* – racial deportees, i.e. Jews.

At the same time, POWs and forced labourers are also returning to France, young men in relatively good health who are greeted with uncomplicated joy by their families. The official ceremonies of welcome are widely covered in the press. In May, a handsome blond POW, Jules Garron, is chosen as the 'millionth' French citizen to be repatriated. Newspaper photos show him landing, saluting, holding flowers. He is young, strong, healthy-looking. His story is widely shown in cinemas.

The Elephant and the Flea

André Weil is another of the team recruited to work with Frenay's Ministry. Weil was one of the co-founders of the umbrella organization COSOR, which in 1944 brought together all the different social services of the Resistance into a national body. A Jesuit priest, Father Pierre Chaillet, is its director, working in close association with Marcelle Bidault from Combat and Marie-Hélène Lefaucheux from the OCM.

André Weil's job is to help organize the practicalities of the return of *les absents* to Paris. In the first instance, this means identifying and securing locations where the returnees can be received and temporarily accommodated. Several centres have already been chosen: army barracks, swimming pools, cinemas, even the Vélodrome d'Hiver, where German women were interned as enemy aliens and foreign Jews were held in the sweltering July heat in the *grande rafle* of 1942. Initially, the plan is for POWs and deportees to be received simultaneously, with the deportees going first to a national reception centre at the Gare d'Orsay and the POWs to a centre in the Tuileries right opposite, on the other side of the Seine. In making this plan, Frenay's team imagined that once everyone had completed the formalities associated with their return they would just go home and get on with their lives. But it soon becomes clear that the preparations they have put in place are woefully inadequate. It is not just the sheer number of people returning at the same time and overwhelming their resources. It is something else.

When André Weil goes to the train station for the first time he and General de Gaulle are the only two people on the platform, 'the elephant and the flea', as he puts it. Troops hold back desperate relatives who are waiting in the hope of seeing their loved ones return. After a brief welcoming wave, de Gaulle departs, leaving Weil and his comrades to help the deportees off the train. He has been allotted a nearby brasserie to receive them. Somehow he manages to get them all inside and has lunch served. The shock is profound: 'They were covered in typhoid lice and had dysentery. It was awful.'

The layers of governmental bureaucracy that render decision-making so painfully slow are not yet in place, so when it becomes apparent that the Gare d'Orsay is an entirely inadequate setting to receive men and women who can barely stand, and that hotels requisitioned in the Alps to serve as convalescent sanatoria are not yet ready, Weil and his colleagues immediately set about seeking a solution. What they need is a reception centre that is big enough to accommodate large numbers of people who need a bed to rest in, a place that can also provide space for the medical services needed to assess their health and the various intelligence and police officers tasked with weeding out the opportunists, collaborators and criminals who fancy getting hold of a certificate stating that they are a 'political deportee', a gateway to various benefits as well as a chance to reinvent themselves as patriotic French citizens.

Once officials in the Ministry are made aware of the scale of the problem, they first show Weil a large building which they deem suitable. It turns out to be semi-derelict, with no windows and cockroaches crawling all over the floor. Rejecting this proposal, Weil starts thinking about alternative buildings that might serve his purpose. He begins with the neighbourhood he knows best, where he was born and brought up: the Left Bank. It is not long before he hits upon an idea.

On the afternoon of 19 April 1945 André Weil, accompanied by Marie-Hélène Lefaucheux and the head of the OCM, Maxime Blocq-Mascart, pay a visit to General de Gaulle. After a brief meeting they walk out with permission to requisition the Hotel Lutetia.

Weil was initially told that the Lutetia is out of the question since it is playing host to officers attached to General Noiret, but de Gaulle grants his request immediately. Perhaps it appeals to the general to choose a hotel with which he is so personally familiar: it was at the

Lutetia, after all, that he spent the first night of his honeymoon, and where he stayed just before he fled Paris for London in 1940. Somewhere in its basement his military trunk lies forgotten.

Weil wastes no time: he and his colleagues go directly to the hotel and pack the officers' trunks themselves.

Dorine, Agnès, Sabine

The Lutetia operation is to be run entirely by volunteers. The staff of the hotel, who remain at the depleted level existing since the Occupation, will continue in post but their role will be limited: chambermaids are to prepare and clean the bedrooms and change the linen; kitchen staff will prepare the food. The manager, Marcel Chappaz, does not interfere. The head concierge, Roger Harrault, has himself just returned from a labour camp. The building is then divided up according to functions: the first floor is reserved for administration, the second for the infirmary. In May, the third floor is reserved for female returnees only.

Although nominally there is a military commander in charge, in reality the Lutetia is run by three women: the reception service is run by Marcelle Bidault, a nurse and General Secretary of COSOR, known by her Resistance name of 'Agnès'. She is also the sister of the Minister of Foreign Affairs. Registration of arrivals is organized by Denise Mantoux, known as 'Dorine', an interior designer who joined the Resistance in 1942 and created the social services department of Combat. In charge of the hotel itself is Sabine Zlatin, whom they call 'the Lady of Izieu'.

After the devastating loss of the children and her husband, Miron, at the Maison d'Izieu in 1943, Sabine Zlatin moved to Paris, where she began working in the social welfare section of the resistance movement MLN. Here she met dynamic, fearless, energetic Denise Mantoux – 'Dorine' – with whom she formed a deep friendship that would last the rest of their lives. 'Of course, I told her about the tragedy of Izieu. Her friendship was of great help to me during those difficult months.' After the Liberation it is Denise who asks Sabine to join Frenay's Ministry. 'Feeling a pressing need to keep busy, to fill my days with tasks that interest me and prevent me from dwelling on the past, I accepted.' Henri Frenay welcomes her into the fold; she is given an office and a typewriter, which she doesn't know how to use, and introduced to Agnès Bidault. When it is suggested that Sabine take charge of the Hotel Lutetia, Denise and Agnès are delighted: 'After what you have suffered and what you have done, this job is for you.' Despite having no experience, Sabine agrees to take on the role. The matter concerns deportees, after all, a subject close to her heart.

The hotel building itself is in good repair, with plenty of bed linen and towels. Olga Jungelson describes the supplies left in the Lutetia as meagre, consisting mainly of tins of biscuits. Sabine Zlatin, on the other hand, recalls that 'in their haste to leave, the Germans had left the fridges full of meat and huge quantities of rice, pasta, and various foodstuffs.' To the relief of Marcel Weber, the new occupants present no novel threat to his treasured wine cellar. 'The cellars were overflowing with wine,' recalls Sabine Zlatin, 'which we did not touch.' The black-market warehouses, those treasure troves of goods so efficiently established and exploited by the occupiers, provide ample booty for the women, who are authorized to go around the city requisitioning clothes, shoes, toiletries, food – anything the returnees might need.

A call goes out for volunteers: teams of doctors, social workers, scouts and soldiers are required around the clock. They come in numbers: from the Resistance, from the Red Cross, from the Quakers, the Salvation Army, as well as scouts of all denominations: Protestant, Catholic, Jewish. General de Gaulle provides the hotel with five chauffeur-driven cars to pick up volunteer nurses as they leave hospital after their shift.

When word gets out that the Hotel Lutetia is to be the main repatriation centre for returning deportees, anxious family members begin to gather on boulevard Raspail, asking questions, hoping for news. Many Resistance members were taken under the Night and

Former deportees consulting photographs of missing
persons at the Hotel Lutetia, May 1945

Fog decree; their relatives have had no news of them in over three
years. Families of Jewish deportees have no idea if their loved ones
are still alive. Crowds of onlookers flock to the hotel: journalists,
people who want to help, people who just want to find out what is
going on. One of the organizers has the bright idea of sequester-
ing all the election boards on boulevard Raspail and putting them
up outside the hotel and in the lobby. The first round of municipal
elections is to take place on 29 April 1945.

When the first lists go up in April, impatient families declare to
Olga Jungelson that they want to go 'there' – to Belsen – to bring their
relatives back. 'Why are they taking so long to return? I've got connections, I can get a car, petrol, they've got no right to stop me going to
find my husband, my son, my wife, because they're still there, alive.'

Alive? Olga has just returned from Belsen, where typhus is rife.
That is why the repatriations are so slow, and why the British forces
there don't want families coming to the camp.

Letters are sent out with information, up to three thousand a day. Lists of survivors go up daily, pinned to the panels outside the hotel. Inside, in the lobby and along the corridors, are hundreds and hundreds of photographs, each with a name and contact details written below, placed there by families hoping for news of their loved ones. Sabine Zlatin puts up photos of her husband, Miron, and of the two older boys who were deported with him, Theo Reis and Arnold Hirsch. Every day, in moments snatched after work or in her break, she comes down to check just in case there is news of them. Only volunteers, staff and those connected to the returnees are allowed inside. Everyone else has to scan the lists outside.

Then the arrivals begin.

What a City!

Springtime in Paris. A fresh breeze stirs the blossom on the chestnut trees that grow along boulevard Raspail. At the Hotel Lutetia, the organizers and their teams of volunteers are readying themselves to receive the first group of returning deportees. It is 26 April 1945, three days before the first round of municipal elections. France has been liberated; the Allies are on the cusp of outright victory in Europe.

On a platform at the Gare de l'Est the bandleader raises his baton and, as the train slowly pulls into the station amid a cloud of steam and screeching brakes, the military band plays the first notes of the 'Marseillaise'. A uniformed delegation waits on the platform ready to greet the returning heroes.

> *Allons enfants de la Patrie*
> *Le jour de gloire est arrivé!*

Officials hold back the crowd as the first concentration camp inmates descend onto the platform.

Aux armes, citoyens
Formez vos bataillons.

Silence falls.

'People looked at these poor creatures and began to weep,' recalls resistance fighter Yves Béon, returning from Buchenwald. 'Women fell to their knees without saying a word. The prisoners move forward, almost as if afraid. They move toward a world they have forgotten, a world they do not understand. They see earthlings, dressed as earthlings. They look at them without saying a word. These beings from a vanished planet see before them other beings whom they do not recognise. There, beneath their feet, there is a border, a passage to cross.'

They are walking skeletons, their skulls covered with skin so thin it is almost transparent. Their heads are shaven, men and women almost indistinguishable. Most wear filthy clothes resembling striped pyjamas.

They are led toward a waiting room where young scouts welcome them and lead them to the buses waiting outside, those same green Parisian buses that took so many from Drancy to Bobigny to be herded on to trains headed east. This time it is seated places only, no standing. The sickest are taken directly to hospital.

The buses depart and head toward the city centre, past the Hôtel de Ville, across the river, there's Notre-Dame, down rue Saint-Jacques, past the Sorbonne, the Jardin du Luxembourg . . . A whirlwind tour of the city sights. The streets are almost empty of cars; passers-by stop to stare at the buses with their strange cargo. Some wave, some sketch a smile, some turn away, some weep, some simply gape. The deportees gaze out of the windows at a sight that, just a few months, years, aeons ago would have seemed quite normal: a spring day in Paris. Some, who have never been to the French capital, cannot believe their eyes. *My God, what a beautiful city!*

★

Later, in June, a young resistance fighter, Simone Alizon, is repatriated in a DC8 military plane. After being liberated from Ravensbrück by the Swedish Red Cross she has spent the past few months in Sweden along with other female survivors, including the anthropologist Germaine Tillion, who was betrayed by Robert Alesch.

Simone spends most of the journey in the cockpit, gazing down at the glittering North Sea. Then, miraculously, the coast of France appears beneath them. They arrive in Paris in glorious sunshine, *C'était un rêve!* It was unimaginable, this return. The first time she had ever seen the capital city. 'Every time I think of it . . . Passing through the *banlieues*, I thought: *C'est ça, Paris . . .*' So this is Paris.

Outside the Lutetia a crowd is gathered, anxious relatives hoping to be reunited with their loved ones. As the first bus pulls up they surge forward, pressing up against the windows. They want to utter joyful words of welcome, but as the first returnees climb from the buses the words catch in their throats and they, too, fall silent. One by one, a series of ghosts in striped uniforms step down into this deep well of silence, strange exiles returning from another planet. The people who are waiting are frozen, only their eyes are moving, scanning the features of the arrivals, searching for a face they once knew, hoping to find in these skeletons some semblance of familiarity. The deportees, in contrast, do not seem to see the waiting crowd. Their gaze is lost in the distance, as if they are somewhere very far away, still absent.

Then the clamour begins. Resistance member Roger Joly returns to Paris after liberation from Neuengamme: 'How to convey to people who are eaten up with anguish that the person whose photograph they are showing us has nothing in common with the person we might have known? They show us a human being, we knew only a remnant . . .'

Good Deeds

When Bertrand Poirot-Delpech and his friends volunteered to help at the Lutetia they thought they would be performing some kind of heroic action. Sixteen years old, studying philosophy at the Lycée Louis-le-Grand (where Alexis Léon completed his *bachot* in August 1941 and Pierre Radványi attended summer school in 1940), Bertrand is a scout at Saint-Sulpice.

'With two or three other scouts from my class, we asked our philosophy teacher, M. Cuvillier, for permission to go and meet the deportees at the Gare de l'Est to accompany them on the bus to the Lutetia.'

They pictured themselves waiting on the platform in their smart scouting uniforms, greeting the arrivals, taking their suitcases – *Here, let me* – leading them to the buses . . .

The reality fractured their youthful illusions.

'The only luggage they had was a package in which they had tied up a few meagre items, their belongings if you can call it that; they clung to it, for them it was a way of rediscovering the pleasure of having something that belonged to them. [. . .] It was their little treasure, like when children bring their dolls with them during air raids.'

It is a lot for young minds to process. Carrying a skeletal man in one's arms, watching a grown man scream from fear at night. André Weil sees young scouts vomit, overcome with nausea. 'A smell of agony mingled with sweat pursued them everywhere.'

The deportees have mostly been liberated just a few weeks earlier. Some have survived death marches, others have remained in camps ravaged by typhus, surrounded by the dead. Some were in the camps just a few months, others for two or three years. At liberation they were given food and water, but the armies or the Red Cross units that freed them lacked the resources to offer the medical treatment or the rest they needed on the spot.

★

They are led inside, through a revolving door and into a lobby, down a corridor lined with faces. The writer Jacqueline Mesnil-Amar records her impressions in the *Bulletin* of the SCDI.[†]

> Hundreds and hundreds of photos hanging on the walls. All these faces of absent loved ones lost in the immense turmoil gaze back with their old eyes, with their cheerful eyes from 'before', smiling with life and youth, photos from weddings or holidays, looking out with their poor paper eyes to see if we will recognise them, if we have glimpsed them once, if we will say what we know about them, this last hope.

And then, another brutal act: a puff of white powder in the face.

DDT

'We arrived in front of this big palace,' writes Maurice Cling, who was sixteen when he was liberated from Auschwitz. 'I'd never been inside the Hotel Lutetia before, to me it was like a palace – and there was a revolving door at the entrance – I'd never seen one in real life – I went round this thing and as I stepped out the other side I received a cloud of white powder almost in my face. It was DDT, for the lice.'

The deportees are used to being treated like animals. But since their liberation there has been a pause: kindly faces, no blows, food, something to drink. Now, as resistance fighter Gisèle Guillemot passes through the door the 'elegant women who welcome us, sympathetic but gloved, you never know . . .' are telling them to undress. They take their rags, and suddenly they are spraying them with ghastly white powder 'everywhere, in the hair, in the mouth, in the nose, in the eyes,

† Le Service Central des Déportés Israélites (The Central Service for Jewish Deportees), a welfare organization founded in late 1944 by Mesnil-Amar with her husband, André Amar, and fellow Resistance member Arnold Mandel.

in the ears . . . enough is enough!' Then a shower, more nakedness. Angry cries from one of the cubicles, a distinguished voice raised in offence: 'Leave me alone! You don't think they made me strip naked enough for two years? You want me to do it again?'

The deportees are caught up in a machine that is intended to be good for them. Hygiene is the first priority: treatment for lice and scabies, removal of clothes, provision of a hot shower, an X-ray; after that, a medical check for wounds, typhus, TB, digestive problems caused by lack of food. More prodding and poking. Doctors asking them questions.

The lice get everywhere. André Weil returns home from his shift at 4 a.m. and brushes the insects off in his bathroom. The first deportees to return are highly contagious, and in the beginning there are two deaths among the staff, a chambermaid and a scout in charge of the cloakroom. 'We hadn't been vaccinated. Nobody warned us.'

Sometimes there are so many buses arriving at the same time the organizers have to use other buildings for the overflow. There is a cinema, the Rey, in a little cul-de-sac, rue Juliette Récamier, just off rue de Sèvres. Volunteers direct the buses to the cinema so that the deportees can sit somewhere comfortable while they wait. A hydrotherapy establishment in the same street is commandeered for the disinfection process.

Volunteers take away the filthy clothes the deportees arrived in, often still the striped uniform of the camps, and replace them with something from the enormous store of garments which Sabine Zlatin and the other organizers have sequestered from the black-market suppliers, augmented by generous donations.

The medical service is run by Dr Toussaint Gallet, an obstetrician and gynaecologist whose Resistance activities landed him in Buchenwald, where, despite the conditions, he continued helping his fellow prisoners. Ignoring his own weakened state, the day after his return to Paris (among the select group of prominent deportees who arrived at Le Bourget on 18 April 1945) he accepted the role of head of the medical service at the Lutetia.

The cursory medical examination can do little, in reality, to address the multiple physical and mental difficulties facing the returnees. This is mere triage, a process to identify those who need urgent medical care, decide who is fit to be discharged with their Red Cross parcel and sent on home to their families, and who needs to spend some time at the hotel to rest.

In theory deportees are entitled to a forty-eight-hour stay in the Lutetia. In reality, some leave immediately, walking out through the revolving door and disappearing into the metro station at Sèvres–Babylone. Many others need to remain longer, either to recover the strength to eat, to walk, to move around, or to locate somebody who can come and meet them. For some, there is no one who will come and no home to go to. These things can take weeks to establish.

Each arrival must be registered and given an identity card that categorizes them correctly as a deportee, a status which will entitle them to various benefits. Volunteers from the Women's Auxiliary Corps keep the records. Known as '*les petites bleues*' (the little blue ones) for their navy uniforms (not to be confused with the '*souris grises*' – the grey mice – of the Nazi occupation), they have two registers, one organized by room number, the other alphabetical. In the chaos many deportees fail to register when they arrive and do not report their departure.

Before an individual can be given the all-important *carte de déporté* there is one vital remaining hurdle to cross.

Interrogations

'They had lost their memory for dates,' writes Olga Jungelson, 'didn't know the names of the *kommandos*, and only knew their torturers by nicknames or incomplete names: "Which comrades did you see die?" They snigger at this stupid question. We feel pathetic in their eyes. They seem to answer out of pity: "There was Maurice, who died of typhus. I think I remember he lived in Niort. His wife was a teacher and he had two children. And the little blond boy, what was his name? His father was a big shot in customs." '

Lieutenant Louis Micard is head of the security and control service at the Lutetia, which includes officers from the intelligence services and the police. Specialists have prepared an arsenal of questions: When were you arrested? Which route did you take to the camp? What sort of work did you do there? Which *kommando* were you in? Who were your bunk mates? Whom did you see die? Were you condemned to death? By which tribunal? Were you tortured? Were you raped? In what circumstances? Resistance fighter Liliane Levy-Osbert, returning from Auschwitz, finds the questioning unbearable:

'He asks: married or single, why, how, who, what happened. Immediately I'm back in the secretive atmosphere of 1940. In reality, I'd never come out of it. The result: rigidity, mouth sewn tight shut . . . Attempt at intimidation by the interrogators: so, you left voluntarily? Now that's a step too far! Offended, I jump up, bang on the table, and walk out.'

The aim is to help the deportees to recover their civil identity, but some, especially those who were in the Resistance, react angrily to these questions. 'We needed other things: food, medical care. We needed to go home.' But without the all-clear from the authorities, the deportees risk leaving without their temporary ID card, which recognizes their status and awards them certain rights, such as free transport. There are different benefits for forced labourers, POWs, political or racial deportees, a source of some conflict among the different groups competing for recognition and support.

An aside: on 2 June 1945 hundreds of former POWs march down the Champs-Élysées not in celebration, but in protest. The demonstration, organized by the Communists together with supporters of an ambitious young political activist, François Mitterrand, is an expression of the anger felt by POWs who, unlike deportees, do not receive clothes or shoes, but must remain in uniform.

'We are soldiers, not beggars!'

They want money for widows of POWs; there's a shortage of socks and shoes. They hold a huge meeting at the Mutualité (where in 1935 the International Writers' Congress took place) before laying symbolic wreaths at the tomb of the unknown soldier. Their anger at Henri Frenay soon threatens to get out of hand as the chants of '*Frenay démission!*' (Frenay resign!) give way to chants of '*Frenay au poteau!*' (Frenay for the chop!). The crowd tries to force its way into the Ministry on avenue Foch until word emerges that de Gaulle has agreed to receive a delegation.

Evidently, there are some among the returnees who are anxious not just to access the 1,000-franc bonus, the tobacco and the clothes, but to wipe clean their wartime slate, to receive the 'certificate of virginity' that would be granted them with the words 'political deportee' written on their repatriation form. Naturally, the intelligence and police officers are focused first on weeding out the fakes. It is an important task, but it goes down badly with Resistance members furious at this line of questioning. Furious but also scared, because the world from which these people have emerged has left them confused, unable to remember dates, places, names . . .

Yves Léon has survived Sachsenhausen and Bergen-Belsen. Liberated in April, now it is 4 June. For almost two months the young resistance fighter has been waiting to go home, convinced that once he is back in France everything will be fine. 'I said to myself: there must be very few of us coming back, and I'm one of them. Everyone knows what we've been through, everyone will finally show some consideration for us . . .'

He arrives at the Lutetia late in the evening, the last group of the day. After passing impatiently through the formalities, the photographs, the medical checks – he is young, he wants to get home to

Brittany – finally he is taken for an interrogation by an officer from the Deuxième Bureau, 'strapped into his uniform'.

'I didn't trust him; I thought he was a former collaborator [. . .] He questioned me as if I were a criminal, a spy, with no regard for my person or even my state of health. I had to answer, give my identity, that of my parents and grandparents, give the reasons for my arrest, with details – including dates – that were frightening for me, who had almost lost my memory [. . .] We hadn't expected this hostile attitude toward us. Perhaps all these people were in a hurry to finish their day? We had nothing to do with it [. . .] Perhaps they were also tired of seeing so many deportees: we were among the last survivors to return to France.'

There is no room to spend the night at the Hotel Lutetia, so Yves is sent to the nearby Hotel Montaigne, where, confronted for the first time in over two years by tables, chairs, plates, spoons, knives and forks, he realizes that he no longer knows what to do with them.

Fakes

Former *kapos* or militiamen are canny in the stories they try to tell. They've purchased themselves a striped costume, perhaps even a fake tattoo, but the mistake they make is to be too precise in their accounts, offering up dates and details which genuine deportees cannot recall. And it is easy enough to cross-check their story: all it takes is to head into the crowd and find someone from the network they claim to belong to.

Officials lock the criminals in a bedroom. Every evening at 6 p.m. a prison car arrives to pick them up. Sometimes, at night, the deportees hear thundering footsteps in the corridors, and shouting. Somebody who hoped to erase the stain of their collaboration is trying to escape.

Among the fakes are women who went to Germany because they'd fallen for the wrong man, or been promised a good job, many of them prostitutes trying to pass themselves off as deportees by borrowing a few names, some camp characteristics gleaned from conversations in the corridors or the hotel dining room. They very quickly become confused when they have to explain the conditions of their arrest.

Not being a member of a known resistance network automatically arouses suspicion. Thérèse Vershueren and two friends escaped during the evacuation of Zwodau, where they had been taken after Ravensbrück. When they try to enter France they are accused of being prostitutes, and are only allowed into the Lutetia after showing their tattoos. After being interrogated all night they end up sleeping on the floor. The miserable experience is compensated for by an excellent breakfast the following morning in the luxurious dining room. Nevertheless, 'Everything would have been easier if we hadn't escaped.'

The interrogations are not just about benefits or criminals. It is also a vital process of beginning to document the scale of Nazi crimes. But the questions, however gently put, elicit terror.

'The hunted look when you ask them too specific questions. We're going to punish them for forgetting a name, for getting the dates wrong. We're going to send them *there* . . . When can they go home? We have to explain that they can help us find the others, locate the mass graves on the evacuation routes, perhaps identify the executioners.'

Olga Jungelson tries hard to piece together the fragments of information, but there is a sense of mutual misunderstanding. She sits patiently, trying to establish a chronology of events – first this, then that – following the logic of normality.

' "You were liberated at Chain? So you're from Dora?"

' "No, I was at Ellrich . . ."

' "You worked at the Heinkel factory? Did you take part in the evacuation to Buchenwald?"

' "Not at all . . . I ended up in Malchow."

' "If you were released from Malchow, did you come from Oranienburg?"

' "I never set foot there – only in Neuengamme."

' "Ah, good! I understand that."

' "You don't understand a thing. I escaped during an evacuation. I walked for days and nights, going in circles . . ."

'It is as if we're faced with the impossible task of reconstructing the frantic meanderings of the inhabitants of an anthill that has been set on fire. But the ants are sizing us up with all the contempt of insiders in a world to which we have no access. Blind strangers in the world of the sighted, trying and pretending to understand what they have suffered without ever having understood: that is what we represent to them.'

Milk, Rice and Jam

Most of the deportees are in a state of near starvation; average weight, 48kg (106lbs). Some are too weak to eat in the dining room and have to be fed by hand in their rooms. Scouts sit patiently with them, spooning soup into their mouths. Food is abundant, prepared by the chefs at the Lutetia, but caution is needed in offering too much to people who have been starved for so long. Dr Gallet has prepared a programme to help the deportees readapt to a normal diet: anything too rich or too fatty could have dire consequences for digestive systems destroyed by near-starvation diets and dysentery. Volunteers have to teach them to eat carefully so as not to overload their weakened and unsettled bodies.

The army delivers the food to the hotel. Officially each deportee is to be provided with a generous daily supply: 125g meat, 15g butter, 200g bread, 10g salt, 5g lime, 200g carrots, 30g coffee, 30g sugar, 60g jam, 150g pasta, 70g cheese, 100g milk, 100g gingerbread, 1kg potatoes, 1 egg.

Most of what is provided is entirely inappropriate for the survivors to eat but can at least be used to feed the volunteers. At one point André Weil receives a visit from a colonel who informs him that he is being taken to the council of war for misappropriation of military supplies. Weil simply laughs. The provisions have the stamp of approval from de Gaulle himself. And if some of what is sent for the deportees is given instead to the volunteers, well, 'I committed the "crime" of giving them military supplies too!'

Among the dozens of individuals who turn up to see what they can do to help is the recently appointed Canadian Ambassador, Major General Georges Vanier, and his wife, Pauline. When told 'We need milk, rice and jam' to make rice pudding for those suffering from dysentery or recovering from typhus, Vanier immediately arranges for a large order of these precious goods to be sent by air freight directly from Canada. Deeply shocked by the conditions they find on their arrival in France in 1944, the Vaniers plunge themselves into the work of helping both French citizens and refugees. At one point they bring thousands of items of clothing for war orphans into France via the diplomatic bag.

In the dining room, girl scouts hover around the deportees, carry plates, lay the table, serve meals, clear up, take fruit juice up to the rooms, note down the lists of arrivals and departures. The two dining rooms are bright and cheerful. There are flowers on the table, wine in carafes which the deportees cannot drink but the volunteers enjoy. After their shift, the scouts sit down to wolf down some food and discuss the day's events.

The previous night, at 3 a.m., Bertrand Poirot-Delpech was asked by a deportee to go and find his wife at their home on rue Lecourbe in the 15th *arrondissement*, and to bring her to him at the hotel, because he was afraid of not recognizing her. When Bertrand went there the woman asked him to accompany her to the Lutetia and stay with her, because she, too, was afraid her husband would not know her.

'I ended up introducing them to one another!'

He does not add that the situation caused him so much distress he did not sleep all night.

Down in the kitchens, young Jacques Desjeunes is confused: despite the enormous quantities of food arriving daily, including so much meat that the cold store is full, the meals they are told to send upstairs

Deportees eating a meal at the Hotel Lutetia, May 1945

consist only of mashed potatoes, pureed vegetables, soft foods that don't need to be chewed, all prepared in huge pans. Jacques is too junior to have any say in the menus or even know who decides what they are going to prepare on any particular day, but the head chef – in co-operation with Dr Gallet and Sabine Zlatin – puts together a daily menu, depending on what has arrived that morning.

Before the war the kitchen of the Lutetia was often required to serve two or three thousand covers for banquets, so providing over a thousand meals per day based on a single dish is hardly a stretch. There are no set mealtimes, so the chefs simply prepare what is needed as and when it is required. Deportees are offered no choice of menu, nor are they in any state to make such decisions. Food is prepared for the volunteers as well, an opportunity to use up some of the supplies of meat.

Ghosts

Once the kitchen staff have finished their shift they venture upstairs to see what all the fuss is about.

Standing at the edge of the lobby, Jacques watches as the deportees are helped down from the buses by the young scout volunteers. As they enter the hotel, his first impression is of the striped pyjamas. But as they pass by him it is something else that embeds itself in his memory:

'They stared right through you. It was very hard to look at them, their gaze was blank, there was no sense of their being happy. I don't think they realized it was over. They were people who had the air of not being people, do you understand? None of them seemed happy – it was a feeling they had completely eliminated. And their physical state was also striking – people with no flesh on them. It's impossible to explain what you feel when you see something like that – it goes beyond you. We couldn't understand – and nobody had warned us.'

'The thing that struck me most was their faces.' Fourteen-year-old Michel Rocard is a member of the Éclaireurs Unionistes de France (the Protestant Scouts of France); he belongs to a group located in the Luxembourg parish, which includes the Hotel Lutetia, a building he and his friends have always regarded with fear because it was requisitioned by the Germans. Michel is tasked with helping the new arrivals off the buses and accompanying them into the hotel. 'The landscape of the faces of these men (I mainly remember the men) had been destroyed by other men. It was frightening. We didn't speak to them. *Le silence s'impose.* It was a sight that marks you for life.'

The arrival of the deportees takes place at a moment in time when the full reality of the concentration camps is still unknown. During the period between the liberation and the end of the war the press published many reports about the camps, but they came mainly from political deportees or escaped forced labourers, rather than Jews. The existence of dedicated death camps is hard for those who are receiving the returnees to comprehend: the notion of gas chambers, the industrial-scale murder of human beings. It is unimaginable. People have no idea how to describe what they are seeing. 'With the influx of survivors at the Lutetia in April and May 1945,' writes Olga Jungelson, 'we had to admit that skeletons could walk, discover a new geography, a new vocabulary.'

There are tables in the dining rooms where the deportees can eat, but many stay in their rooms and are served there by volunteers, two of them accompanying them everywhere. Jacques Desjeunes stares, mesmerized, from his vantage point at the edge of the lobby. *Ils étaient déshumanisés.* 'They had been dehumanized.' Like ghosts, evanescent. *Ils étaient autre part. Ils ne s'étaient pas rendu compte qu'ils soient revenus.* 'They were elsewhere. They hadn't realized that they'd returned . . . You can't explain it in words.'

The kitchen staff never discuss it among themselves.

Going Home

Now comes the most difficult part, the search for loved ones, the long-awaited, much-feared return. Those who were deported under the Night and Fog edict as resistance fighters most often still have families to meet them and homes to go to. Of the 90,000 political deportees, over half returned to France after the war. By contrast, out of the 75,000 Jews who were deported, only 2,500 were liberated, around 3 per cent. While a liberated *résistant* would naturally phone home, for many Jews the idea is unthinkable, because the likelihood is that everyone is dead. Unlike the volunteers and the crowds waiting outside the Lutetia, Jewish survivors have no illusions. They know that Jews over the age of fifty were gassed on arrival in the death camps; they know that children, too, were killed immediately. Their only hope is that others like them have survived:

those who are relatively young, fit, healthy, strong, determined, lucky. The act of returning home requires a terrible courage.

'I'm off to look for those who didn't come to find me,' writes Liliane Lévy-Osbert. 'I reach rue de la Tour d'Auvergne. My heart is pounding, I know, I know very well that in a few moments I will know . . . I no longer listen to the warning my heart is giving me: in this minute, everything about this truth that I dread so much will be said [. . .] I go up and come down again. Nobody there. I cross the street. I enter the bakery. She recognises me. I ask the question . . . The blow came, brutal, painful, irreversible. Careless, almost naive, ill-informed, she said: "But the Germans took them . . ." [. . .] I am alone. I met my sister in Auschwitz and I'll never see her again. But my parents, my poor parents, I still had hope. That's it, it's over, it is finally over.'

Maurice Cling arrives in Paris at 8 a.m. on a beautiful spring day in May 1945. The bus journey to the hotel is overwhelming – people wave at them, tears in their eyes. They're home! And then, in the Lutetia, after the DDT and the medical examination, he finds himself in a big hall, with heavy leather armchairs – the kind that were fashionable in the 1920s – there's a bar, and lots of panels with photos on them.

'I wander through the rooms of this grand hotel – scouts, photos, families, waiters, deep armchairs – not daring to go outside into the city, stepping back before the moment which must come, torn between hope and anguish. The moment of truth is approaching.'

When he takes the metro from Sèvres–Babylone to his parents' apartment on rue Monge he sees the sinister Nazi seal on the door: the eagle with its outspread wings, the swastika. 'The apartment is empty, terribly empty.'

Maurice goes back to the hotel and is later hospitalized for tuberculosis, then sent to a sanatorium. He is just sixteen years old. Deported with his parents and brother to Auschwitz in 1944, he was liberated from Dachau just under a year later. During that short period of time he lost everything: his parents were gassed on arrival, his brother killed a few months later, leaving Maurice with no one to protect him. He survived thanks to a few people whose kindness kept him alive – a fellow camp inmate who had the incredible audacity to reprimand the German *Unterkapo* who was beating him; after liberation, a girl who offered him a piece of bread and honey; women who gave him sandwiches; a man who took him to a bistro near the station to drink a beer. 'I try to refuse – knowing that I will need this money in Paris if I can't find anyone – but it's hard. Never mind.' People feel sorry for him because of his age.

When school starts again in October 1945, he says nothing about his deportation.

You're here!

Charles Palant is twenty-three years old when he returns to Paris. The son of Polish Jews and a member of the Communist resistance, he was arrested in Lyons in August 1943. Palant is lucky to be in relatively good health. After questioning at the Lutetia he is given a package containing cigarettes, biscuits and a pair of trousers. At the hotel he meets a few other Parisians and makes friends with a young man who lives in the same area as him.

'It was midday, we had nothing planned. "Okay then, let's go home."'

They emerge onto the deserted boulevard Raspail. It is a Sunday afternoon, 29 April 1945, the day of the first municipal elections. They stop one of the few passing cars. When the driver discovers they are deportees he offers to drive them home, to Arts et Metiers in the Marais district on the other side of the Seine.

The two men are in a state of such tense anticipation they can barely speak: Palant's friend has left behind a wife and three daughters and is terribly afraid that he will not find them again. Palant himself has no idea whom he will find at home. Realizing that his friend is putting off the moment of return, Palant suggests they go first to his place to get their bearings.

'At rue Pastourelle, my concierge almost fainted when I knocked on her door.

' "My God! My God! You're here!" she cried, which was also a way of saying, "You're here all alone . . ."

'This wonderful woman could sense my urgent desire to know who from my family had survived, and she said to me immediately: "Your brother is upstairs, he's living at your place." Kind Madame Prinet.'

Charles Palant's brother had returned from the southern zone with his wife and child but there were refugees living in their apartment (a common situation at the Liberation), so they were staying at the family home. The brothers embrace, and for the first time Charles meets his eighteen-month-old nephew, Gérard.

'And then immediately came the problem of what to say, and how to say it. How to tell my sister-in-law that her older brother, Albert, one year older than me, who was also deported to Buna, died there, and that I had seen him perish, that I had even kept watch over him for several days before the fear of a selection had forced the Polish doctor of the Krankenbau to throw me out of the infirmary . . . Can one say that to someone who is clinging on to hope, all the more so after my return?' So he delays the moment. 'I told her that I didn't know where Albert was, that we had lost sight of one another by chance during a change in Kommando. I even went to wait for him at the Hotel Lutetia so that Lily could still have something to hope for, at least for a while. For her mother, as for our own, there was not much hope, but for the youngest ones people allowed themselves to wait, until time took it upon itself to put the truth in place.'

Palant is not the only one to lie out of kindness. When Jacques Debord arrives at the Lutetia he is confronted by a woman showing him a photograph he recognizes as a friend who was killed during the bombing of Buchenwald. The woman is so desperate that when she asks, 'Do you think he will return?' he replies, 'Yes, madame, he will.'

Years later, Debord cannot forgive himself for lying to her. 'It was the biggest lie I've ever told. Even today I don't know if I did the right thing. She must have waited a long time.'

For resistance fighters, the fact that they had chosen to fight their enemy in the name of something they believed in – call it France, call it freedom – gave them something to hold on to in captivity. To be captured while fighting made it easier to survive than for people who had been seized without warning and for no reason, even if some of the fighters were, like Charles Palant, also Jewish. Within the camps, belonging to a resistance network meant comradeship, it meant organized action, and this enabled some people, particularly young men and women who were blessed with robust physical health, to retain some part of their former energy on their return. Their determination propelled them forward, although sometimes their youthful self-confidence blinded them to the reality of what their bodies had been through.

'On the first night of my return, Lily, my sister-in-law, frightened by how thin I was, placed next to my bed a thermos of tea and a baguette.

' "Why are you putting that there?"

' "Well, in case you get hungry in the night."

'I only remember sleeping, but in the morning there was no tea and no bread. I must really have been hungry.'

Mum, it's me

When Jacques Debord returns from Buchenwald with a group of fellow resistance fighters they are given a room on the fourth floor of the Lutetia. Some volunteers from the Red Cross bring them breakfast. When they enter the room one of them drops her plate and cries out, 'What's wrong? They're ill! Careful, they're ill!'

She calls the doctor, who arrives to find the three lads lying on the floor. They had tried to sleep on the big, comfortable hotel beds but had lost the habit, so they ended up on the floor.

Physically robust, mentally undaunted, Jacques savours the moment of return, eating his breakfast while admiring the view of the Eiffel Tower from their bedroom window. 'Paris! It symbolized everything we had fought for, everything we'd experienced, to return to a free Paris, a free France.'

Impatient to be getting on with his life, Jacques walks out of the hotel and takes the metro alone, defying a rule which decrees that deportees are not to go anywhere without a companion.

'I was heading toward place Clichy and a man in uniform comes up to me, a lieutenant, and he says, "You've left the hotel without authorization, I've been ordered to accompany you."

'So I said, "Fine."

'It was a good thing he did. We arrive at my place on rue de Caillou. I knock on the door, the lieutenant is with me. My mother opens the door. She looks at me. She says,

' "Hello sir, have you come to bring me news of my son?"

[He pauses]

'There is a moment of emotion and I say, "Mum, it's me."

'Then, well . . . Even the lieutenant couldn't help himself. We were all in tears.'

Cherries

Resistance fighter Yves Léon is so eager to get home to Brittany that when the doctor at the Lutetia wants to have him hospitalized in Paris he categorically refuses, so the doctor provides him with a certificate of emergency admission to the hospital near his home town in Lannion, and another granting him the right to travel first class by train. 'With my cardboard luggage and a repatriation card as identification, I was ready to return to Brittany that very evening.'

He travels alone to Gare Montparnasse, seated in the bus with his cardboard box. The ticket inspector keeps him company, helping him off the bus and taking him to the station entrance. Yves is headstrong, and young, but in his weakened state it takes him a long time to make it up the station steps. It is evening and the station is busy. Feeling dizzy, he sits down, noticing that when people pass close to him they move aside, looking at him as if he is 'an abnormal and strange being'. Aided by a railwayman who tells him that the train to Brest isn't ready yet, he allows himself to be led to another reception centre for repatriates, this one inside the station. Here he sees lots of returnees, mainly prisoners of war. Everyone is eating. Yves isn't hungry, but then he sees that there are cherries for dessert.

'I started to eat without paying any attention to anyone. The waitresses quickly realised this and went to get me some baskets from the other tables where the occupants had left. I continued to enjoy these extraordinary cherries until I realised that I was alone. One of these attentive women came to ask me which train I was supposed to take, and told me that, if it was the one to Brest, I should get going. I replied, "But I haven't finished the cherries." She and her companions stuffed my pockets with the precious fruit.

Every year since then, when this season arrives, or when I hear "Le Temps des cerises", I remember arriving in Paris in June 1945.'

Charles Palant's friend is reunited with his wife and daughters. Palant himself finds both his brothers. But in the district where they live, the 3rd, which is the smallest in Paris and which before the war had a sizeable Jewish minority, many of them immigrants, their absence is felt everywhere. Over two thousand Jews are missing from the area. Only a few dozen will return. Palant is often accosted in the street by people holding photos, asking if he knows this or that person. Some of those who are waiting are kind to the survivors. 'Others could not prevent a kind of anger from invading their gaze, as if those who had returned had made the journey in place of their loved ones.'

A Light

When Marcel Bercau returns to Paris the first thing he does is go to his parents' apartment.

'I went there in my striped jacket, my German soldier's trousers, with hardly any hair – my hair had regrown a little bit – and I turned up at the concierge's office and she says, "Hello, M. Bercau, here's your post and your keys," as if I were coming back after a weekend. When I went into the apartment . . . You can imagine the scene. Having come back from such hell and to go up to the apartment and find the kitchen table set just as it must have been at the moment when my mother was arrested . . .'

As he contemplates the emptiness of his home, Marcel finds something. A tiny glimmer in the darkness. Among the letters given to him by the concierge is a message, written in pencil on a scrap of paper. It is from his sweetheart, Josepha. The message says, 'If you come back, drop by and see me.' He remembers her address, she lives nearby.

'When I saw him arrive – I'll never forget the image of him in his little striped outfit and yellow skin, and his hair all shaved. He had just come back from the Lutetia [. . .] I said to him, "It's a good thing I was in love with you before because you're not very handsome now."'

For a long time Marcel leaves the light on in the apartment just in case his parents come home, with the shutters open, so that if they return they will see that someone is there.

The Children of Buchenwald

One week in May or June some children arrive at the hotel, Jewish orphans or semi-orphans from Poland, Hungary, Romania, Czechoslovakia. They have been brought here in a convoy and will remain in France in rural centres run by Sabine Zlatin's former employers, the humanitarian organization OSE, until relatives willing to take them can be located, or places are arranged for them in centres in Palestine. There are around 150 of them, aged between four and seventeen, the same age as Sabine's young charges at Izieu. There are few young people at the Lutetia for the simple, brutal reason that Jewish children were generally gassed immediately on arrival in the camps. Most of these survivors come from Buchenwald, a few from Bergen-Belsen and Auschwitz. They speak no French. Instead, they have a common language – the language of the camps. It is a version of German understood by all the deportees. Having no other vocabulary, the children use it to describe the new world in which they find themselves: the hotel is a *lager* (camp), a Red Cross nurse a *blokova* (head of block), the infirmary is the *revier*. A man is a *stück* (a unit); to eat is *fressen* – to feed, as animals do.

It haunts the adults, too, this mangled German that has got inside their heads. Decades after his escape Marcel Bercau can recite his tattoo number in German. And yet – it bothers him – he cannot recall the face of the man with the next number who always stood behind him in the queue for soup. After the time he spent in the camps Roger Abada ended up with a good understanding of German and cannot bear to hear it spoken. Some will never speak German again as a point of principle.

The children are the centre of attention among the adults, who gather around them, wanting to spoil them. But these children know nothing of affection. Many have witnessed their parents' deaths. Their faces are solemn, their skin hard and dark, large eyes set against shaven heads. These are the survivors. They have been starved on a diet of *rutabaga* and dried bread. The younger ones have never tasted normal food: they have never eaten meat, or fresh fruit; they have never drunk milk. They are not noisy or rowdy. They gather in little groups by the windows and spend hours looking out at the city without seeming to notice the curious onlookers who gather behind them.

★

Jacques Stanlow is a fourteen-year-old volunteer scout, a member of the EIF (Les Éclaireurs israélites de France – the Jewish Scouts of France). When the leaders of the EIF learn that orphaned children are arriving from the camps, they decide that these survivors should have contact with young people of their own age. The scouts are given strict instructions not to ask the children questions and to be very careful in what they say.

The first attempt at contact goes badly: the children react with horror at the sight of the scouting uniforms – the khaki shirt, the scarf and cap. Once the youngsters change into civilian clothes the children calm down. The volunteers are tasked with going to the bedrooms where the children, physically weak, lie on the bed. The scouts sit next to them.

'The most important thing we had to do was, in the most natural and simplest way, to gradually give them back a sense of freedom, to let them become themselves again. Far more important than asking questions was this warmth. They needed to rediscover the feeling of human warmth. To know that people were listening to them, understanding them, offering them affection . . . Like a friend, like a real friend. Then, if all went well, we would take another step and say to them: "Don't worry, things are alright now. You've been liberated, you're safe. We're going to look after you, just keep calm." And once they felt a little reassured they would take your hand . . . Not right away. Not right away. But once we had established some kind of relationship, sitting there in our civilian clothes, then they would take your hand. They were rediscovering a kind of human relationship that had been lost to them for several years. And it was incredible and comforting when they took your hand, because we felt that we'd achieved what we'd set out to do. Because from the moment they took your hand it meant they had become reconciled with life.'

Decades later, as he recalls the experience, tears slide silently down Jacques's cheeks.

The young people who volunteer at the Lutetia will carry the experience with them throughout their adult lives. When he returns to school that autumn, the fourteen-year-old Protestant scout Michel Rocard learns in his history lessons that Hitler came to power democratically, that it was not the army that was responsible for the war but politicians, chosen by the people. 'I realised that politics is a very important and serious business. A lesson I have never forgotten . . .' It was at this moment in his life that Rocard decided to become a political activist. He later served as Prime Minister of France in the government of François Mitterrand between 1988 and 1991. 'I became a fervent European very early on precisely to prevent such an abomination from happening again.'

The writer Bertrand Poirot-Delpech, reflecting on what it meant to him to be involved with helping the deportees, observes: 'It was stupid, but you felt like somebody. To be of service is a kind of engagement. Many years later, one of them said to me, "You were my goy-scout!" I liked that.'

The children who survived the camps had spent their formative years in a world of terrifying cruelty and brutality, isolated from the outside world. They had seen their parents perish, and had witnessed the worst of humanity. That darkness, that violence, penetrated deep into their young souls, an inner exile from which some never emerged.

After liberation from the Auschwitz sub-camp Neustadt, Edith Davidovici arrives at the Lutetia with a friend. 'We were given a wonderful bedroom in this luxury hotel. And my friend Miriam said, "Shall we nick the towels so we have something to sell to buy food?"

'I said to her, "Miriam, it's over. That was before. Now we're back to normal life."

'She was fifteen or sixteen years old. A child. I was already an adult. I was twenty-one. In a normal life you don't take stuff.'

The Photograph

There is a photograph, one of the few taken inside the Lutetia during this period. A man and a youth are seated together on a deep leather armchair. Both still wear the striped jackets that denote their status as deportees, but underneath the jackets are signs of a different life. The man looks quite at home in the smart hotel; he wears a silk cravat, a V-neck pullover and white shirt, flannel trousers, shiny leather shoes; in one hand he is holding a hat. The boy wears a Basque beret and a pair of woollen plus-fours. Beside them, on the floor, is an open leather case; it is hard to see what is inside it. The man averts his head, smiling slightly, but the boy gazes directly at the lens, his dark eyes confident, almost challenging, a smile playing in one corner of his mouth. They have obviously both been through the formalities at the Lutetia: they have been questioned, disinfected, given fresh clothes. It is entirely possible that the photographer has asked the pair to don their striped jackets again specifically for the photograph.

Eric Breuer is thirty-three, from a well-off Jewish family in Vienna which, before the war, owned a business making ties. After the Anschluss Eric fled to Belgium, then ended up in France in 1940, where he was interned. In August 1942 he was rounded up, sent to Drancy, then transported to Auschwitz in October 1943.

Zenek Schwarzbaum is from an Orthodox Jewish community in Silesia and grew up speaking Yiddish at home and Polish at school. At the outbreak of war his family were enclosed in the Zawiercie ghetto. His two younger brothers were taken to Auschwitz and gassed; then, on 17 October 1943, Zenek too was taken, along with his parents. His mother was gassed immediately, his father put to work. Zenek was only thirteen years old, but he said he was eighteen and an electrician, two lies that saved him from immediate death. At first, he and his father worked together as slave labourers, carrying rocks. When his father was transferred to Golleschau, a sub-camp of Auschwitz, Zenek found himself alone.

Zenek is a resourceful lad. As the number of selections went up relentlessly, he decided to hide himself somewhere within the camp. He chose the worst barracks, where the *Sonderkommando* lived. These were the prisoners who took the bodies from the gas chambers to be burned in the crematoria. Zenek managed to persuade the guard to let him stay in the barracks during the day and return to his own block at night. He spent the days sweeping the floor. The *Sonderkommando* men adopted him and looked after him.

As the Red Army approached, both Zenek and Eric were evacuated to a camp near Stuttgart, an old aircraft hangar where they joined a group of French prisoners planting fence posts in the snow. Eric and Zenek were lucky: they were chosen to work indoors. Being a native German speaker saved Eric here as it did on several other occasions. He was put in charge of record keeping, writing reports for the uneducated young SS officer who ruled there, while Zenek was employed to clean the officer's living quarters and keep the stove going. Their friendship began one evening when Eric slapped Zenek in front of the SS Commandant. It happened like this:

One day the phone rang in the SS barracks. Zenek answered but, since he didn't understand German, replied in Polish. The caller rang off, then called again. Again, it was Zenek who answered. The person at the other end, clearly irritated, started shouting in German, so Zenek put the phone down. It was a display of quite astonishing nerve – all the more extraordinary since it turned out that the call was a summons to a meeting for all the SS officers responsible for the camps in the region. That evening, in the presence of the commandant, Eric made a show of slapping Zenek to spare him a worse punishment. The boy was incredibly lucky not to have been shot on the spot.

From this moment on Eric took Zenek under his wing and the pair became inseparable. When they were evacuated on a death march, Eric's knowledge of German saved them once again when he overheard their guards discussing their orders to liquidate stragglers. He and a group of friends decided to make a run for it before they were shot.

★

Zenek Schwarzbaum and Eric Breuer at the Hotel Lutetia, May 1945

Eric and Zenek arrive at the Gare de l'Est on 26 April 1945. They are taken to the Lutetia where, since neither has any family, they remain for six weeks, an unusually long stay. During this time Eric discovers that his parents were gassed at Auschwitz; Zenek already knows that his family are dead. They stick together, and when someone asks Zenek something Eric replies for him, 'He's a little Pole who doesn't speak French,' a formula which Zenek learns off by heart and thereafter repeats in a loop. Eric is part father, part older brother to Zenek, who is now fifteen years old. It is Eric who teaches the youngster how to use a knife and fork at table, who celebrates his birthday with him for the first time in his new life. And it is Eric, finally, who teaches Zenek what it means to be a human being.

After leaving the Lutetia, Eric and Zenek are sent to a sanatorium near Lourdes at the foot of the Pyrenees. One morning they decide to take a walk in the mountains. High up on a peak, Zenek stands gazing down at the tiny figures going about their business in the valley below.

'You could just put a machine gun here,' he says idly, 'and kill all those people down there in one go.'

Eric is appalled. 'Listen, Zenek,' he says. 'You're in the mountains. Look at nature, admire its beauty and don't think about causing harm.'

Many years later Zenek, established in the world with a family and a job, remembers Eric's words: 'It was so typical of his way of reacting at the time,' he says, then adds, 'I owe so much to that man.'

Jacques and Madeleine

No reunion is simple, when viewed in its context. The gap of one, two, three years yawns like a chasm filled with the darkness of what has passed. At some point, inevitably, the trauma of the past will infect and affect the future. But the moment of reunion itself, that simple, single moment when a person rediscovers a loved one, is delicious and must be savoured, because it is, in itself, a symbol of all that is remarkable in the mere fact of survival.

The volunteers at the Lutetia try not to become disheartened by the terrible mismatch in numbers between people waiting outside for relatives and those inside who have returned. Of course, what every deportee wants, what all the families outside want, is to find one another again.

Sometimes, just occasionally, there is a moment of joy, its rarity so great it is seized by the entire team of volunteers and shared around like chocolate.

Jacques Goldsztein was on the point of death with typhoid and dysentery and a temperature of 41°C (105°F) when the Americans picked him up. Despite the medical care he received in a US hospital, on arrival in Paris one month later he still weighed barely 32 kilos (70 lbs). He is taken first to the cinema on rue Recamier, then two scouts come to fetch him to accompany him across the road to the Lutetia. He is led to one of the various booths where the deportees are questioned.

'So, sir,' says the female volunteer, 'were you deported with someone?'

'Yes, my wife.'

'Right. And what is your name?'

'Goldsztein.'

'Ah! We have a Madame Goldsztein on our list!'

Jacques is unimpressed. 'Listen,' he says, 'where I come from there are as many Goldszteins as there are Durands and Martins. It's just not possible.'

'Alright then, what was her first name?'

'Madeleine.'

'Yes, we have a Madeleine Goldsztein who has returned.'

Jacques is still not prepared to allow hope to enter the conversation.

'I'm sorry, Madame, but it's just not possible.'

'Well, how about you tell us her maiden name?'

'Before becoming Mrs Goldsztein my wife's name was Elphand.'

'Yes! She's here! She's gone to fetch your daughter near Lyons.'

Jacques smiles and promptly passes out.

He wakes to find himself lying naked in a bed, with a doctor and two nurses by his bedside. As soon as he regains consciousness he wants to leave.

'My wife is here. I'm going to Lyons to find her.'

'Don't be crazy,' replies the doctor. 'You can barely stand.'

'I don't care, pass me my trousers. I'm off.'

'Please, sir, be reasonable.' The doctor pauses. 'Alright. Look, do something for me, will you? Swallow this first. It will give you strength.'

When Jacques awakes the next day he is alone. He grabs his trousers, his old shirt and a bag with a heel of bread in it. He goes downstairs to get a train ticket.

'And there was my wife.'

★

When Madeleine Goldsztein returned from Auschwitz she immediately searched the boards for some sign of her husband, Jacques. There was nothing, so when her mother-in-law came to fetch her from the Lutetia and told her she had news that Jacques was alive, Madeleine – like her husband – refused to indulge in a hope that would surely be cruelly disappointed. She is about to go to Lyons to fetch their daughter, who was hidden there by friends during the war, but at the last minute she decides to leave word at the Lutetia, just in case. As she passes through the revolving door into the lobby there he is.

'The poor man, he looked terrible.'

There is laugher, tears. Volunteers look on in delight, deportees stare in bewilderment at the two weightless ghosts who are clutching each other, crying and laughing.

'I can't tell you – our reunion in the lobby of the Hotel Lutetia . . .'

Jacques – retelling this story sixty years later – is so emotional he cannot go on. Both he and Madeleine remember the exact date: it was 2 June 1945, the day their lives began again.

Waiting

Every day, no matter how busy she is, Sabine Zlatin finds the time to go downstairs and check on the boards to see if there is news of Miron or the boys.

One day, a man wearing a brown Russian hat approaches her and asks if she is Madame Zlatin.

'These three men,' he says, pointing to the photographs of Miron, Theo Reis and Arnold Hirsch, 'I knew them. We were in the same fortress.' He tells Sabine that her husband and the two boys first worked in a flour-mill, then in another factory near Tallinn. When the Russians were near, an SS detachment came to the barracks and chose a group of twenty-one men: 'Today, you are not going to the factory, you're going to chop wood.' The man learned later that they were shot in a nearby forest on 31 July 1944. For three weeks the same pattern was repeated, with those chosen each day having to bury their comrades who had been killed the previous day. Miron was thirty-nine years old. Theo Reis, aged sixteen, and Arnold Hirsch, aged seventeen, were both born in Germany.

Desolate, Sabine returns to her work. 'My wait for the return of Miron and those two boys was over. Despite the many friends who surrounded me, I felt very much alone.'

So long as there was no news there was room for hope. With the hard facts comes a pain so profound the heart is sealed off. Each person stands alone: they can see that there are others nearby, people who are trying to communicate something to them. But in their grieving exile they cannot hear the words of comfort nor see the arms held out to them in love.

Outside the hotel, the families wait behind white barriers. It is June now, many weeks after the first returnees arrived. The numbers are steadily dwindling, the buses come less frequently, but still one cannot give up hope. Some families come every day, taking turns to stand sentinel, anxiously watching each bus that delivers up its cargo of deportees, with their suitcases wrapped in string, their boxes, their little parcels, their bags.

The night is mild. Behind the white barrier, a boy is still waiting for his father. His sister will come and take over at 8 a.m. Couples pass by, embracing. It is a lovely night.

The windows of the Lutetia are shining. Behind one of them, a silhouette is visible of someone walking up and down. The headlamps of a Jeep momentarily illuminate a poster: *Pétain for the chop*. The boy leans on the barrier so as not to fall asleep standing up.

All over the country, families stand at railway stations waiting for the trains to come in. Some come every day for weeks. Hundreds, thousands of families are waiting, waiting, waiting . . .

Inside the Lutetia, Olga Jungelson watches with compassion those whom no one has come to find: 'After all, they can't all be dead! – Maybe they've moved house – Even if they were hiding, why don't they come back now?'

Outside, among the crowds on boulevard Raspail, it is the children who exhibit the most steadfast patience, whose hope is extinguished last.

Christiane

Every morning Christiane Umido listens to the radio in her aunt's house when they broadcast a list of the names of the people who have arrived at the Lutetia. Eleven years old when her parents were deported for their resistance activities, she is hoping – longing – to hear her mother's or her father's name read out. On Friday 8 June, the day of her fourteenth birthday, her patience is rewarded: her father's name is on the list. Saying nothing to her aunt, Christiane decides not to go to school. Instead, she goes to the Hotel Lutetia alone, anxiously waiting in the crowd holding a photo of her mother, just in case.

When she sees her father, her first thought is that he must have arrived the night before because he is wearing normal clothes – trousers and a shirt – and he looks clean: his hair combed, his chin freshly shaved. He comes toward her, tears streaming, smiling, and he says: 'My feet were bleeding, they hurt so much, but what kept me going was the idea of getting here in time for your birthday. How you've grown!' he adds. 'You've changed so much!'

'I wanted to say "So have you," but I stopped myself. Because he really had changed a lot. He was so thin, lots of his teeth were missing . . . But above all it was his thinness. He seemed smaller, but I'd grown so I suppose that was normal. A man came and drove us through Paris in a tiny little car to Bois-Colombes, where we had lived before. My father said, "You'll see, we'll start a new life." I was happy because I wouldn't have to live with my aunt any longer. It was a feeling of joy but also of pain – I felt very small, as if these events were much bigger than me. There was no news from my mother, you see. The third person was missing. So my joy was not complete. We never spoke about it, either of us. We didn't want to broach the subject. I think it was too painful for him, and for me too. So we stayed silent. I asked no questions, he didn't want to answer, and years went by in this way. He must have known. I kept on hoping for a long time. And whenever I pass the Hotel Lutetia I say to myself, *My God! What a story.*'

Seventy-eight years later, in the basement of their office on boulevard Saint-Germain, a tiny, sweet-faced woman attends a meeting of the Paris section of the AFMD (Les Amis de la Fondation pour le Mémoire de la Déportation – the Friends of the Foundation for the Commemoration of Deportation), an organization dedicated to the memory of deportees. Christiane Umido is ninety-two years old now, still a regular at these meetings, smiling and joking with the assembled company as they wrap up their business before the long summer break. Papers are passed around, the agenda swiftly dispensed with. There's a birthday to celebrate: somebody has brought champagne and biscuits; they distribute glasses, a toast is proposed, everyone sips politely in the sticky summer heat. Afterwards, as they disperse, wishing one another a relaxing summer, Christiane waits until the others have gone up so that she does not hold anyone back. She is frail. One of her fellow committee members helps her up the stairs.

When she tells her story again, the same details are still vivid, etched in her memory: a child who waited for her parents, only one of whom returned.

Serge

Serge Klarsfeld was eight years old when his father was arrested in 1943. The family were staying in an apartment in Nice when an edict went out declaring that Jews could no longer leave the area.

'My father created a false partition in a cupboard in our flat. He told us that if the Germans caught us he would survive because he was strong, but we (my mother, my sister and me) would not. We spent several days practising how to hide in the cupboard to make it look as if my father was living alone in the flat.

On 30 September, at midnight, we saw the searchlights on the ceiling. There were German trucks in the street. We realized that it was a round-up.'

Serge's father hurried his wife and two children into the cupboard, then went to open the door. Serge could hear the questions: *Where is your wife? Where are your children?* His father replied that they were disinfecting the flat and that his family were in the country. The soldiers didn't insist, but they searched the flat. One of them even opened the cupboard.

'We got down on all fours behind the false back. He pushed aside the clothes, but he didn't touch the partition, which saved our lives. We remained there, drenched in sweat. My sister, who was coughing a bit, put a handkerchief in her mouth. We understood that we had to keep quiet, that discovery meant death.'

Serge's mother went to see the transport depart, around a hundred Jews. She told Serge later that his father had signalled with his eyes to her that she should leave, fearful that the Germans might arrest the people who were watching.

For another four months Serge, his sister and their mother managed to avoid the round-ups, returning to Paris in 1944. In the spring of 1945 they are staying in a flat near Porte Saint-Cloud when they make the short journey to the Hotel Lutetia, carrying a photograph of Serge's father to ask if anybody has news of him. They go many times, and with each visit the anguish grows greater because he does not return. After a few weeks it becomes painfully clear that he is not going to come.

'I remember the hotel with all the pictures, the notices, the crowds. From time to time people found each other, they were crying, telling each other their stories. I don't resent the Hotel Lutetia because my father didn't return. It's nothing to do with the place, it's just a backdrop. I imagine that for an officer of the Abwehr returning there in 1970 the Lutetia was a good memory. As Stendhal said, "Every landscape is a state of mind."'

Numbers

On Thursday, 26 April 1945, the first deportees arrive at the Lutetia.

On 29–30 April, the hotel receives over 800 survivors of Neckar, Buchenwald, Dora and Bergen-Belsen camps.

From 10 May, the hotel registers an average of 300–400 entries daily.

Between 20 May and early June, sometimes over 500 returnees a day pass through the Lutetia's doors.

After 10 June the numbers drop significantly.

From 12 July, the fall in returns is even more marked.

The last returnees arrive on 29 and 30 August.

The Lutetia repatriation centre closes officially on 1 September 1945.

At the peak of the arrivals there are almost 600 volunteers, although by June this number has halved.

The Hotel Lutetia was not the only repatriation centre to receive deportees – there were about forty centres set up, located mainly in the north and east of France, and in Paris. The Lutetia is the best known, partly because of its splendour but also because it received the largest numbers of returnees. Although it is impossible to give exact numbers, it has been estimated that between 18,000 and 20,000 deportees passed through the Lutetia in total, i.e. more than a third of the total who returned.

Aftermath

'And now here I was, alone in my room,' writes Charlotte Delbo after liberation from Auschwitz. 'Despair overwhelmed me. Throughout the deportation I had dreamed of freedom. Was this freedom, this intolerable solitude, this room, this fatigue . . . ?'

The return home is something all deportees longed for. It is this dream, above all, that has sustained them throughout their incarceration and the arduous journey across Europe. And yet the return, when it comes, proves far more complicated than they could ever have imagined.

Micheline Maurel, Resistance member and survivor of the Ravensbrück sub-camp Neubrandenburg: 'This decision, to want to live, is the only thing that kept me going until the Liberation. Surviving meant fighting, it meant not accepting what they wanted to do to us. Survival: our ultimate sabotage. At the Liberation, no longer in danger, people whose vital resources were broken could no longer hold up. Existence seemed empty as a desert to them.'

For some members of the Resistance the close bonds they formed with their comrades have become more important than family. The loss of this companionship is almost unbearable as they return to a world that seems cold, indifferent, even hostile.

'I was happy to see my mother, whom I had not seen since 1942,' recalls Germaine Bonnafon, just twenty-two when she was deported to Ravensbrück for her resistance activities, 'but where were we going to go? What was to become of us? My father was no longer with us. I had left home at eighteen, when I returned I was twenty-three. The group I was with, like me they met their families – one was reunited with her husband, another was lucky enough to find both parents – but we had been such a close group, we had sustained one another, we had created a sense of solidarity: at times when you felt you were about to collapse all it took was a hand on the shoulder, just that, it gave you warmth, raised your spirits. We became a close-knit little family. So with all the relief of being liberated, of no longer having to fear the SS, or having to do everything in secret with the French police at our backs, we found it hard to believe in it all. So it was hard to be separated from that little group. We all promised to write to one another, but each one went off to try to take up their normal life again . . . And suddenly, brutally, it was all over. Finished.'

And then there is the reaction of others. As soon as they leave the Hotel Lutetia the camp survivors are suddenly exposed to a world where many people have spent the war carrying on with relatively normal lives and show little desire to understand what the deportees have been through.

Resistance fighter Marcel Debrouwer: 'They pitied us. They didn't speak to us and we didn't want to speak to them about it. [. . .] I remember once, I missed the step getting off the metro and I fell. Five or six people immediately helped me up, but without saying a word, as if I was sick or old, or a stranger, someone who had returned from far away. People didn't speak to us. We found that later, too.'

'They gave us 5,000 old francs and a special metro ticket,' recalls Edith Davidovici. 'We got on the metro with our pockets stuffed full of fruit – I admit we took as much fruit as we could carry. I had an apple and ate it on the metro. There was a man checking tickets and he said, "What's this then?" I explained that we were deportees returning from Auschwitz. He said, "Oh, you look well. You must have had a good life there."

'I said to Miriam, "It's all I can do not to throw this apple core in his face." But I let him say his bit, because you couldn't talk to anyone about it.'

Silence

After the war comes the great silence.

Those who have not experienced concentration camps cannot imagine it. Those who have survived soon learn that others are not willing to hear what they have to say. What people want to do, more than anything else, is forget. Forget the shame of collaboration, the lack of solidarity, the betrayal of foreigners, the betrayal of Jews, the poverty, the hunger, the suffering.

'Even my parents,' recalls Edith Davidovici, 'I couldn't tell them what had happened. It would not come out of my mouth. Everything they'd heard they hadn't wanted to believe. Everything they believed they didn't want to tell me, in order to spare me pain. How could we speak of all the awful things we saw there? Who would have believed it? It was impossible. For years and years I said nothing. And not just me. It was beyond my strength. And people didn't really ask. They didn't want to know. And since I looked alright, and I'd been fattened up a bit, they said it can't have been as bad as all that.'

Trauma expresses itself in different ways, pursuing survivors through their lives in dreams, nightmares, compulsions, anxieties, ill health. Marcel Bercau always has the same nightmare: always in a labyrinth, being pursued, unable to escape. Different variations but always the same theme.

'For many months after our return,' writes Jean-Claude Vogel, 'I dreamed almost every night of our arrival at the camp. I would see my mother getting into a truck with my brother, the truck would start up and my mother would abandon me. I would start crying and run after the truck; I would be stopped by one of the SS men hitting me on the head with a truncheon. I'd wake up in the camp and the nightmare would start all over again.'

For some, silence is the only way to carry on with a 'normal' life. Raymond Huard was deported to Buchenwald for his resistance activities: 'As soon as I was liberated I said to myself, I want to stamp out all that misery . . . Lots of my friends were affected by it for years. They would wake up at night with nightmares. I wanted to free myself from that. I went back to my life quite easily.'

To survive deportation is to find oneself in a particular kind of exile: separated from the rest of society by experiences that others cannot begin to understand.

The discovery of the reality of the Nazi concentration camp system and the Final Solution casts a cruel shadow over the end of the war for people freshly liberated from years of occupation. But this knowledge sits uneasily with the narrative of national resistance put forward by General de Gaulle in the name of unity. The deportees are an unwelcome reminder that it was the French themselves who had rounded up and interned Jews and resisters. They are a living reproach.

After the war many of those who fought in the Resistance became disenchanted by those who rose to power claiming a much greater involvement in the anti-Nazi struggle than they played in reality. They found it hard to reintegrate into civilian life. The social and political renewal they hoped for never arrived. After the clarity of the fight against Nazism, the return to the grey half-truths of politics-as-usual was hard to accept.

For Jews, the return meant emptiness, decimated families. Questions with no answers. Feelings that will not settle. Isolation. A legacy of fear, ill health, depression, fear again. The fear of not being believed by those who did not experience the horror of the camps. The fear of plunging those whose loved ones had perished into the horror. Léopold Rabinovitch, a resistance fighter who managed to escape from Dachau in April 1945: 'My wife has always refused to know exactly when and how her mother died, having to imagine her undressing and then running naked as blows rained down upon her, into the gas chamber.'

And above all, a sense that nobody wants to know what happened to them. Simone Veil: 'One often hears that the deportees wanted to forget or preferred to remain silent. It is undoubtedly true for some but not for most. In my case, for example, I would have liked to have spoken about it, to bear witness. But nobody wanted to listen to us.'

It would be decades before this terrible moment in France's history was fully opened up and examined. Most of the survivors started talking and writing about their experiences only in old age, attempting to understand what they had gone through and pass it on to others. Maurice Cling felt compelled to share his experiences as a child in Auschwitz before it was too late: 'The experience of rational barbarism in the mid-twentieth century is a vital warning.'

Amicales

Immediately after the war, medical or social support for survivors of concentration camps was almost non-existent, leading some of the most active among them to set up their own organizations, known as *amicales* (associations). Groups of survivors from different camps arranged meetings and get-togethers, offering warmth and solidarity to their members, a chance to step in from the isolation which so many experienced and to share their thoughts and feelings with people who truly understood what they had been through. The *amicales* campaigned on behalf of their members for the right to benefits and medical treatment, they published newsletters, organized commemorations. Groups of survivors would pay an annual visit to the Hotel Lutetia to eat a meal in remembrance of their return to France, and in 1985 they persuaded the hotel to allow them to place on its façade a commemorative plaque which can still be seen today:

> From April to August 1945, in this hotel transformed into a reception centre, some of the survivors of the Nazi concentration camps were received, happy to regain their freedom and the loved ones from whom they had been torn. Their joy could not erase the anguish and sorrow of the families of the thousands of missing people who waited in vain for their loved ones in this place.
>
> 40th anniversary of the liberation of the camps, 21 May 1985

For the deportees, the Hotel Lutetia represented a brief moment of unexpected warmth in a cold, unfathomable world. They returned to France as exiles returning from a strange planet whose landscape of cruelty and violence was unimaginable to those they had left behind. It was at the Lutetia that their faith in humanity began slowly to reassert itself. It is also where they recovered their identity: after so long being treated as something less than animals, they were given official papers, they were fed, they were approached with gentleness. Edith Davidovici: 'They welcomed us with such warmth, with such luxury, such kindness, after all the humiliation we had been through . . .'

A Handbag

It is a short walk from the Lutetia to the Bon Marché department store across the little square, but it takes Margot Rauch what feels like an age to get there. She has some money, the first she has held in her hand in – how long is it? It's hard to tell. It seems a generous amount but when she sees the prices she understands, vaguely, that things have changed since she last purchased anything. Recently she has been given many things – clothes to wear, food to eat – but this cash is the first she has received that is hers to do with as she wants. And what she wants, right now, is to feel like a normal woman again.

The store assistant has seen a few of these ghosts recently: they are not like the usual customers who linger around the perfume counter trying on the scents, gossiping and giggling. Everyone is underfed, that's inevitable after six years of war, but these women are different: some hide their mouths when speaking, ashamed of missing teeth; some stare when spoken to, as if the sound is coming to them across a very great distance. They move like shadows, and nobody really wants to look at them, because there is something about them that evokes in others a feeling of repulsion, or is it shame?

Margot buys three things. First, a comb and a toothbrush. Then, a handbag, the cheapest one she can find because the money, it turns out, is worth little and she needs to save some of it for other necessities. The store assistant watches as the dark-haired lady in the ill-fitting clothes carefully opens the handbag. From her coat pocket she takes a document – *carte de déporté* she reads, upside down – and tucks it carefully into the little zipped pocket inside the bag. 'That will do,' she says, in strongly accented French. She holds out her hand with several notes and allows the woman to take the amount needed.

The shop assistant watches Margot as she walks toward the exit, a middle-aged woman with a handbag tucked over her arm. She can have no idea of the significance of this moment for Margot Rauch. She cannot know that these small gestures are the first steps on a journey back from a brutal exile toward something other people call normality. To be a woman, a human being rather than a dog, is to be able to comb your hair, brush your teeth, and carry your identity documents safe inside a handbag.

She returns to the Lutetia, makes her way slowly past the crowds of people gathered outside asking *Have you seen . . .? Do you know . . .?* She walks up the carpeted stairs to her room and lies down, exhausted.

Margot Rauch, the German pianist who fled the Nazis for Rome and then France with her daughter, Ruth, and who was interned in Gurs camp where she entertained her fellow German internees with piano concerts, survived Auschwitz and returned to France in 1945, alone. Her daughter was dead, her mother and ex-husband too. One of a tiny number of German Jewish refugees to return to France after the war's end, when Margot arrived at the Lutetia and was given a small sum of money, along with the all-important *carte de deporté*, her first independent act was to go to Le Bon Marché and buy a cheap bag, a toothbrush and comb. Because, as Eva Tichauer's mother knew when she was ordered from the train at Auschwitz, a handbag is more than just an item of luggage: it is the safe place where a woman can keep important documents. The German exiles had been deprived first of their German nationality and then denied the right to be considered French. What they knew, better than anyone, was that without identity documents you not only have no rights and no country to protect you – you simply do not exist.

Eva Tichauer was fifteen when her parents fled Berlin for Paris, twenty-one when war broke out, twenty-six when she embarked on the death march from Auschwitz to Ravensbrück in 1944, and twenty-seven when she was finally liberated from Ravensbrück by Russian soldiers. Despite everything she had endured, her joy at liberation was youthful and wholehearted. 'Freedom gave us wings,' she recalled, as she and her friends made their way back across Europe toward France. 'I remember a tree in blossom on the road.'

The Russians gave them bicycles. 'I didn't immediately understand that you had to pedal backward to brake, but I managed to get back without falling off.' American soldiers helped them find a train which took them to an airport somewhere near Halle. Here, amid hundreds of displaced people waiting, she and her friends were moved to the front of the queue (deportees were given precedence over prisoners of war) and soon Eva was one of a group of twenty-five deportees being flown in a small transport plane to Paris. The pilot made a special detour over the Eiffel Tower before landing at Le Bourget airport, just a couple of miles from Drancy camp, whence she and her mother had been transported to Auschwitz in 1942. At the airport a band played the 'Marseillaise' while a doctor sprayed the new arrivals with DDT. She arrived at the Lutetia on 18 May 1945, where she stayed in what seemed to her a 'luxury room' and was given 'a full-on interrogation at the hotel. On the same day I received refugee papers and the clothing and financial aid I had been promised.'

Like Margot Rauch, Eva Tichauer's most vivid memory of her return to France is the re-establishment of her identity. 'I'm not sure what the first document was, I think it was a *carte de deporté*, but a little later they gave me back my certificate of naturalization.'

This all-important document had been granted in 1937 to Eva and her parents as political refugees, bringing with it the right to work and the assurance that they would now be safe in France. In 1940 this right was revoked by Marshal Pétain.

'They had taken it from us and now they had to give it back. It was sitting folded up at the bottom of some official's drawer . . . There it was, neatly folded in four.'

★

Eva survived thanks to the determination of her parents, notably her mother, Erna, who did everything in her power to create future possibilities for her only surviving child. It was Eva's medical training, above all, that saved her life, along with her fluency in French, which brought her close to a group of French Communist resisters in the camp. After she was separated from her mother at Auschwitz, Eva was able to work in the infirmary at Birkenau. Then, she was moved to a sub-camp of Auschwitz-Birkenau named Raisko, where inmates were employed in scientific research for the Kaiser Wilhelm Institute (of which Albert Einstein, before fleeing Germany, was director of the physics section). Their main task was to cultivate an Asian plant called kok-saghyz under European conditions. Its roots contain latex, and the Nazis wanted to develop a strain that could be used to produce rubber. An SS doctor, Joachim Caesar, was in charge of the project, but since Caesar had no idea how to go about the task, he placed an inmate in charge, a Frenchwoman named Claudette Bloch-Raphaël. The *kommando* was made up of many different nationalities, and many of the women had degrees in biology, chemistry, or agronomy. Claudette Bloch did her best to find jobs for many of her fellow French inmates. One of these was Eva Tichauer, whose German origins had by now faded so thoroughly she was seen by others – and considered herself – as French. It was the solidarity of the Frenchwomen she met in the camp that held her up and pulled her through; and it led to a lifelong commitment to Communism.

As she tried to rebuild her shattered life, Eva returned to her medical studies, qualifying as a doctor four years later than she had originally planned. She worked as a doctor in France for her entire career and lived to the age of one hundred.

'During our whole time in France my mother was the most dynamic of the family, the one we could all count on, the most solid figure in our lives in France.'

Eva's last image of this dynamic woman is of her walking away in the dusk toward a waiting truck, knowing that death awaits her because she has been told to leave her handbag behind on the train.

Margot Rauch provides the mirror image of this memory: a mother who has survived when her child has perished. A woman who buys a handbag in order to reassert her existence.

The End of the Return

July comes, then August. The flood of returnees dwindles to a stream, then a trickle. The crowd waiting outside the Lutetia becomes sparse. The photographs grow yellow and fade. The war, which ended in Europe in May, finally draws to a close in August with mushroom clouds rising above Japan.

The panels are taken away, the barriers are gone. In September the hotel is closed for a month while it is put back in order. Louis-Hippolyte Boileau, architect, draws up a list of the damage to be sent to the Ministry:

'Paint: stained, damaged and dirty. Flagstones: broken. Locks: don't work. Mirrors: broken. Doors: handles and fittings missing. Parquets: stained, strips loose. Chandeliers and lamps, in good condition. Moulding: mosaic on steps pulled up, brass borders of steps smashed. Corridor walls: scratched in several places. Bedrooms: stained carpets, paper ruined and ripped off, painted wood needs to be washed.'

The war is over. The Lutetia must prepare to welcome a new generation of guests.

Coda

Endings – Irène Némirovsky

It wasn't the Germans who were coming but *one* German: the first. From behind closed doors, through half-closed shutters, from attic windows, the entire village watched him arrive. He stopped his motorcycle in the deserted village square. He had on a green uniform, gloves and a helmet with a visor. When he raised his head, you could see a rosy, thin, almost childlike face. 'But he's so young!' murmured the women. Without actually realising it, they were expecting some vision from the Apocalypse, some terrifying, foreign monster.

Irène Némirovsky died of typhus in Auschwitz on 17 August 1942, just one month after she was taken from France. Her husband, Michel Epstein, was deported to Auschwitz on 6 November 1942 and gassed on arrival.

Their two daughters, left in the care of their nanny, Julie Dumot, spent much of the time after the disappearance of their parents in Bordeaux, where they attended school under false names. When the war came to an end, the girls made several trips up to Paris with Julie to wait for their parents, whom Julie was trying to track down.

Years later, Irène Némirovsky's final, unfinished novel, on which she had been working at the time of her arrest, was published as *Suite Française*, sixty-two years after the author's death. The incomplete manuscript was preserved in the suitcase that Michel had urged his daughters to keep safe. The subject of the novel was the fall of France, the flight from Paris, the Occupation. Everything that Irène and her family experienced had been transformed into fiction. Written in two parts, Irène's intention had been to conclude the book with a third part, which presumably would have taken the reader to the end of the war. We will never know what it would have contained.

Paul Léon, Theodor Tichauer

It wasn't until the end of the war that Lucie Léon met a survivor who had been on her husband's transport and was able to tell her what happened to Paul. He was killed on 4 April 1942, only ten days after Lucie and Alexis saw him off on the railway platform: 'They were building Birkenau, an extension of Auschwitz, and during the march to that site he fell behind and was shot because he couldn't keep up.'

Eva Tichauer's father, Theodor, died two days after Paul Léon, on 6 April 1942.

From that very first transport of 27 March 1942, only 20–30 men returned out of a group of 1,112.

A Poet in Mauthausen

'Thomas, you have to save Péron!'

'But Commandant, I'm sneaking him food. You know the risk I'm taking.'

For months, all of us had been protecting, supporting, defending, shaking, watching over and loving the only pure heart in our miserable troupe, who had descended into Mauthausen like Orpheus into the underworld, a lost lamb in a cage of wolves. We pulled Dick Péron away from the SS and the *kapos*, stole back the bread he'd just let be taken from him, got him out of his shifts and took blows on his behalf. He would have died a hundred times if we hadn't dragged him clear of the hundred catastrophic perils he stumbled into. [. . .] He was forty years old, looked fifty, and he was our child. One day, because of all his blunders, his carelessness, his general air of astonishment, his disconcerting and comical kindness in the midst of all the savagery, the entire camp finally woke up to the fact that he was a poet. The word went round the barracks, the latrines, the watchtowers and the factory: there was a poet in the coal *kommando*, a poet black with coal dust, threatened with purulent conjunctivitis, who picked up coke with his bare frozen hands because he couldn't lift a shovel; a sickly, gentle man, who had studied at the École Normale Supérieure, who was a specialist in all sorts of things. Whenever he found the strength he would recite love sonnets he'd written himself that were always a little bitter, or classical odes that we listened to like a kind of revenge, even the people who understood nothing of his words listened. Péron was persecuted by the SS, beaten by the *kapos* for lateness, for unpunctuality, for daydreaming, but he radiated kindness, and he took great pains to give us this amazing spectacle: he demanded friendship from the Poles, who came to his aid as much as we did, and we saw Otto, the super-*kapo* before whom the gang of black caps bowed and trembled, Otto who had beaten him up and hunted him down with threats of the crematorium, yes, we saw Otto, on the evening of his anniversary as a murderer, come begging him to recite some poetry.

– *Wo ist der Dichter, der Franzose!* (Where is the poet, the Frenchman?)

I will never forget the gawping faces of those monsters as they listened to Verlaine.

Alfred Péron, he of the fashionable Irish plus-fours, tennis partner to the young Samuel Beckett, translator and teacher, courageous member of the Resistance, betrayed by a priest, ended up in Mauthausen. His presence in the camp is recorded in vivid detail by his fellow prisoner, Georges Loustaunau-Lacau, a right-wing politician who used his position in the Vichy government to cover his resistance activities. Like Walter Benjamin clutching his briefcase as he stumbled across the Pyrenees, like Paul Léon scribbling instructions for the proper education of his son, Alfred Péron was a man whose only real home was a room filled with books, a gentle soul ill-suited to survival amid the brutality of twentieth-century war.

Samuel Beckett was in Ireland when he learned of the death of his friend. Alfred Péron survived Mauthausen, only to die in Switzerland, on his way home, on 1 May 1945. Two accounts of Péron's last months by Georges Loustaunau-Lacau were published shortly after the war. It is entirely likely that Alfred's widow, Mania, showed them to Beckett. Anyone familiar with *Waiting for Godot*, written in 1948–49, will find there the imprint of the war years. Had Mania Péron not warned Beckett of Robert Alesch's betrayal, he, too, would have ended up in a concentration camp.

Saved by a German

Germaine Tillion, the anthropologist at the Musée de l'Homme whose arrest in August 1942 came about as a result of Robert Alesch's betrayal, was deported to Ravensbrück in October 1943. Here she was held in the *Nacht und Nebel* (Night and Fog) section of the camp, together with Geneviève de Gaulle, niece of Charles de Gaulle. Germaine's mother, Emilie, was sent to the same camp, where she would later die in March 1945.

It was a German friend who saved Germaine Tillion's life: Margarete 'Grete' Buber-Neumann, sister of Babette Gross. Grete was married to one of the shining stars of the German communist firmament, Heinz Neumann, who was later accused of 'deviating' from the Party line and fell from grace. When Heinz was arrested by the Swiss police in late 1934 and Moscow offered to take the couple in, Heinz and Grete ignored the advice of Willi Münzenberg and Babette Gross not to go. They set sail on a Soviet freighter, arriving in Moscow in the early summer of 1935, where they stayed at the Hotel Lux and watched as their friends gradually fell victim to Stalin's Terror. It was only a matter of time before they, too, heard the knock on the door and received the summons to Lubyanka prison. After Neumann's arrest and murder in 1937, Grete was sent to a Siberian Gulag, where she survived three years only to be handed over to the Nazis and deported to Ravensbrück after the German–Soviet pact.

Grete was sick in the *revier* at Ravensbrück when a rumour passed around the camp that all 'Night and Fog' prisoners, Jews and gypsies were to be sent to Mauthausen, where they would be gassed. It was Grete who came up with the plan to save 'Kouri' – the resistance name of Germaine Tillion. Her friends smuggled her into the infirmary and hid her under Grete's blankets, where she curled up and tried to make herself as small as possible as they waited, listening to the siren sounding outside for the prisoners to assemble, the bellowing of orders by the SS Overseers and the noise of lorries starting up and driving off. When three SS doctors came in, one of them asked Grete how many sick were in the room.

'"Two, Herr SS Doctor," I answered in a weak voice.

'"What's the matter with you?" he asked.

'I told him and he gave one look at the dying woman below me and went out with the two others. The door closed behind them. We were saved.'

Robert Alesch

On trial in a French court in May 1948, the priest Robert Alesch was charged with treason and threatened with the death penalty. The indictment listed thirty-four deportations and twenty-eight executions for which he was believed responsible. During the proceedings the priest insisted on presenting his own case. He spoke for over an hour, claiming that he was always faithful to his religion and 'never stopped preaching goodness'. He invoked his German nationality and stated that he was mobilized as a nurse and then as a hospital porter. His service, he added, was a duty to his country. After four days in court, the verdict was death. Alesch declared, with Christ-like fervour: 'I am innocent, but I forgive you your mistakes!'

Testifying in Alesch's favour was his former liaison officer, Major

Karl Schäfer, now a wine merchant in Bingen, who came to court to claim that Alesch was 'a good agent' who carried out his duties properly. Schäfer confirmed that he gave 3,000 francs monthly to Alesch for a female informer, Claude, who in turn claimed she never received a penny. It seems he pocketed the money, perhaps to give to one of his two mistresses, Renée André and Geneviève Guillemin, also on trial. Oscar Reile sent a sworn statement to the court from his home in Trier asserting that Alesch was a *Volksdeutscher* who took German nationality in 1941, was called up to serve in the medical service, and that Reile had himself proposed to Alesch that he work for the Abwehr as a German soldier.

Alesch remained calm throughout the trial, posing counter-questions to witnesses, implying that it was they who were guilty of involvement with Germans. Immaculately dressed, phlegmatic, his little grey eyes watchful, Alesch seemed unaware that the more he denied the evidence against him, the greater the public's hostility toward him.

On 28 May 1948 Robert Alesch was sentenced to death by the Seine Court of Justice.

On 25 January 1949 he was shot at Montrouge Fort.

Scholars

As the war came to an end, Pierre Radványi, now nineteen, decided to leave Mexico and return to France to study. 'From a distance I saw France as a utopia to be built, where everything would be possible, where I dreamed of finding my friends again.' His mother, Anna Seghers, explained to him that she understood, but that she must return to Germany because – as a writer – she could not work in a language that was not her own. Pierre could not imagine returning to the country of his birth – 'Sitting at university next to boys who had worn Nazi uniforms? It was inconceivable.'

This is the legacy of their exile: the handful of younger men and women who returned to France after the war did so because they saw themselves not as Germans, but as French citizens: Gisèle Freund established herself as a distinguished French photographer, Pierre Radványi as a French scientist, Eva Tichauer as a French doctor.

When Pierre officially became a recipient of a French grant and registered at the Science Faculty of the Sorbonne to become a physicist, as a scholarship-holder he was given lodgings that were paid for by the French state. The rooms were in the Hotel Lutetia, where the top two floors were reserved for students. Tourists were thin on the ground in Paris after the war, and the hotel had to take what guests it could find. Pierre's neighbours were Yugoslavs, some of whom had fought as partisans.

In 1954, a group of American scholars of James Joyce arrived in Paris to examine Sylvia Beach's papers. They spent several months at the Hotel Lutetia while studying the archive. It was not an expensive stay.

Memory Lane

Ten years after the war, Friedrich Rudolph makes a trip to Paris. He is on a pilgrimage: he wants to revisit the places that made such an impression on him when he was stationed in the city. Paris holds happy memories for Rudolph, and the visit would be incomplete without returning to the building where he spent four years of his life.

Rudolph walks up and down boulevard Raspail in front of the hotel. He is hesitant. Is it appropriate for a former German officer to revisit a part of history so filled with pain for the French? What kind of welcome is he likely to receive? But then he cannot help himself. He enters by the familiar revolving door. The very first person he meets in the lobby is the manager, Marcel Chappaz.

'How delightful to see you again and to welcome you, Colonel!' exclaims Chappaz, unflappable as ever. 'Unfortunately, your favourite table is currently occupied . . . But if you don't mind waiting a few minutes it will be free, and then I'd be delighted if you would be my guest.'

Oscar Reile reflects: 'We Germans can only try to emulate such urbane fluency and French charm.'

The German Past

The pianist Margot Rauch is a striking figure in her early eighties: her hair dyed dark brown, styled in a huge, curly bouffant, eyebrows pencilled thin, arched high above her eyes. She is well turned out: red lipstick, dark eyeshadow, wearing a smart white shirt and a dark jacket. It is 1980 and Rauch is being interviewed by a young German filmmaker who is documenting the Hotel Lutetia's 'German chapter'. She tells him about her time in Auschwitz, her liberation and her arrival at the hotel. About how she cried for an entire year after the liberation, and how she ate day and night during that year before the insatiable hunger finally abated.

The tiny percentage of German and Austrian Jews who survived deportation and settled in France after the war did so mainly because they had nowhere else to go: returning to their place of birth was out of the question, and France was at least familiar, a European country that had once welcomed them, offering some fragile thread of continuity in the fractured history of their existence. Not everyone could face a new beginning in the new world, in brash New York or Tel Aviv. And Paris was still Paris.

'The Hotel Lutetia remains an unforgettable memory,' Margot Rauch tells the filmmaker. 'A warm one and a very sad one. The many desperate people to whom we couldn't give any answers, that was deeply painful to us. But it was impossible to give them information and we didn't want to talk about life in Auschwitz either. The people waiting at the window with their pictures were all crying out to us – *Do you know my mother, do you know my daughter, do you know my wife?'*

Most of those who fled Germany in 1933 never returned from their second exile – Gustav Regler remained in Mexico, Fred and Lilo Stein in New York, Lion Feuchtwanger and others elsewhere in the US. But a few – particularly those who had maintained faith in the communist project – were tempted to return, not to the old Germany but to its newly born twin, the German Democratic Republic. In 1950, Heinrich Mann was about to turn his back on the failed years of his exile in California, where Nelly had committed suicide in 1944 and his career had come to a painful halt. He had been offered a prestigious role as director of the Deutsche Akademie der Künste in Berlin but died, aged seventy-eight, just before he was due to leave. Shortly afterwards, his good friend Alfred Kantorowicz was invited to become director of the newly founded Heinrich Mann Archive, a role which would become the main focus of Kantorowicz's attention in a busy career at the head of various cultural institutions in East Germany. Out of all the returnees, Kantorowicz seemed to have made the most successful transition to life in the GDR, until he caused a sensation by fleeing to the West in 1957.

Anna Seghers settled in East Berlin, where she remained, along with László and Ruth (now a doctor) until her death in 1983. Anna believed in the project of East Germany and devoted herself to building a new society in opposition to the values of Nazism. In her early letters after her return, she expressed her surprise and disappointment at the narrowness of mind of those she met, but she remained embedded in the cultural life of East Berlin and – over the years – was sometimes criticized for not speaking up on behalf of writers who fell foul of the politics of the GDR. She continued writing and dedicated a great deal of time and energy to encouraging young writers. She often visited France, where her son Pierre had grown up to become an eminent French physicist.

During the 1950s and 60s, the KPD leaders Walter Ulbricht and Wilhelm Pieck between them took the helm of the German Democratic Republic, running it as a Soviet satellite and imposing one of the most enthusiastically hardline regimes in the whole of the Eastern Bloc.

Residue

After the war the Left Bank of Paris slowly began to rediscover its *joie de vivre* with a new generation of polo-neck-wearing philosophers and jazz enthusiasts, whose preferred hang-out was not the Café le Dôme or the Coupole but Les Deux Magots on the corner of boulevard Saint-Germain. Publishers, actors, musicians and politicians continued meeting and drinking in the Lutetia's bar. There were concerts and annual balls. The famous *chanteuse* Juliette Gréco, who had waited among the crowd outside the Lutetia for her mother and sister to return (they were reunited), performed there regularly.

But the Lutetia was still short of guests, and the hotel was looking increasingly tired. In 1955 it passed to a new owner, Pierre Taittinger, founder of the well-known champagne brand and head of the Paris Municipal Council between May 1943 and August 1944. The same Taittinger who went to the Hotel Meurice to beg General von Choltitz not to leave Paris in ruins. An ambiguous figure, Taittinger collaborated with the Nazis for a large part of the war and made a fortune selling them his champagne, but he later shifted his allegiance. After the liberation of Paris, he was temporarily imprisoned at Drancy – which found a new role as a camp for collaborators – but was later released. He bought the Lutetia for a song. Over the next few decades the Lutetia managed to stay afloat ('Tossed by the waves but does not sink'), its glamour gradually fading.

In 2014, after uninterrupted service of over a hundred years, the Hotel Lutetia closed for renovation, and its new owners, a wealthy real estate consortium, auctioned off its tatty old furniture and old-fashioned art collection. Hundreds of Parisians flocked to take a look inside one of their city's best-known and most beloved institutions. When the Lutetia reopened in 2018 it was as a modern luxury hotel, its rooms priced to tempt not locals but the global 'elite'. Yet still, the Lutetia retains something of its old appeal: its position on the Left Bank, the entrance giving directly on to the street, encourages a sense that one has the right to enter without permission, to walk through the doors and survey the domed ceiling of the lobby and reflect on what remains of the history that took place within it and around it. Out of all the grand hotels in Paris, the Lutetia was the only one to be offered the 'redemption' of receiving the returning deportees after the compromises of the Occupation. It is a complex legacy for a hotel that sells itself on luxury, for who wants to be reminded of such horrors? The little plaque on the outside wall is there for those who care to read it, but it is easy to miss.

The staff who serve in large hotels are invisible. It is their duty and their role to serve as silent witnesses to the dramas that unfold around them. *Il n'y a pas de livre écrit par un concierge.* There is no book written by a concierge. The discretion of service is also a vow of silence.

Like Jacques Desjeunes, Jean-Luc Jean began his career at the Lutetia as a young boy, working his way up to become head concierge in the 1990s. Concierges, he explains, are experts at assessing those who enter their hotel. They learn to recognize the regulars, they can spot adulterers and con men, famous actors travelling incognito, businessmen who are down on their luck. Sometimes, Jean-Luc recognized former deportees returning to the Lutetia. He knew them because they entered the lobby with their eyes lowered, as if they felt they did not belong here. He experienced a powerful sense of sympathy for these increasingly elderly visitors, moved by their shy presence, and always made a point of approaching them and asking them, tactfully, why they had come. Then he would show them around, following the path they took in those spring and summer days of 1945. One former deportee from Bordeaux became a friend – he sent Jean-Luc Jean a copy of the map of the journey he made to escape the death march and find his way home to France.

*

Some people believe that there is such a thing as 'emotional resi-due' – that the memory of human actions and feelings is absorbed or held within the walls of a building. The truth, of course, is that the walls of a building tell no story. It is only the words and memor-ies of those whose paths led them to occupy these spaces for a brief moment in time that create in our imaginations a world filled with meaning. And yet, that brief moment carries within it a shadow, a reflection, an echo of one of the most complex and devastating periods in twentieth-century history.

Notes

Unless otherwise specified, where there is no published translation available all translations into English are mine.

Part I Before: 1933–1939

p. 5 **Not everyone's life:** Erich Maria Remarque, *Arch of Triumph* (London, 1998), 144.

p. 7 **It is a cold night in the early spring:** Gisèle Freund, *Le Monde et ma caméra* (Paris, 2006), 11–14.

p. 9 **The author Heinrich Mann:** Evelyn Juers, *House of Exile* (New York, 2008).

p. 12 **The novelist Anna Seghers:** the story of the Radványi family's escape from Germany and exile in France is principally told in Pierre Radványi, *Au-delà du fleuve, avec Anna Seghers* (Paris, 2014) and Christa Wolf, *Anna Seghers: eine Biographie in Bildern* (Berlin, 1994).

p. 14 **Hitler and Goebbels speed to the scene:** Joachim Fest, *Hitler: A Biography* (London, 1974), 396.

p. 16 **Gustav Regler is a journalist:** Gustav Regler, *The Owl of Minerva* (London, 1959), 155–60.

p. 21 **Don't worry about money:** Regler, *Owl of Minerva*, 161.

p. 22 **After the children have gone to bed:** Wolf, *Anna Seghers*, 73.

p. 22 **It's only an excursion:** Alfred Döblin, cited in Gilbert Badia et al., *Les Barbelés de l'exil* (Grenoble, 1979), 66.

p. 24 **At the French border:** Freund, *Le Monde et ma caméra*, 15.

p. 25 **Those who arrived in France:** detailed information concerning the German exiles in France in the 1930s can be found in Badia et al., *Les Barbelés*, as well as in Jean-Michel Palmier, *Weimar in Exile* (London, 2006).

p. 26 **In 1933 alone:** Badia et al., *Les Barbelés*, and Vicki Caron, 'The Politics of Frustration', *Journal of Modern History* 65 (June 1993), 311–56.

p. 27 **The Tichauer family are lucky:** Eva Tichauer, oral testimony recorded for La Fondation pour la Mémoire de la Déportation (FMD), 1995.

p. 29 **Everything in it was of modest ugliness:** Manès Sperber, *Until my Eyes are Closed with Shards* (New York, 1994), 43–4.

p. 29 **I was now in Paris:** Ludwig Marcuse, *Mein zwanzigstes Jahrhundert* (Berlin, 1960), 206.

p. 30 **In January 1934:** Badia et al, *Les Barbelés*, 70.

p. 33 **You have to remember:** interview with Pierre Radványi, *Portraits: des histoires singulières*, Musée de l'histoire de l'immigration (online).

p. 33 **Opened in 1910:** Pascaline Balland, *Hôtel Lutetia Paris* (Paris, 2009).

p. 36 **For the great Austrian writer:** Joseph Roth, *The Hotel Years* (London, 2016).

p. 38 **The return to the city:** Sperber, *Until my Eyes are Closed*, 66.

p. 38 **Gisèle's first home in Paris:** Freund, *Le Monde et ma camera*, 17.

p. 42 **Fred Stein is twenty-four years old:** Fred Stein, Letter to friends and relatives, 1946 (courtesy of Peter Stein).

p. 43 **Despite having all the correct paperwork:** Tichauer, oral testimony for the FMD, 1995.

p. 44 **In my hotel the typewriters crackle:** Hans Sahl, *Die Wenigen und die Vielen. Roman einer Zeit* (Frankfurt, 1959), 167–9.

p. 45 **Well, then it happened:** Sperber, *Until my Eyes are Closed*, 134.

p. 47 **Since their arrival in Paris:** Dossier Willi Münzenberg, Archives de la Préfecture de Police, Paris.

p. 47 **Münzenberg's inner circle:** accounts of Willi Münzenberg's activities in Paris appear in several works, including Arthur Koestler, *The Invisible Writing* (London, 2005); Regler, *Owl of Minerva*; Sperber, *Until my Eyes are Closed*; Babette Gross, *Willi Münzenberg* (Michigan, 1974); and Helmut Gruber, 'Willi Münzenberg', *International Review of Social History* 10 (2008). See also Willi Münzenberg's dossier at the Archives de la Préfecture de Police in Paris.

p. 48 **Write to Feuchtwanger:** Arthur Koestler, *The Invisible Writing* (London, 2005), 250–51.

p. 50 **We had to rely on guesswork:** Koestler, *Invisible Writing*, 249.

p. 51 **At his regular table:** Juers, *House of Exile*, 158.

p. 53 **The government subsequently introduces legislation:** Badia et al., *Les Barbelés*, 35–6.

p. 55 **At the annual dinner of the British Legion:** The *Chicago Tribune* and *New York Daily News*, 25 November 1934.

p. 56 **Gisèle Freund has finally finished:** Freund, *Le Monde et ma caméra*, 61–3.

p. 58 **The great triumph of the Congress:** Regler, *Owl of Minerva*, 230–33.

p. 58 **Freund observes:** Freund, *Le Monde et ma caméra*, 73.

p. 60 **Alfred Kantorowicz, a close friend:** Alfred Kantorowicz, *Nachtbücher* (Hamburg, 1995), 84–7.

p. 60 **Aldous Huxley returns:** Sybille Bedford, *Aldous Huxley* (London, 1993), 303.

p. 60 **A short report in a French newspaper:** *L'Action française*, 12 July 1935.

p. 61 **Gisèle Freund arrives:** Freund, *Le Monde et ma caméra*, 77–8.

p. 62 **I have received an expulsion order:** Hellmut von Gerlach, *Pariser Tagebuch* no. 213, cited in Badia et al., *Les Barbelés*, 38.

p. 62 **Are you a Communist?:** Maximilian Scheer, *So war es in Paris* (Berlin, 1964).

p. 62 **My situation is as difficult:** Letter to Max Horkheimer, Paris, 16 October 1935 in *The Correspondence of Walter Benjamin 1910–1940* (London, 1994).

p. 64 **An informal circle:** Willi Jasper, *Hotel Lutetia* (Paris, 1995).

p. 65 **It is a mild day in late September 1935:** information on the Lutetia Committee's meetings can be found in Jasper, *Hotel Lutetia*; Willi Jasper, *Der Bruder, Heinrich Mann* (München, 1992); Gross, *Willi Münzenberg*; Gruber, 'Willi Münzenberg'; Gilbert Badia, 'Une tentative de Front Populaire Allemand à Paris (1935–1939)', *Marxisme et Histoire* 7 (1981); and Ursula Langkau-Alex, *Deutsche Volksfront 1932–1939* (Berlin, 2004–5).

p. 68 **He writes to his brother Thomas:** Heinrich Mann, *Letters of Heinrich and Thomas Mann 1900–1949* (London, 1998), 189.

p. 69 **Lion Feuchtwanger, in the capital:** Lion Feuchtwanger, *Ein Möglichst Intensives Leben – Die Tagebücher* (Berlin, 2018), 381–2.

p. 71 **He had a face stiff with malice:** Regler, *Owl of Minerva*, 175.

p. 72 **Gustav Regler's girlfriend:** Regler, *Owl of Minerva*, 165–7.

p. 75 **When Eva Tichauer returns home:** Tichauer, oral testimony for the FMD, 1995.

p. 75 **One of the German émigrés selected:** Badia, *Les Barbelés*, 57.

p. 76 **Anna Seghers takes her children:** Radványi, *Au-delà du fleuve*, 36.

p. 77 **It is at one of Adrienne's dinners:** Freund, *Le Monde et ma caméra*, 124.

p. 77 **That autumn, Sylvia Beach:** Sylvia Beach, *'Your friend if ever you had one'* (Leiden / Boston, 2021).

p. 78 **It is at this inconvenient moment:** see note for 'Münzenberg's inner circle' above, p. 304.

p. 79 **In no country, he declares:** André Gide, *Retour de l'U.R.S.S.* (Paris, 1936), 38.

p. 79 **As soon as Willi Münzenberg returns:** Dossier Willi Münzenberg, C-283, Archives de la Préfecture de Police, Paris.

p. 80 **Nearly three hundred delegates:** see note for 'It is a mild day in late September 1935' above, p. 305.

p. 81 **'You see,' he says wearily:** Alfred Kantorowicz, *Exil in Frankreich* (Frankfurt, 2016), 17.

p. 81 **Despite everything, Mann and Münzenberg:** Gross, *Willi Münzenberg*, 297.

p. 84 **Anna Seghers takes an evening walk:** *Tagebuchseiten*, June 1938, cited in Wolf, *Anna Seghers*, 88.

p. 85 **Joyce, whose eyesight is severely damaged:** Freund, *Le Monde et ma caméra*, 126–131.

p. 87 **The playwright Theo Balk:** Theodor Balk, *Das Verlorene Manuskrit* (Mexico, 1943), *Préfecture, fünfte Etage*.

p. 88 **In May 1938 Willi Münzenberg:** Dossier Willi Münzenberg, C-283, Archives de la Préfecture de Police, Paris.

p. 88 **And still Walter Benjamin writes:** Momme Brodersen, *Walter Benjamin: A Biography* (London, 1996), 238.

p. 89   **I do not know how long:** Letter 109, 4 October 1938, *Theodor Adorno and Walter Benjamin, The Complete Correspondence 1928–1940* (Cambridge, 1999), 277.

p. 89   **And yet:** Juers, *House of Exile*, 228–32.

p. 91   **The night before the final meeting:** interview with Willy Brandt by Günter Gaus for ZDF, 25 September 1964, cited in Jasper, *Hotel Lutetia*, 174–5.

p. 91   **I tried in vain:** Heinrich Mann letter to Klaus Pinkus, 3 January 1939, cited in Jasper, *Hotel Lutetia*, 115.

p. 92   **Municipal carts deposit:** Alexander Werth, *The Twilight of France* (London, 1942), 240.

p. 93   **Adorno later writes to Benjamin:** Letter 110, 10 November 1938, *Adorno and Benjamin Correspondence*, 280.

p. 94   **After *Kristallnacht*:** Caron, 'The Politics of Frustration'.

p. 94   **Writer Hans Marchwitza:** Gilbert Badia et al., *Exilés en France* (Paris, 1982), 19.

p. 95   **Throughout the years of her Paris exile:** Peter Gross, 'Memories of Willi Münzenberg', *Quadrant Magazine* (2010).

p. 96   **In early March 1939, *Time* Magazine:** Freund, *Le Monde et ma caméra*, 127–31.

p. 99   **Once again they are forced:** Sperber, *Until my Eyes are Closed*, 150.

p. 99   **You had only to repeat it:** Koestler, *Scum*, 26.

p. 100   **At the end of July:** Gross, 'Memories'.

p. 100   **No death is so sad:** Koestler, *Scum*, 31.

p. 101   **The following morning *L'Humanité*:** Koestler, *Scum*, 32.

Part II During: 1939–1944

p. 105   *All this trouble:* Anna Seghers, *Transit* (London, 2021), 9.

p. 107   **Pierre Radványi goes out to the kiosk:** Radványi, *Au-delà du fleuve*, and Wolf, *Anna Seghers*.

p. 109   **The first (and, as the event:** Regler, *Owl of Minerva*, 333.

p. 110   **He collapses on the five-mile walk:** Hans Sahl, *Walter Benjamin im Lager*, in *Zur Aktualität Walter Benjamins* (Frankfurt, 1972).

p. 110   **The camp doctors gave me the following order:** Letter to Adrienne Monnier, 21 September 1939, in Benjamin, *Correspondence*, 613.

p. 112   **The experience of being interned:** Letter to Max Horkheimer, 30 Nov. 1939, Benjamin, *Correspondence*, 618.

p. 113   **Fellow photographer Fred Stein:** Fred Stein, Letter to friends and relatives, 1946.

p. 113   **Since his return from Spain:** Kantorowicz, *Exil in Frankreich*.

p. 114   **It is mid-October:** Richard Ellmann, *James Joyce* (New York/Oxford, 1959), 728–9, and Richard Ellmann (ed.), *Selected Letters of James Joyce* (London, 1975).

p. 116   **They share much in common:** Ellmann, *James Joyce*, 728.

p. 116   **The stooping, scholarly:** the principal source for the story of Paul Léon is Alexis Léon, Anna Maria Léon and Luca Crispi (eds.), *James Joyce and Paul L. Léon: The Story of a Friendship Revisited* (London, 2022). This includes Lucie Noel's 1948 memoir of her husband, *James Joyce and Paul Léon: The Story of a Friendship*, reflections on his family by Alexis Léon, Paul Léon's writings on Joyce, and Paul Léon's letters to Lucie from Drancy.

p. 117   **On arrival at Saint-Gérand:** Maria Jolas, *Joyce in 1939–1940*, cited in N. R. Davison and K. Ahearn, 'With Joyce in Saint Gérand-le-Puy: Maria Jolas's *Joyce en 1939–1940* in Translation', *James Joyce Quarterly* 52, 1 (2014), 129–42.

p. 118   **First the central heating:** Koestler, *Scum*, 155.

p. 119   **With László still in Le Vernet:** Radványi, *Au-delà du fleuve*, 52.

p. 120   **It was a dirty trick:** Lion Feuchtwanger, *The Devil in France* (London, 1942), 8.

p. 121   **In Paris, the famous indoor cycle track:** Lisa Fittko, *Escape Through the Pyrenees* (Evanston, Illinois, 2000), ch. 2.

p. 122   **The chaos of the Nazi invasion:** Hanna Schramm and Barbara Vormeier, *Vivre à Gurs* (Paris, 1979), 35.

p. 122   **Where do you come from?:** Fittko, *Escape*.

p. 122   **The panic induced by the German advance:** Feuchtwanger, *Devil in France*, p. 95.

p. 123 **When, during one of the train's frequent stops:** Kantorowicz, *Exil in Frankreich.*

p. 126 **When she moved south with her school:** Maria Jolas, *Joyce,* and Lucie Noel, *James Joyce and Paul Léon.*

p. 128 **The night before his first visit:** Philippe de Gaulle, *Mémoires accessoires* (Paris, 1997).

p. 128 **At de Gaulle's first visit to London:** Julian Jackson, *A Certain Idea of France* (London, 2018).

p. 129 **The bombing of the petrol dumps:** Richard Cobb, *French and Germans, Germans and French* (London, 1983), 153–4.

p. 130 **Across the street, the American Embassy:** David Pryce-Jones, *Paris in the Third Reich* (London, 1981), 5.

p. 130 **With his resignation letter:** Jackson, *A Certain Idea.*

p. 131 **The following morning, de Gaulle:** Charles de Gaulle, *Mémoires* (Paris, 2000), 71.

p. 132 **The first addresses to be snapped up:** Pierre Assouline, *Lutetia* (Paris, 2005), and Pryce-Jones, *Paris.*

p. 133 **We couldn't believe our eyes:** interview with Marcel Weber, *Per Adresse: Hotel Lutetia, Paris,* dir. Hans-Rüdiger Minow (WDR, 1980).

p. 134 **So, it is true, they were there:** Weber, in *Per Adresse.*

p. 134 **Colonel Friedrich Rudolph:** The National Archives (TNA) KV-2-266_1,_2 and_3.

p. 135 **The Lutetia Section is to be set up:** The main source of information on the Abwehr at the Hotel Lutetia is Colonel Oscar Reile's two books about his four-year-posting in Paris: *Treff Lutetia Paris (1939–45)* (München, 1973) and *L'Abwehr, le contre-espionnage allemand en France, de 1935–1945* (Paris, 1970).

p. 135 **Reile is an odd character:** Dossier Oscar Reile, Archives du Service historique de la Défense, GR 28 P 9 5579.

p. 136 **Reile's physical appearance:** TNA KV 2/3016.

p. 136 **Would I be able to fulfil it:** Reile, *Treff,* 45.

p. 138 **Colonel Rudolph looked good:** Reile, *Treff,* 46; Reile, *L'Abwehr,* 76.

p. 138 **His sturdy build is less courteously depicted:** TNA KV-2-266_2.

p. 139 **My driver had already found a place to stay:** Reile, *Treff,* 47; Reile, *L'Abwehr,* 76.

p. 140   **The French waiters served us:** Reile, *Treff*, 49; Reile, *L'Abwehr*, 76.

p. 142   **As the Germans grow merry:** Weber, in *Per Adresse*.

p. 143   **During the invasion Weber thought:** Weber, in *Per Adresse*.

p. 145   **It is at this moment:** Juers, *House of Exile*, 280.

p. 146   **The sculptor Arno Breker:** Arno Breker, *Paris, Hitler et Moi* (Paris, 1970), 97–110.

p. 150   **In the summer of 1940:** Reile, *L'Abwehr*, 81.

p. 151   **Signs pop up:** Pryce-Jones, *Paris*, 38.

p. 151   **Paris is of such importance:** Melanie Gordon Krob, 'Paris Through Enemy Eyes', *Journal of European Studies* (2001).

p. 151   **They are placed:** Pryce-Jones, *Paris*, 35.

p. 152   **Although all soldiers:** Krob, 'Paris Through Enemy Eyes'.

p. 153   **How much more reassuring then:** Cobb, *French and Germans*, 142.

p. 154   **Lothar Gunther Buchheim:** Krob, 'Paris Through Enemy Eyes'.

p. 154   **One evening at the Lutetia:** conversation with Hotel Lutetia staff member Romuald Cotillon, July 2023.

p. 155   **In this summer, Victory:** Reile, *L'Abwehr*, 77.

p. 155   **Reile's secretary, Käthe Winkler:** Dossier Käthe Winkler, Archives du Service historique de la Défense, GR 28 P 9 4884.

p. 156   **At the beginning, everything was very strict:** Weber, in *Per Adresse*.

p. 156   **As soon as German troops entered Paris:** Curt Riess, 'Le Secret de l'Amiral Canaris', *Die Weltwoche* (Zürich) 27 July 1951.

p. 158   **When Admiral Wilhelm Canaris was asked:** Heinz Höhne, *Canaris* (München, 1979), ch. 6.

p. 160   **The admiral was a good listener:** Reile, *Treff*, 69.

p. 161   **Every morning, at around eleven:** Lucie Noel, *James Joyce and Paul Léon*.

p. 163   **As naturalized French citizens:** Tichauer, oral testimony for the FMD, 1995.

p. 163   **Anna Seghers, too, has decided to return:** Radványi, *Au-delà du fleuve* and Wolf, *Anna Seghers*.

p. 165   **I should understand:** Anna Seghers, *Transit* (London, 2021), 212.

p. 166   **They meet one another:** Kantorowicz, *Exil in Frankreich*, ch. 12.

p. 166   **What is this fancy dress?:** Koestler, *Scum*, 229.

p. 167   **Six months later, Breitscheid and Hilferding:** Rudolf Breitscheid later died in Buchenwald camp in 1944; Rudolf Hilferding was taken to a prison in Paris, where he was tortured; he died of his injuries toward the end of 1941.

p. 167   **When Alfred Kantorowicz:** Kantorowicz, *Exil in Frankreich*, ch. 13.

p. 168   **We ate and drank in silence**: Kantorowicz, *Exil in Frankreich*, ch. 12.

p. 168   **Heinrich, Nelly and Heinrich's nephew:** Juers, *House of Exile*, 281–2.

p. 169   **Thus begins his second exile**: Heinrich and Nelly later moved to California. Living nearby were Lion and Marta Feuchtwanger and many other German exiles, a little corner of Weimar Germany in the US.

p. 169   **Lisa Fittko is asleep:** Fittko, *Escape*, ch. 7.

p. 172   **Walter Benjamin's death:** Brodersen, *Walter Benjamin*, 254–60.

p. 172   **Finding myself with no way out:** Walter Benjamin, letter to Henny Gurland (and Adorno?), 25 Sept 1940, *Lettres françaises* (Caen, 2013).

p. 173   **Benjamin asked him, 'If anything goes wrong:** Koestler, *Scum*, 244. This is the original English-language edition of *Scum of the Earth*. The German edition differs slightly: 'He possessed fifty morphine tablets, which he intended to take if captured. He told me it was enough to kill a horse, and gave me half of his tablets – "just in case."'

p. 173   **The possessions handed over:** Brodersen, *Walter Benjamin*, 254–60.

p. 173   **Walter Benjamin, author and critic:** Koestler, *Scum*, 244.

p. 173   **Not long after Benjamin's death:** Kurt Kersten, *Das Ende Willi Münzenberg*, cited in Gross, *Willi Münzenberg*, and Gruber, 'Willi Münzenberg'.

p. 175   **Meanwhile, Juhl runs:** Count Josef von Ledebur-Wicheln in TNA KV-2-266_2.

p. 176   **One day staff at the Hotel Lutetia:** Weber, in *Per Adresse*.

p. 176   **Admiral Canaris's expensive tastes**: Höhne, *Canaris*, 493.

p. 177   **Hermann Brandl, known as Otto**: for details of Bureau Otto, see TNA KV-2-266_2 and Dossier Friedrich Rudolph, Archives du Service historique de la Défense, GR 28 P9 1214.

p. 179–180   **In their freezing studio apartment**: James Knowlson, *Damned to Fame: The Life of Samuel Beckett* (London, 1996), 303.

p. 181   **That evening, in Paris**: Lucie Noel, *James Joyce and Paul Léon*.

p. 181 **Not long afterwards, Paul Léon discovers:** Lucie Noel, *James Joyce and Paul Léon.*

p. 182 **It is cold in Le Vernet:** Radványi, *Au-delà du fleuve;* Wolf, *Anna Seghers.*

p. 184 **Alfred and Friedel Kantorowicz are here too:** Kantorowicz, *Exil in Frankreich,* ch. 17.

p. 185 **Even for this small number:** Koestler, *Scum,* 243.

p. 186 **After the flurry of departures:** Schramm and Vormeier, *Vivre à Gurs.*

p. 187 **It is a warm summer's day when Samuel Beckett:** Knowlson, *Damned to Fame,* 304.

p. 188 **Acts of sabotage, once rare, become more frequent:** Reile, *L'Abwehr,* 111.

p. 188 **At the same time, repressive policies:** Laurent Joly, 'The Parisian Police and the Holocaust', *Journal of Contemporary History* 55 (July 2020), 557–78.

p. 188 **In Paris, life went on:** Reile, *Treff,* 112.

p. 189 **Things are going well for Colonel Reile:** for information on Porto, Interallié, etc. see Reile, *L'Abwehr,* also TNA KV-2-166_01, TNA KV-2-164, and Archives du Service historique de la Défense, dossier Hugo Bleicher GR 28 P 9 1782, dossier Andreas Folmer GP 28 P 9 11796.

p. 191 **The candidate is short, dark-haired:** for information on Robert Alesch see Reile, *L'Abwehr,* also TNA KV-2-166_02; AN F/7/15306, rapport sur Robert Alesch, 1946; Archives de la Préfecture de Police, dossier Robert Alesch.

p. 193 **A 1944 SOE report:** cited in Knowlson, *Damned to Fame,* 307.

p. 193 **When he returned to Paris:** Knowlson, *Damned to Fame,* 153.

p. 194 **The network to which Alfred:** for information on Gloria SMH see Knowlson, *Damned to Fame,* 305–15; also Germaine Tillion, *La Traversée du Mal* (Paris, 1997); TNA KV-2-1313 on Jeannine Picabia.

p. 194 **They would bring this information:** Knowlson, *Damned to Fame,* 308, interview with Samuel Beckett.

p. 196 **How is Alexis:** Paul Léon's 'Letters from Hell: Drancy and Compiègne', transcribed, translated and edited by Mary Gallagher, in Léon, Léon and Crispi (eds.), *James Joyce and Paul Léon: The Story of a Friendship Revisited,* ch. 5, 119–216. Reproduced by kind permission of Anna Maria Léon.

p. 198 **On 12 December 1941:** Tichauer, oral testimony for the FMD, 1995.

p. 199 **Lucie and Alexis Léon are there**: interview with Alexis Léon, *Irish Times*, 29 October 1998, and Lucie Noel, *James Joyce and Paul Léon*.

p. 199 **The arrival of Carl Oberg:** Reile, *L'Abwehr*, 173.

p. 200 **We were warned:** Tichauer, oral testimony for the FMD, 1995.

p. 201 **On a beautifully sunny**: see Olivier Philipponnat and Patrick Lienhardt, *The Life of Irène Némirovsky* (London, 2011), and Susan Suleiman, *The Némirovsky Question* (New Haven, 2016).

p. 202 **I am sitting on my blue cardigan:** Irène Némirovsky, *Suite Française* (London, 2006), Appendix I, 362. Extracts from *Suite Française*, copyright © Editions DENOËL 2004, translation copyright © Sandra Smith, 2006, are reprinted by permission of the Random House Group Ltd.

p. 202 **My dearest love:** Némirovsky, *Suite Française*, Appendix II, 374.

p. 203 **My dearest love, my cherished children:** Némirovsky, *Suite Française* Appendix II, 374.

p. 203 **I know, Ambassador:** Némirovsky, *Suite Française*, Appendix II, 380.

p. 203 **In August 1942, Robert Alesch asks permission:** Reile, *L'Abwehr*; TNA KV-2-166_02; AN F/7/15306, rapport sur Robert Alesch, 1946; Archives de la Préfecture de Police, dossier Robert Alesch; also Sonia Purnell, *A Woman of No Importance* (London, 2019), ch. 6.

p. 206 **Robert Alesch's success:** Reile, *L'Abwehr*; TNA KV-2-166_01, TNA KV-2-164; Archives du Service historique de la Défense, dossier Hugo Bleicher GR 28 P 9 1782, dossier Andreas Folmer GP 28 P 9 11796.

p. 209 **The first transport departs:** brief information on Ruth Rauch can be found in the *Biographisches Lexikon der Theaterkünstler* and on the Holocaust Survivors and Victims Database, United States Holocaust Memorial Museum (USHMM).

p. 210 **My mother was exactly fifty years old:** Tichauer, oral testimony for the FMD, 1995.

p. 211 **Three hundred miles away:** see Philipponnat and Lienhardt, *Life of Irène Némirovsky,* and Susan Suleiman, *Némirovsky Question*.

p. 211 **Between June 1942:** Barbara Vormeier, *La Déportation des juifs allemands et autrichiens de France 1942–44* (Paris, 1980).

p. 212 **At the beginning of the Occupation:** Richard Vinen, *The Unfree French* (London, 2006), 110.

p. 212 **In early December 1942 Admiral Canaris:** Reile, *L'Abwehr*, 262.

p. 213 **We ought to open a little coffee shop:** Höhne, *Canaris*, 469.

p. 214 **The streets were busy:** Reile, *L'Abwehr*, 271.

p. 215 **When Admiral Canaris visits:** Reile, *Treff*, 318.

p. 217 **Canaris, now almost unrecognizable:** Höhne, *Canaris*, 488.

p. 218 **On 6 April 1944, a group:** Sabine Zlatin, *Mémoires de la 'Dame d'Izieu'* (Paris, 1992).

p. 218 **In the same month the pianist:** Documentation on Margot Rauch is available at the Centre de Documentation du Mémorial de la Shoah, Paris.

p. 219 **At the Lutetia, Oscar Reile:** Reile, *L'Abwehr*, 298.

p. 219 **In Berlin, Admiral Canaris has retreated:** Höhne, *Canaris*, 565.

p. 220 **After repeated arrests, trials and interrogations:** see TNA KV-2-266_2.

p. 222 **Reile has the impression:** Reile, *Treff*, 383.

p. 222 **Marcel Weber, who hid the Lutetia's best wines:** Weber, in *Per Adresse*.

Part III After: 1945

Much of the detailed information about the return of deportees to the Hotel Lutetia in 1945, including many oral depositions, was gathered by the Paris section of Les Amis de la Fondation pour la Mémoire de la Déportation (AFMD) for their travelling exhibition, *Lutetia, 1945: Le Retour des Déportés*, first opened in 2014. I have noted individual testimonies, but unless otherwise referenced, information concerning the organization of the Lutetia can be found in the pamphlet accompanying the exhibition (edited by Catherine Breton), or on their website: https://lutetia.info.

p. 228 **We entered the lobby:** Germaine Bonnafon, oral testimony recorded for La Fondation pour la Mémoire de la Déportation (FMD), 2000.

p. 229 **In October 1944 a seventeen-year-old boy:** Conversation with Jacques Desjeunes, June 2023, and oral testimony recorded for the Mémorial de la Shoah, Paris, 2014.

p. 233 **Olga Jungelson is a history teacher:** The book which resulted from Olga Jungelson's work was published under her married name of Olga Wormser-Migot as *Nuit et Brouillard: Quand les alliés ouvrirent les portes* (Paris, 1965), later expanded and republished under the title *Le Retour des déportés* (Paris, 1985).

p. 234 Information provided for the exhibition *Lutetia 1945* by Arnaud Boulligny, historian at the FMD.

p. 234 **Paris martyrisé:** Speech made by Charles de Gaulle on 25 August 1945 at the Hôtel de Ville, Paris.

p. 235 **At the same time:** Alain Navarro, *1945, Le Retour des Absents* (Paris, 2015), 16–17.

p. 236 **André Weil is another of the team:** interview with André Weil conducted by La Fédération Nationale des Déportés et Internés, Résistants et Patriotes (FNDIRP), Archives nationales de France 72AJ/NC_FNDIRP/211.

p. 238 **After the devastating loss of the children:** Zlatin, *Mémoires*, 63.

p. 240 **When the first lists go up:** Wormser-Migot, *Le Retour des déportés*, 365.

p. 242 **People looked at these poor creatures:** Yves Béon, *Retour à la Vie* (Paris, 2003), cited in *Lutetia 1945: Le Retour des Déportés – Témoignages* (Paris 2104) [from now on: *Lutetia 1945*].

p. 243 **Later, in June, a young resistance fighter:** Simone Alizon, oral testimony for the FMD, 2000.

p. 243 **How to convey to people:** Roger Joly, testimony cited in *Lutetia 1945*.

p. 244 **When Bertrand Poirot-Delpech and his friends:** interview with writers François Nourissier and Bertrand Poirot-Delpech by Pierre Assouline, *Magazine Littéraire*, 2005.

p. 245 **Hundreds and hundreds of photos:** Jacqueline Mesnil-Amar, *Bulletin du SCDI*, no. 9, July 1945, cited in *Lutetia 1945*.

p. 245 **We arrived in front of this big palace:** Maurice Cling, oral testimony for the Paris section of the AFMD, 2014.

p. 245 **Elegant women who welcome us:** Gisèle Guillemot, oral testimony for the AFMD, cited in *Lutetia 1945*.

p. 246 **Leave me alone:** Wormser-Migot, *Le Retour des déportés*, 343.

p. 246 **André Weil returns home:** interview with Weil conducted by FNDIRP, Archives nationales de France 72AJ/NC_FNDIRP/211.

p. 247 **They had lost their memory for dates:** Wormser-Migot, *Le Retour des déportés*, 343.

p. 248 **He asks: married or single:** Liliane Levy-Osbert, testimony cited in *Lutetia 1945*.

p. 248 **An aside: on 2 June 1945:** Navarro, *1945, Le Retour*, 56–7.

p. 249 **Yves Léon has survived Sachsenhausen:** Yves Léon, *Bergen-Belsen* (Paris, 1999), cited in *Lutetia 1945*.

p. 250 **Among the fakes are women:** Wormser-Migot, *Le Retour des déportés*, 311.

p. 251 **Not being a member:** Thérèse Vershueren, oral testimony for the FMD, 1994.

p. 251 **The hunted look when you ask:** Wormser-Migot, *Le Retour des déportés*, 343

p. 251 **You were liberated at Chain:** Wormser-Migot, *Le Retour des déportés*, 332.

p. 252 **At one point:** interview with Weil conducted by FNDIRP, Archives nationales de France 72AJ/NC_FNDIRP/211.

p. 253 **The previous night:** interview with Poirot-Delpech by Pierre Assouline, *Magazine Littéraire*, 2005.

p. 253 **Down in the kitchens:** Desjeunes, oral testimony, Mémorial de la Shoah, 2014.

p. 255 **The thing that struck me most:** Michel Rocard, oral testimony for the AFMD, 2014.

p. 256 **With the influx of survivors:** Wormser-Migot, *Le Retour des déportés*, 69.

p. 256 **Of the 90,000 political deportees:** Arnaud Boulligny, information for the exhibition *Lutetia 1945*.

p. 257 **I'm off to look for those:** Liliane Levy-Osbert, *Le Grand Livre des Témoins* (Paris, 2005), 330.

p. 257 **Maurice Cling arrives in Paris:** Maurice Cling, *Un enfant à Auschwitz* (Paris, 1999), 226.

p. 258 **Charles Palant is twenty-three years old:** Charles Palant, *Je crois au matin* (Paris, 2010), 219–20.

p. 259 **When Jacques Debord arrives:** Jacques Debord, oral testimony for the FMD, 1999.

p. 260 **On the first night of my return:** Palant, *Je crois*, 222.

p. 260 **When Jacques Debord returns:** Debord, oral testimony for the FMD, 1999.

p. 261 **Resistance fighter Yves Léon:** Yves Léon, *Bergen-Belsen*, cited in *Lutetia 1945*.

p. 262 **Others could not prevent:** Palant, *Je crois*, 222.

p. 263 **I went there in my striped jacket:** interview with Marcel Bercau, *Auschwitz Lutetia*, 2000, dir. Pascal Magontier, France 3 INA.

p. 265 **Jacques Stanlow is a fourteen-year-old:** Jacques Stanlow, oral testimony for the AFMD, 2014.

p. 265–6 **When he returns to school:** Michel Rocard, oral testimony for the AFMD, 2014, and *Si ça vous amuse* (Paris, 2010), 29.

p. 266 **It was stupid, but you felt:** interview with Poirot-Delpech by Pierre Assouline, *Magazine Littéraire*, 2005.

p. 266 **Edith Davidovici arrives**: Edith Davidovici, oral testimony for the FMD, 1994.

p. 267 **Eric Breuer is thirty-three:** Navarro, *1945, Le Retour*, 146–65.

p. 270 **Jacques Goldsztein was on the point of death:** Jacques and Madeleine Goldsztein, oral testimony for the Mémorial de la Shoah and the Mairie de Paris, 2004.

p. 272 **One day, a man wearing:** Zlatin, *Mémoires*, 64.

p. 273 **Outside the hotel, the families wait:** *Les Lettres françaises*, 19 May 1945.

p. 274 **Every morning:** Christiane Umido, oral testimony for the AFMD, 2014.

p. 275 **Serge Klarsfeld was eight:** Serge Klarsfeld, oral testimony for the AFMD, 2014.

p. 277 **On Thursday, 26 April 1945:** Arnaud Boulligny, information for the exhibition *Lutetia 1945*.

p. 277 **And now here I was:** Charlotte Delbo, *Mesure de nos jours* (Paris, 1971) cited in *Lutetia 1945*.

p. 278 **This decision, to want to live:** Micheline Maurel, testimony cited in *Lutetia 1945*.

p. 278 **I was happy to see my mother:** Germaine Bonnafon, oral testimony for the FMD, 2000.

p. 279 **They pitied us:** M. Debrouwer, oral testimony for the FMD, 2000.

p. 279 **They gave us 5,000 old francs:** Edith Davidovici, oral testimony for the FMD, 1994.

p. 279 **Even my parents:** Edith Davidovici, oral testimony for the FMD, 1994.

p. 280 **For many months after our return:** Jean-Claude Vogel, *Le Grand Livre des Témoins* (Paris, 2005), 336.

p. 280 **As soon as I was liberated:** Raymond Huard, oral testimony for the AFMD, 2014.

p. 281 **My wife has always refused:** Léopold Rabinovitch, testimony cited in *Lutetia 1945*.

p. 281 **One often hears that the deportees:** interview with Simone Veil 1990, in Annette Wieviorka, *Déportation et génocide, entre la mémoire et l'oubli* (Paris, 1992).

p. 281 **The experience of rational barbarism:** Cling, *Un enfant à Auschwitz*, 229.

p. 283 **They welcomed us with such warmth:** Edith Davidovici, oral testimony for the FMD, 1994.

p. 284 **Margot Rauch, the German pianist:** interview with Margot Rauch, *Per Adresse: Hotel Lutetia, Paris*, dir. Hans-Rüdiger Minow (WDR, 1980).

p. 284 **Eva Tichauer was fifteen:** Eva Tichauer, oral testimony for the FMD, 1995.

p. 287 **Paint: stained:** Pascaline Balland, *Hôtel Lutetia Paris, 100 years* (Paris, 2009).

Coda

p. 291 **It wasn't the Germans:** Irène Némirovsky, *Suite Française* (London, 2007), 93.

p. 292 **They were building Birkenau:** interview with Alexis Léon, *Irish Times*, 29 October 1998.

p. 292 **Thomas, you have to save Péron:** Georges Loustaunau-Lacau, *Mémoires d'un français rebelle: 1914–48* (Paris, 1948). Translation Jane Rogoyska / Natasha Lehrer.

p. 294 **It is entirely likely:** Knowlson, *Damned to Fame*, 381.

p. 295 **Grete was sick in the *revier*:** Margarete Buber-Neumann, *Under Two Dictators, Prisoner of Stalin and Hitler* (London, 2008), 265–6. After liberation in July 1945, Germaine Tillion provided vital testimony in the trial of Robert Alesch, and then embarked on a decade of research on the camps, publishing widely on the subject. Encouraged by Arthur Koestler, Margerete Buber-Neumann wrote a memoir, *Under Two Dictators*, about her unique experience as a prisoner of both a Soviet Gulag and a Nazi concentration camp.

p. 295 **Never stopped preaching goodness:** *Combatant*, 25 May 1945.

p. 295 **Testifying in Alesch's favour:** Robert Alesch appeal dossier 1948, Archives de la Préfecture de Police, Paris.

p. 296 **From a distance:** interview with Pierre Radványi, *Portraits: des Histoires singulières*, Musée de l'Histoire de l'Immigration [online].

p. 297 **When Pierre officially became a recipient:** Radványi, *Au-delà du fleuve*.

p. 297 **In 1954, a group of American scholars:** conversation with Professor Luca Crispi, February 2024.

p. 298 **Oscar Reile reflects:** Reile, *Treff*, 401.

p. 298 **The pianist Margot Rauch:** interview with Margot Rauch, in *Per Adresse*.

p. 301 **Like Jacques Desjeunes, Jean-Luc Jean began:** conversation with Jean-Luc Jean, July 2023.

Sources

Archives

The National Archives, Kew (TNA)
Centre de Documentation du Mémorial de la Shoah, Paris
Archives nationales, site Pierrefitte-sur-Seine (AN)
Service historique de la Défense, Paris
Archives de la Préfecture de Police, Paris
Fondation pour la Mémoire de la Déportation (FMD)
Fédération Nationale des Déportés et Internés Résistants et Patriotes
   (FNDIRP)
Deutsches Historisches Institut Paris
Das Bundesarchiv, Berlin
Brandenburgisches Landeshauptarchiv, Potsdam
Yad Vashem, Jerusalem
Leo Baeck Institute, London

Online Resources

Art in Exile – https://kuenste-im-exil.de/KIE/Web/EN/Home/home.html
United States Holocaust Memorial Museum – https://collections.ushmm.org

Select Bibliography

Alizon, Simone, *L'exercice de vivre* (Paris, 1996).
Amouroux, Henri, *La grande histoire des Français sous l'Occupation: les Beaux Jours des Collabos, juin 1941– juin 1942* (Paris 1976–93).
Arendt, Hannah, *The Jewish Writings* (New York, 2007).

Arendt, Hannah, *Men in Dark Times* (New York, 1958).

Assouline, Pierre, *Lutetia* (Paris, 2005).

Badia, Gilbert et al., *Les bannis de Hitler: acceuil et luttes des exilés allemands en France 1933–39* (Paris, 1984).

Badia, Gilbert et al., *Les barbelés de l'exil : études sur l'émigration allemande et autrichienne (1938–1940)* (Grenoble, 1979).

Badia, Gilbert et al., *Exilés an France: souvenirs d'antifascistes allemands émigrés (1933–1945)* (Paris, 1982).

Balk, Theodor, *Das Verlorene Manuskrit* (Mexico, 1943).

Balland, Pascaline, *Hôtel Lutetia Paris, 100 years* (Paris, 2009).

Bauer, Walter, *Tagebuchblätter aus Frankreich* (Dessau, 1941).

Beach, Sylvia, *Shakespeare and Company* (New York, 1959).

Beach, Sylvia, *'Your friend if ever you had one': Letters of Sylvia Beach to James Joyce* (Leiden / Boston, 2021).

Beckett, Samuel, *Lettres, vol. I. 1929–1940* (Paris, 2014).

Bedford, Sybille, *Aldous Huxley: A Biography* (London, 1993).

Benjamin, Walter, *Briefe* (Frankfurt, 1996).

Benjamin, Walter, *The Correspondence of Walter Benjamin 1910–1940* (London, 1994).

Benjamin, Walter, *Lettres françaises* (Caen, 2013).

Berr, Hélène, *Journal* (London, 2008).

Bobkowski, Andrzej, *Wartime Notebooks, France 1940–44* (New Haven, 2018).

Bowker, Gordon, *James Joyce* (London, 2010).

Brodersen, Momme, *Walter Benjamin: A Biography* (London, 1996).

Breker, Arno, *Paris, Hitler et Moi* (Paris, 1970).

Brissaud, André, *Canaris: The Biography of Admiral Canaris* (London, 1973).

Bruttmann, Tal, Laurent Joly and Annette Wieviorka, *Qu'est-ce qu'un déporté? Histoire et mémoires des déportations de la Seconde Guerre mondiale* (Paris, 2009).

Buber-Neumann, Margarete, *Under Two Dictators: Prisoner of Stalin and Hitler* (London, 2008).

Buchheim, Lothar-Gunther, *Mein Paris: Eine Stadt vor dreissig Jahren* (Munich, 1977).

Canteloube, Marie-Laure, *Anna Seghers et la France* (Paris, 2012).

Carter Hett, Benjamin, *Burning the Reichstag: An Investigation into the Third Reich's Enduring Mystery* (Oxford, 2014).

Charpak, Georges, *La vie à fils tendu* (Paris, 1993).

Chauvy, Gerard, *L'Abwehr* (Paris, 2023).

Cheniaux, Martine (ed.), *Le camp de Gurs – 1939–1945: Un ensemble de témoignages, dont celui d'Hanna Schramm* (Navarrenx, 2009).

Cling, Maurice, *Un enfant à Auschwitz* (Paris, 1999).

Cobb, Richard, *French and Germans, Germans and French* (London, 1983).

Collins, Larry, and Dominique Lapierre, *Paris, brûle-t-il?* (Paris, 1964).

Delbo, Charlotte, *Aucun de nous ne reviendra* (Paris, 1965).

Delbo, Charlotte, *Le convoi du 24 janvier* (Paris, 1978).

Dessarre, Eve, *Mon enfance d'avant le Déluge* (Paris, 1976).

Döblin, Alfred, *Berlin Alexanderplatz.* (London, 2019).

Döblin, Alfred, *Destiny's Journey: Flight from the Nazis* (New York, 1992).

Drost, Wolfgang et al., *Paris sous l'Occupation* (Heidelberg, 1995).

Duras, Marguerite, *La Douleur* (Paris, 1985).

Eisner, Lotte H., *Ich hatte einst ein schönes Vaterland: Memoiren* (Heidelberg, 1984).

Ellmann, Richard, *James Joyce* (New York/Oxford, 1959).

Ellmann, Richard (ed.), *Selected Letters of James Joyce* (London, 1975).

Fest, Joachim, *Hitler: A Biography* (London, 1974).

Feuchtwanger, Lion, *The Devil in France: My Encounter with him in the Summer of 1940* (London, 1942).

Feuchtwanger, Lion, *Ein möglichst intensives Leben: Die Tagebücher* (Berlin, 2018).

Feuchtwanger, Lion, *The Oppermanns* (London, 2020).

Fittko, Lisa, *Escape through the Pyrenees* (Evanston, Ill., 2000).

Frenay, Henri, *La nuit finira* (Paris, 1973).

Freund, Gisèle, *James Joyce in Paris: His Final Years* (London, 1966).

Freund, Gisèle, *Mémoires de l'œil* (Paris, 1977).

Freund, Gisèle, *Le Monde et ma caméra* (Paris, 2006).

Freund, Gisèle, *Trois jours avec Joyce* (Paris, 1982).

Fry, Varian, *Surrender on Demand* (New York, 1945).

Furet, François, *The Passing of an Illusion: The Idea of Communism in the 20th Century* (Chicago, 1999).

de Gaulle, Charles, *Lettres, notes et carnets*. Vol. 1: 1905–1941 (Paris, 2010).

de Gaulle, Charles, *Mémoires* (Paris, 2000).

de Gaulle, Philippe, *Mémoires accessoires* (Paris, 1997).

Gide, André, *Retour de l'U.R.S.S.* (Paris, 1936).

Gmeyner, Anna (as Reiner, Anna), *Café du Dôme* (London, 1941).

Gmeyner, Anna, *Manja* (London, 2003).

Green, John, *Willi Münzenberg: Fighter against Fascism and Stalinism* (Oxford, 2019).

Gross, Babette, *Willi Münzenberg: A Political Biography* (East Lansing, Mich., 1974).

Hartlaub, Felix, *Clouds Over Paris* (London, 2022).

Heller, Gerhard, *Un Allemand à Paris* (Paris, 1981).

Höhne, Heinz, *Canaris* (Munich, 1979).

Humbert, Agnès, *Résistance: Memoirs of Occupied France* (London, 2009).

Jackson, Julian, *A Certain Idea of France: The Life of Charles de Gaulle* (London, 2018).

Jackson, Julian, *France: The Dark Years 1940–44* (Oxford, 2001).

Jasper, Willi, *Der Bruder, Heinrich Mann: eine Biografie* (Munich, 1992).

Jasper, Willi, *Hotel Lutetia: Un exil allemand à Paris* (Paris, 1995).

Joly, Laurent, *La rafle du Vel d'Hiv – Paris 1942* (Paris, 2022).

Josephs, Jeremy, *Swastika over Paris* (London, 1990).

Juers, Evelyn, *House of Exile: The Life and Times of Heinrich Mann and Nelly Kroeger-Mann* (New York, 2008).

Jünger, Ernst, *A German Officer in Occupied Paris* (New York, 2019).

Kantorowicz, Alfred, *Deutsches Tagebuch* (Munich, 1959).

Kantorowicz, Alfred, *Exil in Frankreich: Merkwürdigkeiten und Denkwürdig-keiten* (Frankfurt, 2016).

Kantorowicz, Alfred, *Nachtbücher* (Hamburg, 1995).

Katz, Otto (ed.), *The Brown Book of the Hitler Terror and the Burning of the Reichstag* (London, 1933).

Kerr, Judith, *Trilogy: Out of the Hitler Time* (London, 2016).

Kersaudy, François, *Les secrets du IIIe Reich* (Paris, 2015).

Kesten, Hermann, *Dichter im Café* (Munich, 1959).

Kesten, Hermann, *Deutsche Literatur im Exil: Briefe europaischer Autoren 1933–1949* (Vienna, 1964).

Kesten, Hermann, *Meine Freunde die Poeten* (Munich, 1959).

Kitson, Simon, *The Hunt for Nazi Spies* (Chicago, 2008).

Klarsfeld, Beate and Serge, *Mémoires* (Paris, 2015).

Klarsfeld, Serge *Adieu les enfants* (Paris, 2005).

Knowlson, James, *Damned to Fame: The Life of Samuel Beckett* (London, 1996).

Kochanski, Halik, *Resistance: The Underground War in Europe, 1939–1945* (London, 2022).

Koestler, Arthur, *The Invisible Writing* (London, 2005).

Koestler, Arthur, *Scum of the Earth* (London, 2006).

Lambauer, Barbara, *Otto Abetz et les Français, ou, L'envers de la Collaboration* (Paris, 2001).

Langkau-Alex, Ursula, *Deutsche Volksfront 1932–1939: Zwischen Berlin, Paris, Prag und Moskau* (Berlin, 2004–5).

Large, David Clay, *Between Two Fires: Europe's Path in the 1930s* (New York, 1991).

Laub, Thomas J., *After the Fall: German Policy in Occupied France, 1940–44* (Oxford, 2010).

Léon, Alexis, Anna Maria Léon and Luca Crispi (eds.), *James Joyce and Paul L. Léon: The Story of a Friendship Revisited* (London, 2022).

Léon, Yves, *Bergen-Belsen: Mouroir des camps de concentration nazis* (Paris, 1999).

Lorenz, Heinz, *Soldaten fotografieren Frankreich* (Paris, 1943).

Lottman, Herbert, *The Left Bank: Writers, Artists and Politics from the Popular Front to the Cold War* (London, 1982).

Loustaunau-Lacau, Georges, *Chiens maudits: Souvenirs d'un rescapé des bagnes hitlériens* (Paris, 2020).

Loustaunau-Lacau, Georges, *Mémoires d'un Français rebelle: 1914–48* (Paris, 1948).

McMeekin, Sean, *The Red Millionaire: A Political Biography of Willi Münzenberg, Moscow's Secret Propaganda Tsar in the West* (New Haven/London, 2003).

Mahler, Alma, *And the Bridge is Love* (New York, 1958).

Mahler, Alma, *Mein Leben* (Frankfurt, 1960).

Mann, Erika, *Escape to Life* (Boston, 1939).

Mann, Heinrich, Thomas Mann and Hans Wysling, *Letters of Heinrich and Thomas Mann 1900–1949* (London, 1998).

Mann, Thomas, *Letters 1889–1955* (London, 1970).

Marcuse, Ludwig, *Mein zwanzigstes Jahrhundert* (Berlin, 1960).

Mauthner, Martin, *German Writers in French Exile, 1933–1940* (London, 2007).

Medvedev, Roy A., *Nikolai Bukharin: The Last Years* (New York, 1980).

Mehring, Walter, *The Lost Library* (London, 1951).

Mesnil-Amar, Jacqueline, *Maman, What Are We Called Now?* (London, 2015).

Michel, Henri, *Paris allemand* (Paris, 1981).

Modiano, Patrick, *Livret de famille* (Paris, 1977).

Moorhead, Caroline, *A Train in Winter* (London, 2012).

Müller, Michael, *Canaris: The Life and Death of Hitler's Spymaster* (Barnsley, 2007).

Navarro, Alain, *1945, Le retour des absents* (Paris, 2015).

Neau-Dufour, Frédérique, *Yvonne de Gaulle* (Paris, 2010).

Némirovsky, Irène, *Suite Française* (London, 2007).

O'Keeffe, William J., *A Literary Occupation: Responses of German Writers in Service in Occupied Europe* (New York, 2013).

Paine, Lauran, *The Abwehr: German Military Intelligence in WWII* (London, 1984).

Palant, Charles, *Je crois au matin* (Paris, 2010).

Palmier, Jean-Michel, *Weimar in Exile* (London, 2006).

Perrault, Gilles, *Paris Under the Occupation* (London, 1989).

Philipponnat, Olivier, and Patrick Lienhardt, *The Life of Irène Némirovsky* (London, 2011).

Philipps, Roland, *Victoire: A Wartime Story of Resistance, Collaboration and Betrayal* (London, 2021).

Potts, Willard, *Portraits of the Artist in Exile: Recollections of James Joyce by Europeans* (Dublin, 1979).

Pryce-Jones, David, *Paris in the Third Reich: A History of the German Occupation, 1940–1944* (London, 1981).

Purnell, Sonia, *A Woman of No Importance* (London, 2019).

Quack, Sibylle, *Between Sorrow and Strength: Women Refugees of the Nazi Period* (Washington, DC, 1995).

Radványi, Pierre, *Au-delà du fleuve, avec Anna Seghers* (Paris, 2014).

Regler, Gustav, *The Owl of Minerva* (London, 1959).

Reile, Oscar, *L'Abwehr, le contre-espionnage allemand in France, de 1935–1945* (Paris, 1970).

Reile, Oscar, *Treff Lutetia Paris (1939–45)* (Munich, 1973).

Remarque, Erich Maria, *Arch of Triumph* (London, 1946).

Rocard, Michel, *Si ça vous amuse: chronique de mes faits et méfaits* (Paris, 2010).

Roth, Joseph, *Briefe 1911–1939* (Berlin, 1970).

Roth, Joseph, *The Hotel Years* (London, 2016).

Roth, Joseph, *What I Saw: Reports from Berlin 1920–1933* (London, 2003).

Sahl, Hans, *Walter Benjamin im Lager*, in *Zur Aktualität Walter Benjamins: Aus Anlass des 80 Geburtstags von Walter Benjamin herausgegeben von Siegfried Unseld* (Frankfurt, 1972).

Scheer, Maximilian, *So war es in Paris* (Berlin, 1964).

Schramm, Hanna, and Barbara Vormeier, *Vivre à Gurs: un camp de concentration français, 1940–1941* (Paris, 1979).

Schwertfeger, Ruth, *In Transit: Narratives of German Jews in Exile, Flight, and Internment during the 'Dark Years' of France* (Berlin, 2012).

Seghers, Anna, *Ich erwarte Eure Briefe wie den Besuch des besten Freunde, Briefe 1924–1952* (Berlin, 2008).

Seghers, Anna, *The Seventh Cross* (London, 2019).

Seghers, Anna, *Transit* (London, 2021).

Semelin, Jacques, *The Survival of the Jews in France 1940–44* (London, 2018).

Semprun, Jorge, *Le grand voyage* (Paris, 1965).

Speer, Albert, *Inside the Third Reich: Memoirs* (London, 2015).

Sperber, Manès, *Until my Eyes are Closed with Shards* (New York, 1994).

Stein, Fred, *Portraits de l'exil, Paris–New York (1933–42)* (Dresden, 2018).

Suleiman, Susan, *The Némirovsky Question: The Life, Death, And Legacy of a Jewish Writer in Twentieth-Century France* (New Haven, 2016).

Sullivan, Rosemary, *Villa Air Bel: The Second World War, Escape and a House in France* (London, 2007).

Tank, Kurt Lothar, *Pariser Tagebuch 1938, 1939, 1940* (Berlin, 1941).

Tillion, Germaine, *Ravensbrück* (Paris, 1997).

Tillion, Germaine, *La traversée du mal* (Paris, 1997).

Sources

Torrie, Julia S., *German Soldiers and the Occupation of France 1940–1944* (Cambridge, 2018).

Vinen, Richard, *The Unfree French: Life under the Occupation* (London, 2006).

Vittori, Jean-Pierre (ed.), *Le grand livre des Témoins* (Paris, 2005).

Vormeier, Barbara, *La Deportation des juifs allemands et autrichiens de France 1942–44* (Paris, 1980).

Weber, Eugen, *The Hollow Years: France in the 1930s* (New York, 1994).

Wegner, Bernd, *Das Deutsche Paris: Der Blick Der Besatzer 1940–1944* (Paderborn, 2019).

Werth, Alexander, *The Twilight of France, 1933–1940* (London, 1942).

Wieviorka, Annette, *Déportation et genocide, entre la mémoire et l'oubli* (Paris, 1992).

Wolf, Christa, *Anna Seghers: eine Biographie in Bildern* (Berlin, 1994).

Wormser-Migot, Olga, *Le retour des déportés: quand les alliés ouvrirent les portes* (Paris, 1985).

Zlatin, Sabine, *Mémoires de la 'Dame d'Izieu', avec sa déposition au procès Barbie et les témoignages de Gabrielle Perrier et de Samuel Pintel* (Paris, 1992).

Articles

Armorin, François-Jean, *Hotel Lutetia, ou les récits du brouillard et de la nuit*, April 1945.

Badia, Gilbert, 'Une tentative de Front Populaire Allemand à Paris (1935–1939): l'Opposition Antihitlerienne en France', *Marxisme et Histoire* No. 7 (1981).

Breton, Catherine (ed.), *Lutetia 1945 – Le Retour des Deportés*. AFMD, Paris 2014.

Caron, Vicki, 'The politics of frustration: French Jewry and the refugee crisis in the 1930s', *Journal of Modern History* 65, 2 (June 1993).

Caron, Vicki, 'Prelude to Vichy: France and the Jewish refugees in the era of Appeasement', *Journal of Contemporary History* 20, 1 (January 1985), 157–76.

Davison, N. R., and K. Ahearn, 'With Joyce in Saint Gérand-le-Puy: Maria Jolas's "Joyce en 1939–1940" in translation', *James Joyce Quarterly* 52, 1 (2014), 129–42.

Gross, Peter, 'Memories of Willi Münzenberg', *Quadrant Magazine*, 1 April 2010 (founded as the journal of the Australian Association for Cultural Freedom).

Gruber, Helmut, 'Willi Münzenberg: propagandist for and against the Comintern', *International Review of Social History* 10, 2 (Dec 2008).

Joly, Laurent, 'The Parisian police and the Holocaust: control, round-ups, hunt, 1940–44', *Journal of Contemporary History* 55 (July 2020), 557–78.

Krob, Melanie Gordon, 'Paris through enemy eyes: the Wehrmacht in Paris 1940–44', *Journal of European Studies* (March 2001).

'Le Lutetia: l'hotel des morts-vivants', *Le Sens de l'Histoire*, Commemorative edition on the Holocaust 70 years on, 2015.

Palant, Charles, 'Au Lutetia, le silence des survivants', *Libération*, 24 January 2005.

Poirot-Delpech, Bertrand, '1945, Lutetia, entretien avec Francois Nourissier and Bertrand Poirot-Delpech par Pierre Assouline', *Magazine Littéraire*, 2005.

Riess, Curt, 'Le Secret de l'Amiral Canaris', *Die Weltwoche* (Zurich), 27 July 1951.

Wieviorka, Annette, 'Rendez-vous á l'Hotel Lutetia', *L'Histoire* 179 (July–August 1994).

Audio-visual

Diamant-Berger, Guillaume, *Souviens-toi, Lutetia*. Documentary film, La Mansarde Cinéma, 2017.

Magontier, Pascal, *Auschwitz-Lutetia*, France 3 INA, 8 May 2000 (interview with Marcel Bercau).

Minow, Hans-Rüdiger, *Per adresse, Hotel Lutetia, Paris*. Documentary film, WDR, 1980.

Stein, Fred, *Report from Exile: Fotografien von Fred Stein*. Exhibition, Deutsches Historisches Museum, Berlin, 2021.

Acknowledgements

I would like to thank the numerous people who have aided me in my research for this book. From the Hotel Lutetia: Romuald Cotillon, Jacques Desjeunes, Jean-Luc Jean, Jean-Marc de Margerie, Patrick Scicard, Pierre Faucet. For their help in answering my questions and most generously sharing their knowledge, Catherine Breton and everyone at the AFMD, Paris; Guillaume Diamant-Berger, Hans-Rüdiger Minow, Professor Luca Crispi, Barbara Lambauer, Peter Stein, Melanie Krob, Pierre Assouline, Julia Torre, Byron Schirbock, Talbot C. Imlay, Annette Antignac, Faye Carney. For help with German research: Dr Carmel Anna Heeley, Joe Wald, Rose Campbell, Anna Seifert-Speck. For time, translation and a lovely lunch, Natasha Lehrer. For archival assistance: Cyrille Le Quellec, Frantz Malassis, Patricia Gillet, Ariel Sion, Karen Taieb, Mark Nixon, Elizabeth White and all the staff at the various archives in Paris. For connections: Hester Abrams, Derek Niemann, Dr Daniel Lee, Eloise Caléo. For their hospitality, Claire Dupuis and Olivier le Marois. For friendship and jokes, Esther Selsdon. And for being themselves, Alex and Hal.

Enormous thanks go to my agent, Andrew Gordon, and my US agent Allison Devereux, editors Simon Winder and Chloe Currens at Allen Lane, John Glusman at Norton and Martha Kanya-Forstner at Knopf, and all the editorial, production, publicity and marketing teams who have made the book possible. I truly appreciate your hard work. Thank you to Cecilia Mackay for picture research.

My extended research trip to Paris was funded by a work-in-progress grant from the Society of Authors, for which I am incredibly grateful. I would also like to warmly thank Anna Maria Léon for permission to quote from Paul Léon's letters from Drancy and Peter Stein for allowing me to use Fred's wonderful photographs.

Index

Index

QUAI

ESPLANADE

DES

INVALIDES

Chambre des Députés

Président

Ambassade d'Allemagne

Pl. d.Pal. Bourbon

Ministère de la Guerre

Mie des Affaires Etrangères

GARE DE

GALLIÉNI

FABER

RUE DE BOURGOGNE

RUE

BOU

RD DE L'UNIVERSITÉ

RUE DE CONSTANTINE

DOMINIQUE

dépôt des fortific.

Service Geographiq de l'Armée

Inst.de Recherches Agronomiq.

Min.du Travail

MARTIGNAC

RUE ST. DOMINIQUE

RUE CASIMIR PERIER

Mairie du 7e Arr.

PALAIS

CASES

BELLECHASSE

RUE DE GRE

Ministère du Commerce et de l'Indust.

Minist. des P.T.T.

Secr. Gen.P.T.T

Ministère de l'Agriculture

Léa. des Pays-Bas

Ambass. de l'U.R.S.S.

INVALIDES

AV. DE TOURVILLE

Place des Invalides

Sq.de la Tour Maubourg

Sq.des Invalides

HÔTEL DES INVALIDES

Musée de l'Armée

Eglise St.Louis

Tombeau de Napoléon Ier

Cour du Dôme

Caserne de la Tour Maubourg

Minist.du Travail

Musée Rodin

RUE DE VARENNE

Ministère de l'Agriculture

RUE BARBET DE JOUY

RUE VANEAU

RUE DE CHANALEILLES

Présidence du Conseil

Missions Etrangères

CITÉ DE VARENNE

RUE VANEAU

BOULEVARD DES INVALIDES

BOUL. DE LA TOUR MAUBOURG

Sq. Lég. du Chili

Sq.de la Tour Maub.

AV. DE VILLARS

Lycée Victor Duruy

Ecole prép. d'apprent.

L'ospice Leprince Filles de Charité

Egl. Pierre Caillou

SAINT

GRENELLE

RUE CLER

CHAMP DE MARS

RUE DUVIVIER

RUE DE GRENELLE

RUE AMÉLIE

PAS.JEAN NICOT

RUE SURCOUF

Marché

RUE COMTE

Bun Cent. d.Recrut.

PICQUET

BOUL. DE LA TOUR

LOWENDAL

AV. DE SÉGUR

Pl. Denis Cochin

D. TOURVILLE

Place Vauban

RUE DE BABYL

Sœurs de St Vincent de

Min. du Trav. Assur.Socle

Pl.de l'Ecole Militaire

AV. LOWENDAL

RUE DE SÉGUR

Ecole Israélite

Pl. du Pres.

Eg. St.François Xavier

Chap.

Mme Cath. Tchéco-Slovaq.

Cas. Babylone

RUE MONSIEUR

Lég.de Chine

OUDINOT

RUE PIERRE LEROUX

RUE VANEAU

Hôpital Laennec

Min. de la Marine Marchde

Pl.de Pomtenoy

Caserne

AVENUE

DE

Millhouard

RUE

Les p.es Sœurs hospitalières

Maison de Santé Ste Jean de Dieu

Ministre des Colonies

R.C.Coquelin

RUE VANEAU

DE BRETEUIL

RUE EBLÉ

INVALIDES

DUQUESNE

RUE

DUROC

RUE MASSERAN

inst.des Jeunes Aveugles

AV.DAN.LESUEUR

SÈVRES

R.L.BAROUILLI

Caisse d'Epargne

GARIBALDI

AVENUE

RUE

PERIGNON

Place de Breteuil

Mⁿˡᵉ de Pasteur P.T.T.

AV. DE SAXE

DUROC

RUE BERTRAND

BOUL.

DU

GARIBALDI

R.FR. BONVIN

R.J. DAUDIN

AV. DE SAXE

Hôpital Necker

Ec. Sudria

Inst. d'Optique

Hôpital des Enfants Malades

BOUL.

VAU